Contents

Acknowledgments

I would like to express my thanks to Andrew Lockett, the former Head of BFI Publishing, who commissioned this volume and to Rebecca Barden and Tom Cabot at the BFI who saw it through to completion. I would also thank the staff at the Academy Motion Picture Library in Beverly Hills, California for their guidance and help. Similarly, I wish to express my gratitude to the students I have taught on my module 'The Politics and Culture of Hollywood' at London Metropolitan University since 1999 and to my former Head of Department Iwan Morgan for suggesting the development of this course. I would finally wish to thank my family and friends who have provided invaluable help within this project through discussions and feedback. I dedicate this book to my mother and to the memory of my father, who encouraged my interest of film in the first place.

Hollywood

Politics and Society

Mark Wheeler

 Publishing

First published in 2006 by the
BRITISH FILM INSTITUTE
21 Stephen Street, London W1T 1LN

The British Film Institute's purpose is to champion moving image culture in all its richness and diversity across the UK, for the benefit of as wide an audience as possible, and to create and encourage debate.
Copyright © Mark Wheeler 2006

Cover image: Robert Redford in *The Candidate* (Michael Ritchie, 1972);
Redford–Ritchie Productions/Warner Bros.

Cover design: Clare Skeats

Set by Servis Filmsetting Ltd, Manchester
Printed in the UK by St Edmundsbury Press, Bury St Edmunds, Suffolk

British Library Cataloguing-in-Publication Data
A catalogue record for this book is available from the British Library
ISBN 1–84457–136–X (pbk)
ISBN 1–84457–135–1 (hbk)

Introduction

At the beginning of the 21st century, the United States' (US) film industry overtook the aeronautics and car industries to become one of the highest exporters of American products.[1] The major studios are important economic, social and cultural institutions that determine the flow of motion picture product in the global film marketplace. Hollywood has acted as a microcosm for the debates which have existed throughout the course of American political history. It is the purpose of this book to provide an interdisciplinary study of the film industry by reviewing the dynamics of the US motion picture trade, the political constituencies in Hollywood and the links between celebrity and campaign politics.

In providing an account of how Hollywood has related to the institutions of American politics, together with the internal dynamics which have defined its conduct as a business, this study covers censorship, labour relations, trade policy and celebrity activism to demonstrate how the US film industry has and always will be an arena for political action and conflicts. The analysis considers the extent to which Hollywood has been characterised by different 'types' of political forces by referring to the range of economic, cultural and ideological imperatives that have shaped the industry's development. To this end, it provides a historical and contemporaneous survey of the trading principles, labour forces and political constituencies existing in the US film community. It should also be noted that while this analysis makes reference to films, it remains outside its remit to provide a detailed discussion of the political, social and cultural content of the motion pictures themselves.[2]

The study begins by considering the political economy of the motion picture industry. As Douglas Gomery has demonstrated, the studio system is worthy of an industrial analysis with regard to its corporate ownership and control over the production, distribution and exhibition of film product (Gomery, 2005b: 3). However, it is also necessary to consider how American governments established the business conditions through which expansion occurred. Upon these foundations, the film industry evolved from fairground sideshow to a global phenomenon.

Chapter 1 considers how the studios in the first half of the 20th century, with the support of the Department of Commerce, established controls over the distribution and exhibition of films in the North American marketplace while expanding into international territories. This cartelism sat uneasily with the US Justice Department's principles of competition. In 1948, the Supreme Court found in favour of the 'Paramount Decrees' which divorced the studios' production and distribution arms from their exhibition chains, leading to the collapse of the studio system.

Chapter 2 traces Hollywood's transformation from an 'industry' into a 'business'. It discusses the US governments' deregulation of the communications markets which encouraged the formation of the global media conglomerates who own the studios. In particular, the Motion Picture Association of America (MPAA) brokered the relationship between the Washington and Hollywood elites. Its international arm, the Motion Picture Association (MPA) operated as a 'little State Department' by removing trade barriers with the support of the State Department and the Office of the US Trade Representative.

In 1966 Jack Valenti, Lyndon B. Johnson's (LBJ) Special Assistant, was appointed as the MPAA/MPA President and proved a zealous lobbyist during his thirty-eight-year reign. He courted Democrats and Republicans, and was aided by several presidents who had close affiliations with Hollywood. Throughout his stewardship, Valenti led the MPA in more than eighty negotiations to liberalise the international film and broadcasting markets. Meanwhile, foreign trade associations objected to Hollywood's expansion on economic and cultural grounds.

The MPAA's other concern was the protection of the studios' intellectual property rights. Although new communication technologies provided Hollywood with opportunities to extract profits from different revenue streams, anxieties arose over their ability to retain control over their distributed product. The increase in the illegal piracy of motion pictures has coincided with the ascendance of the Internet as the perfect copying medium in which there is no deterioration in second-, third- or nth-generated material. These problems remain Valenti's legacy to his successor, former Agricultural Secretary, Dan Glickman.

However, in considering Hollywood's role in US politics, this analysis cannot be confined to matters of trade. It also focuses on the questions the film industry raises about America's history, culture and self-image. Although the MPAA has promoted motion pictures' trading interests, most visibly it developed censorship and ratings systems as US films were deemed to have a unique influence over the public. Chapter 3 discusses why Will Hays, the Post-Master General for President Harding, was appointed to run the Motion Picture Producers and Distributors of America (MPPDA). Hays, a Presbyterian picked by the Jewish moguls to offset the anti-Semitic accusations directed against Hollywood, was committed to the development of a Production Code to ensure the moral content of films. He reasoned with the moguls that if they did not agree to a self-enforced code, Washington would establish a federal form of censorship. From 1934 to 1967, the Production Code Administration (PCA) applied the 'Hays' Code so that every Hollywood film was vetted for sex, violence and language.

When Valenti became president of the renamed MPAA he replaced the Code with the Ratings system and films were allowed to handle issues of sex and violence. Graphic representations remain controversial as fears have grown about copycat violence. Alternatively, liberal positions suggest that all forms of censorship are retrogressive. These divisions have been exacerbated by the widening gulf between religious fundamentalists and civil libertarians.

Consequently, a political survey of the US film industry must locate itself in wider debates about Hollywood's place in America's cultural life. The studios are key institutions which reflect 'a definable and relatively cohesive social leadership cadre in American society' (Powers, Rothman and Rothman, 1996). This study will review the political correlations between the backgrounds, attitudes and beliefs of the motion picture elite. Ironically, Hollywood, the quintessential American institution, was created by 'Eastern European Jews who themselves seemed to be anything but the quintessence of America' (Gabler, 1988). On one hand, the entrepreneurial Jewish immigrants who established the US film industry represented the American Dream in which meritocracy and tolerance are prized. Conversely, the intolerance expressed towards them, their products and film artists by White Anglo-Saxon Protestant (WASP) elites brings into question the notion of the US as a melting pot of cultures and ideals.

Chapter 4 shows how the moguls' relations with US politicians allowed them to gain acceptance into the American elites who had treated them with suspicion owing to their Jewish origins. It discusses how the Semitic background of many writers, directors, actors and artists led to a growing political consciousness reflecting the conditions of the era, notably Franklin D. Roosevelt's (FDR) New Deal, the establishment of trade unionism and the emigration of refugees from Nazism. Moreover, it was associated with the Gothamisation of Hollywood as New York-based writers settled on the West Coast and were attracted to liberal and Communist causes.

Chapter 5 considers the extent to which this radicalism characterised the labour struggles in Hollywood during the 1930s and 1940s. Until the 1930s, the moguls controlled the working conditions owing to the largely disparate nature of the film workforce. They were naturally reluctant to recognise the guilds – the Screen Actors Guild (SAG), Screen Writers Guild (SWG) and Screen Directors Guild (SDG) – and unions such as the International Alliance of Theatrical and Stage Employees (IATSE) and the Conference of Studio Unions (CSU). The guilds' formation was accompanied by strikes and jurisdictional disputes emerged between the rightwing IATSE which was connected to organised crime and the CSU, whose organisers had associations with the Hollywood Communist Party.

The political divisions in Hollywood intensified when rightwing activists established the Motion Picture Alliance for the Preservation of American Ideals to offset the perceived leftist bias within the guilds. Once the battle lines were drawn, a catalyst was required to make these divisions conspicuous. Thus, a fury of 'Red baiting' was unleashed in the 1946 CSU strike enabling the studios to crush the union. The fallout from the dispute provided the conditions for Washington's attack on Hollywood liberals, trade unionists and Communist Party members during the anti-Communist witch-hunts of the 1940s and 1950s. The divisions between those who did or did not testify in front of the House Un-American Activities Committee (HUAC) and the blacklist have underpinned Hollywood's attitude to politics to this day.

Since the blacklist, the 'above-the-line' (writers, directors, actors) screen guilds and the 'below-the-line' (crews, technicians, painters, carpenters) craft unions have concentrated on industrial rather than ideological matters. Chapter 6 demonstrates how contemporary labour issues have focused on disputes over residual fees and possessive credits. These issues further point to the changes in the studios' ownership as global media corporations have used foreign production centres to cut costs leading to a decline in the number of films being made in Hollywood. The guilds and unions have been concerned by the growth of runaway productions filmed in Canada, Australia and Eastern European states which offer cheaper locations, facilities and labour costs through devalued currencies, subsidies and tax incentives.

Another area of importance was the guilds' attempts to effect changes in the film studios' employment practices on diversity. The SAG has advocated equality, fair representation and inclusion since the negotiation of a non-discrimination clause in its 1963 Theatrical Agreement. However, for many minorities, Hollywood remains impenetrable and the National Association for the Advancement of Colored People (NAACP) has proposed greater equality for African-Americans in front of and behind the camera.

Finally, it is necessary to consider Hollywood's symbolic worth in US politics. In an age of mass media-led political communication, there has been a growth of star activism and a blurring of the distinction between celebrity and political behaviour. Stars' access to television coverage has led to them being considered legitimate representatives of causes within the political process. Moreover, close affiliations were established between Hollywood and political elites as campaign-funding became a centrifugal force in US politics.

Chapter 7 considers how politicians have been cultivated by Hollywood and the extent to which star activism has enabled celebrities to become politicians. Film executives such as the Music Corporation of America (MCA) chairman Lew Wasserman promoted gatherings to raise campaign funds. These close relationships have invariably been between the leaders of the Democratic Party and the Hollywood elites. For example, Wasserman and United Artists' chief Arthur Krim were invited by LBJ to sit on his Cabinet. However, it should be noted that shrewd industry players cultivated rightwing politicians to advance their interests.

Politicians have realised the worth of star support in appealing to the electorate. Roosevelt invited film celebrities to luncheons and birthday balls to enhance his standing. In modern US politics, such affiliations occurred in the presidencies of John F. Kennedy and Bill Clinton. In this way, stars are sought out to endorse candidates on campaign stops, organise inaugural events or participate in the electoral process.

Simultaneously, celebrity activists have a symbolic worth in US politics. A legacy of the witch-hunt was the creation of a liberal political consensus in modern Hollywood. Typically, stars have opposed wars and engaged in environmental activism, civil rights struggles and liberal causes. However, since 9/11, the centre-leftist sensibility in celebrity politics has been a source of conservative vilification as activists, such as Tim Robbins, Sean Penn and Susan Sarandon, have been damned over their attacks on the American justice system, support for pro-choice abortion rights and their doubts about President George W. Bush's 'realist' foreign policies.

Hollywood's paradoxical role in US politics has been exacerbated as celebrity and image have become greater forms of capital. Style has dominated over substance and stars have become politicians. During the era of the blacklist, Ronald Reagan was elected onto the SAG board and became a virulent anti-Communist. Reagan used his terms as SAG president (1947–52, 1959–60) to establish his leadership and communications skills. He attained the support of industry powerbrokers, notably the original MCA chairman, Jules Stein. Reagan's convictions reflected the values of individualism, family, community and Judeo-Christianity which underpinned his films. Ultimately, he became Governor of California and the President of the United States.

Most recently, Arnold Schwarzenegger campaigned for the Californian governorship during the 2003 recall vote. In contrast to Reagan who followed a more traditional route into politics, the 'Governator' used his stardom as his sole form of political capital. The use of fame in politics leads to questions about whether the electorate has been unduly influenced by the merging of imagery, glamour and ideology. Commentators argue that style has impoverished the rights of citizens and Hollywood's role in politics has been condemned.

It is the purpose of this volume to analyse, assess and explain the role of Hollywood in US political, cultural and social life. It will take a holistic approach to the material by touching on a variety of subjects, from the political economy of the industry to its internal politics, and from the labour rights won by the guilds to the use of film celebrities in campaigns. Looking at these issues, it seeks to understand how Hollywood has reflected and informed societal debates in the US. It asks why the American film industry has been celebrated and vilified by political elites in equal measure. Finally, the book surveys the historical and contemporary political trends associated with Hollywood, thereby contributing to readers' understanding of the industry's unique position in the American body politic.

Notes

1. The Hollywood film industry refers to the major studios which are owned by global media corporations and located in Los Angeles. It should be noted that a thriving independent sector has emerged since the 1990s and there are other film production centres in America.

2. There are many significant studies of the political and social content of film including Brian Neve (1992), *Film and Politics in America: A Social Tradition*, London and New York: Routledge.

1

'Trade Follows Film': The History of the US Film Trade from 1900 to 1950

Introduction

Throughout the first half of the 20th century, Washington became increasingly interested in the value of the American film industry both locally and internationally to the economy. As a result, the studios formed an alliance with the United States' (US) Department of Commerce, which supported Hollywood through its Bureau of Foreign and Domestic Commerce (BFDC). And American presidents, from Woodrow Wilson on, realised the economic and cultural worth of Hollywood not only as a vibrant national industry, but also in its international distribution of US film product.

For American governments there were many advantages in the international exploitation of film. At one level, the export of film product aided the balance of payments figures in the US economy. It was also appreciated by US governments that 'Trade follows film' (Woodrow Wilson) and films provided an international means through which to advertise products. The ideological worth of films became apparent to politicians when America entered World War I in 1917, as pictures were used to propagate the war effort and to project US values into occupied countries.

The realisation of the economic, political and ideological worth of the US film industry within governing circles established the context for the emergence of effective trade representation. In 1922, the major studios jointly backed the creation of the Motion Picture Producers and Distributors of America (MPPDA) which was headed by former Postmaster General Will H. Hays. While the body was established in response to those organisations campaigning for the state censorship of films (see Chapter 3), it proved to be a potent trade body by gaining the ear of government (Jarvie, 1992: 279). Such access would be useful, as the studios sought to maintain an iron grip over the distribution and exhibition of films in the North American and international marketplace. This was effected through block- and blind-bidding practices and the chain ownership of first-run movie theatres.

However, this cartelism sat uneasily with US principles of competition. From the 1920s, the Justice Department pursued a series of anti-trust investigations which culminated in the

dismantling of the studios' control over production, distribution and exhibition in the 1948
Paramount Decrees. Also, despite attaining its status as America's fifth largest business by
1929, the film industry was treated with suspicion by White Anglo-Saxon Protestant (WASP)
political elites because of the predominantly Jewish complexion of its talent base, ranging
from the moguls to the stars (Horne, 2001: 26).

This chapter will consider the contradictory history which emerged between Hollywood
and Washington from 1900 to 1950. It will focus on the economic and political factors that
allowed Hollywood to establish itself as the world's premier film industry, while its value to
American political elites was complicated by the industry's anti-competitive practices.

The characteristics of the Hollywood film industry: 1900 to 1948

From the 1910s to 1948, the US film industry was defined through the development of vertically integrated major film studios who controlled the production, distribution and exhibition of product both domestically and internationally. To supply cinemas with the requisite
amount of films, the studios employed 'Fordist' industrial practices in which a workforce held
on a series of long-term contracts produced features. They were run by moguls who controlled their domains from their front offices. Yet these showmen initially had to battle for
their ascendancy in the embryonic film industry.

ORIGINS

At its inception, the US cinema was dominated by the Edison Company's exclusivity over
film production through its patent on motion picture cameras. This control was extended by
the establishment of the Motion Pictures Patents Company (MPPC), known as the 'trust',
in 1909, wherein a patents pooling agreement was adopted between the major industry
players: Armat, Biograph, Edison and Vitagraph. Each MPPC member retained an exclusive
arrangement with the Patents Company concerning the use of film stock and cameras in
return for a royalty payment (Allen, 1976: 120–4). Exhibitors were also licensed projection
machinery for a fee.

The trust often employed violent goon squads to enforce its control of the patent. In particular, it tried to exclude the immigrant Jewish showmen who had seen opportunities for
profit in the film industry. In 1905, Pittsburgh-based vaudeville tycoon, Harry Davis, hap-
pened upon a profitable idea: the Nickelodeon. This was a tiny theatre made up of 199 seats,
which charged cinemagoers a nickel a time to watch a short, single-reel film. This simple
innovation spread throughout the immigrant, slum districts in the Eastern cities. It attracted
other Jewish entrepreneurs, such as Carl Laemmle, who set up his film exchange for distributors so audience demand could be catered for in 1906. By 1907, the number of film
exchanges had mushroomed to over one hundred across thirty-five cities.

However, with the establishment of the MPPC, both the small-time exhibitors and the
owners of the film exchanges were forced to sign a patent trust document or face a lawsuit.
They demonstrated their opposition when Laemmle employed advertising agent Robert
Cochrane to campaign against the trust through satirical cartoons in the trade press.
Furthermore, when the MPPC created its General Film Company to control the independent

film exchanges in 1910, it inadvertently forced distributors, including Laemmle, William Fox and Adolph Zukor, to establish a rival exchange and move into film production. These entrepreneurs stole audiences from the MPPC when Zukor produced, marketed and exhibited feature films, thereby superseding the trust companies who were still producing one-reelers. He reasoned that films shown in the comfort of a movie theatre would attract a wider range of American audiences (Kerrigan and Culking, 1999: 5–8).

In 1912 the MPPC lost a vital court case to the studio IMP, which was judged free to use non-patented movie cameras to film its productions. The trust was dismantled when the Supreme Court found in favour of the US government's anti-competitive suit against it in 1915. This was a significant victory for the showmen, who now included Samuel Goldfish (later Goldwyn), Louis B. Mayer, Marcus Loew and Jesse L. Lasky.

The court case was accompanied by the Jewish showmen's decision to relocate the production centre of US film from New York to the small farming community of Hollywood in Southern California to circumvent the influence of the trust in the first half of the 1910s. Their success inculcated in the embryonic studio chiefs the belief that a 'monopoly . . . was a terrible thing [unless] you had one of your own' (Puttnam, 1997: 73).

THE MOVE WEST TO HOLLYWOOD

The move to Hollywood occurred by accident when Samuel Goldwyn developed a partnership with his brother-in-law Jesse Lasky and Cecil B. De Mille to produce feature films for their Famous Players Company. The first production was *The Squaw Man* which was directed by De Mille in 1913. When seeking locations, De Mille looked at Flagstaff in Arizona, but deemed it unsuitable for his purposes. Having heard that several film crews had used California as a location, he moved the production to the Hollywood hills.

In the wake of De Mille, it became apparent to the infant film studios that the westward shift to Hollywood would have many advantages. First, the climate proved ideal for filming outdoors and meant costs could be kept to a minimum. Los Angeles' geographical basin, with its range of landscapes, provided the pioneers with ideal locations to shoot films. Second, the companies were attracted to Southern California due to the 'open shop' labour rules, meaning workers could be employed at half the rate of their New York counterparts (Sklar, 1975: 68). Third, for the immigrant entrepreneurs, the westward move held a tremendous symbolic value. The physical and intellectual remoteness of Los Angeles from the Eastern seaboard enabled them to bypass the traditional arbiters of American culture and taste (Puttnam, 1997: 79). Finally, the Hollywood farmland provided another vital resource for the fledgling industry – a vast amount of acreage for the new tycoons to establish a studio system.

THE STUDIO SYSTEM

In 1914 Carl Laemmle purchased a 230-acre ranch in the San Fernando Valley and on 15 March 1915 opened the first studio complex, entitled Universal City. This included a front office for the management and a backlot with several interior stages and outdoor sets. By the 1920s, four major studios with large backlots existed – Paramount (incorporating Famous

Players/Lasky), Metro–Goldwyn–Mayer (MGM), Warner Bros. and Radio-Keith-Orpheum (RKO), alongside smaller companies such as Universal, Columbia Pictures and United Artists.[1] In 1935, a further studio was added to the majors when Fox merged with Darryl F. Zanuck's Twentieth Century, to create 20th Century-Fox.

The classic studio system, which defined the US film industry from the 1920s to 1940s, followed a Fordist model of production in which a dedicated workforce made movies. Stars, writers, directors and technicians would be held on binding seven-year contracts. The Jewish entrepreneurs, showmen and risktakers who had established the US film industry, transformed themselves into moguls. The power of the front office was non-negotiable as the studio chiefs dominated their businesses and were only answerable to their holding companies on the Eastern seaboard.

The star system meant studios built up stars in their vehicles, which were easily marketable to home and international audiences, and placed them in recognisable genres (musicals, Westerns, gangster films, comedies and costume dramas). Each studio was known for a certain type of product. For instance, the poorer studios such as Universal and Columbia became associated with horror films and the work of directors such as Frank Capra respectively, while MGM's Louis B. Mayer boasted that his studio held on to more stars than there were in the heavens!

The other major factor to dramatically shape the studio system concerned the introduction of sound in films with Warner Bros.' production of *The Jazz Singer* in 1927. The change from silent to talking pictures had major ramifications for stars, technicians, directors, producers and moguls alike. Initially the revolution heightened costs and ruined the careers of such performers as John Gilbert and Vilma Banky whose voices were considered unsuitable. As the technology was improved, the system settled down but according to Jesse L. Lasky:

> . . . With many more craftsmen and auxiliary mechanical devices, less teamwork, more complex organisation, less pioneering spirit, more expense, less inspiration, more talent, less glamour, more predatory competition, less hospitality, more doing, less joy in doing . . . Hollywood would never be the same again (Lasky, 1957).

VERTICAL INTEGRATION: CONGLOMERATION BLOCK-BOOKING AND BLIND-BIDDING

The studios developed a monopolistic control of the production, distribution and exhibition of their features in cinemas across the US. This occurred when Zukor merged Famous Players and Lasky in 1916. He then renamed the conglomerate studio, Paramount, when it combined with a dozen other companies in 1917. Through this amalgamation, Zukor controlled the first vertically integrated motion picture studio, which produced over 100 feature films per annum. With this aggregate number of films, Zukor realised he could sell films to exhibitors in packages. This meant that when a cinema chain wanted to show an expensive A-picture, it would be required to purchase several inferior B-pictures.

Zukor originated the practice of block-booking, which guaranteed a market for even the most mediocre movie, as exhibitors had to buy all the films offered sight-unseen. Over time the practice became more sophisticated, as the blocks not only included features but short subjects, cartoons and newsreels. This mature form of block-booking, called full-line forcing, gave the studios a pre-sold market for their pictures, and kept the production departments working at capacity. Since the films were usually blocked before they were produced, theatre chains had to book movies on the barest of information provided by the distributor. This practice became known as blind-bidding and forced exhibitors to buy films knowing no more than the title, cast and tagline.

The studios insulated their profits by fixing admission prices, developing unfair runs and clearances of their films, and determining the pricing and purchasing arrangements to favour the movie chains that they owned. Again, Zukor was at the forefront of these developments, by buying out the pool of exhibitors and by developing a consortium which bought the first-run theatres in the downtown areas in major American cities. These cinemas were well appointed and the right size to showcase new productions at inflated prices.

FOREIGN MARKETS AND INTERNATIONAL TRADE

During the 1920s and 1930s, the costs of production escalated as the studios competed for audiences with more lavish movies. This led them to look beyond their shores to recoup this expenditure. At first, the income from exports remained marginal, however, by the end of the 1920s, it represented a significant percentage of the majors' profits.

The studios realised that, through the international distribution of product, they could dominate the rival film markets, such as Italy, Germany and France, which had competed with them before World War I (Thompson, 1985). The collapse of these industries because of the war meant the international competition was stymied. This was borne out by the increase in the US exports in Hollywood product from 36 to 159 million feet of film between 1915 and 1916, a year before America entered the war. Simultaneously, imports declined from 16 million feet of film before 1914 to 7 million feet by the mid-1920s (Miller *et al.*, 2001: 24). Other lucrative European markets such as the United Kingdom, where domestic production had been virtually annihilated by the mid-1920s, and regions including Latin America and Asia, were sought for fruitful exploitation.

To aid their development, the studios adapted their domestic, vertically integrated strategies on an international scale. Paramount moved into the chain ownership of cinemas across Canada in 1920, while Marcus Loew, the financial backer of MGM, took over the Gaumont cinema chain in France through the formation of Gaumont-Metro-Goldwyn (GMG) (Segrave, 1997: 27). By 1924, Paramount had 100 offices worldwide and controlled 125 distribution branches in seventy countries (ibid.: 28).

Meanwhile, Universal attempted to buy into the cash-strapped German film conglomerate UFA in 1925, which owned 150 cinemas. However, the deal was thwarted by Paramount and MGM who set up a joint company with UFA to guarantee that they would distribute a sizeable number of films per annum to the German market. In return, they agreed to distribute ten German films on a yearly basis as long as they were deemed 'suitable for American taste' (ibid.: 35). Yet, UFA's hopes were quickly dashed as Paramount and MGM exported 250 films to Germany, while only importing five German films in the first year of the agreement.

In the 1920s, the studios benefited from films being silent, meaning there were no linguistic barriers. However, in the sound era, the common international market appeared to have broken down. For a period of time, Hollywood made foreign-language versions of their films, such as a Spanish version of *Dracula* (1936), to appeal to international markets. This trend was complimented by the use of dubbing tracks when sound equipment became more sophisticated and the introduction of subtitles for films distributed abroad. As the Hollywood companies held a dominant international position, by 1926 they were sufficiently financed and placed to exploit sound technology. They could buy the requisite patents to fight foreign-rights holders, thereby standardising sound systems and ensuring English became the accepted language within the American mass media (Jarvie, 1992: 7).

FOREIGN RESISTANCE TO HOLLYWOOD

Unsurprisingly, there was resistance to the US film industry's international dominance from several countries who protected their film industries through tariffs and trade embargoes. For instance, the British government passed a quota law in 1927, determining a specific number of domestically produced films to be shown on UK screens. France followed by imposing sanctions in response to French films' failure to crack open the American film market. This had been due to what the authorities believed to be the discriminatory nature of the US marketplace (Ulff-Moller, 2001: 48). Therefore, the majors faced a range of laws designed to stop their international growth.

There was also a growing criticism concerning Hollywood's stereotyping of other cultures. For instance, Miguel Cruchaga Tocornal, the Chilean Ambassador to the US, complained at a dinner for the Associated Motion Picture Advertisers in 1927: 'Imagination in the production of moving pictures has clothed the men from other American countries with a mental and material garb which only belong in the property room of a wandering musical comedy' (Segrave, 1997: 54).

This dinner was attended by two figures who had proved pivotal in establishing the foreign dominance of the US film industry in the 1920s – Will H. Hays and Herbert Hoover. These 'modern' men shared the post-World War I corporatist conviction that business provided the moral foundation to society. To this end, they believed the US film industry and the governments' interest were one and the same (Jarvie, 1992: 282).

'Trade follows film': the Hollywood–Washington link between 1915 and 1950

From the 1920s to 1940s, Will Hays as the head of the studios' trade body, the Motion Picture Producers and Distributors of America (MPPDA) was an assiduous representative for Hollywood. He had been picked for his Presbyterian religious beliefs to offset the growing calls from often anti-Semitic constituencies for state censorship (see Chapter 3). Yet, his political connections, as a former chairman of the Republican National Committee and member of President Harding's cabinet, were priceless. This meant he formed strong ties with the Department of Commerce in the 1920s, for whom future President Hoover was the Secretary of State between 1920 and 1928.[2] Hays' lobbying benefited from the government's realisation that the distribution of Hollywood films abroad had many economic, cultural and ideological advantages for the US's international interests.

EARLY FORMS OF CONTACT

Initially, the relationship between Hollywood and Washington was confined to the 1915 Supreme Court's decisions against the MPPC trust and the Mutual case which determined that the First Amendment (governing freedom of speech) could not be used to protect a film's content (see Chapter 3). Otherwise there had been only sporadic contact between the two, owing to the political establishment's disinterest in Hollywood.

However, the first signs of an alliance between the industry's leaders and the political classes occurred when Carl Laemmle, largely for reasons of personal aggrandisement, contacted President Woodrow Wilson in 1915. In his letter of introduction, Laemmle suggested Wilson might speak directly to the public by being shown on screens across America. While Wilson declined the offer, he realised the populist opportunities afforded by the cinema. Subsequently he viewed Hollywood's latest feature, D. W. Griffith's groundbreaking and controversially racist *The Birth of a Nation* (1915). Wilson responded by commenting 'It's like writing history with lightning. My only regret is that it is all so terribly true' (Puttnam, 1997: 88–9). In that moment, he bestowed upon Hollywood an asset which had been elusive – respectability.

'It's like writing history with lighting': D.W. Griffith's *The Birth of a Nation*

WORLD WAR I
Propaganda and persuasion
A change in attitude became palpable within US governing circles, as the political value of cinema was understood when the US entered World War I. With Hollywood on its side, the government realised it held the means through which to disseminate a persuasive ideological message to the nation. In accordance with this realisation, the Hollywood film companies lobbied to support the war effort. William A. Brady, the president of the studios' trade body, the National Association of the Motion Picture Industry (NAMPI), commented 'the motion picture can be the most wonderful system for spreading the National Propaganda at little or no cost . . . [and] in two weeks to a month [it is possible] to place a message in every part of the civilised world' (ibid.: 90). In turn, Wilson proclaimed film 'has come to rank as the very highest medium for the dissemination of public intelligence and since it speaks a universal language it lends itself importantly to the presentation of America's plans and purposes' (ibid.: 91).

To mobilise public support for the war, Wilson established the Creel Committee on Public Information in 1916 (chaired by George Creel, a former journalist who had organised public speakers to provide patriotic messages between reel changes known as the 'Four Minute Men'). The committee spread Wilson's views on liberal democracy and turned 'the pacifist population into a hysterical, war-mongering population which wanted to destroy everything German' (Chomsky, 2002: 11–12). It established a film division in 1917 and commissioned a series of documentaries on American industry.

To co-ordinate links between the Creel Committee and the studios, bosses such as Zukor and Loew were assigned to government departments. This arrangement institutionalised the relations between Hollywood and Washington in a manner that would prove harmonious in successive administrations. From then on, for the American political establishment, films provided a potent set of economic goods and ideological tools through which to disseminate US values to the public (Puttnam, 1997: 90).

Economic opportunity
During the war, Hollywood's worth to the US's international trading position also became apparent. The State Department printed a general instruction to US consuls on 15 December 1916 stating officials should report on the number of theatres and film-supplying agencies and make recommendations to improve opportunities for US film manufacturers, not only with regard to film, but other accessories (Jarvie, 1992: 276). NAMPI mobilised the US Foreign Service to collect economic intelligence which would aid the studios' exploitation of foreign markets.

Through the collection of data, the industry streamlined a reliable supply of product to the war-torn countries. The importance of film to the US economy became clear in 1918 when the Wilson administration defined it as an 'essential business' and declared, 'the government, while it cannot create trade, can give to trade the environment in which it can develop' (Puttnam, 1997: 93). Yet, despite this accord between Hollywood and Washington, US trade officials remained concerned about: overseas restrictions on American films; organisation by foreign firms and government to promote locally made films at home and abroad;

and disarray and lack of cooperation between the US motion picture industry and the federal government (Jarvie, 1992: 279).

TRADE REPRESENTATION: THE FORMATION OF THE MOTION PICTURE PRODUCERS AND DISTRIBUTORS OF AMERICA (MPPDA)

Early attempts to strengthen the relationship between the political classes and the studios had been brokered by NAMPI, the industry's first trade body set up in 1916. However, NAMPI had provided insufficient leadership to withstand the Volstedt Act's attacks on the movie industry which were designed to facilitate federal regulation on film content. Furthermore, NAMPI was ineffective owing to its dependence on the powerful companies it represented as it held no control over them. Instead, the US film industry required a trade body founded on 'persons familiar with politics, business, and law but not themselves former or present employees of the major members of the organisation' (ibid.: 286). By establishing the MPPDA in 1922, the studios demonstrated their adherence to the corporatist principles of free enterprise and transparency which had predominated in contemporary business practice (ibid.: 285).

The choice of Hays as president of the MPPDA was crucial in this process. He felt that, for Hollywood to achieve its true worth, it would be necessary to establish interlocking contracts between the association and the companies, and among the studios themselves. It was, however, made immediately clear that the organisation could not interfere with the internal affairs of its members. Similarly, the studios were told that they held no control over the MPPDA.

Even more tellingly, Hays was co-opted by Hollywood before the MPPDA had been established and the moguls gave him *carte blanche* to shape the body's structure. They had been impressed by Hays' administrative capacities when he turned around Harding's failing campaign in 1920, and reorganised the US Post Office between 1921and 1922. He had the managerial experience to forge an autonomous trade body and an appreciation of those public relations strategies required to benefit the industry.

The MPPDA consisted of twenty-three members, from which all exhibitors were excluded, and power rested with its inclusion of the studio chiefs. Operating out of New York, it was responsible for the creation of standard contracts, the enforcement of self-censorship rulings and for advocating Hollywood's interests to government. To administer its responsibilities, ten departments were created including Public Relations and the Foreign Relations Committee.[3]

THE MPPDA AND FOREIGN MARKETS

From 1922 to 1941, Frederick L. Herron chaired the MPPDA's Foreign Relations Committee, which would become the International Department (Segrave, 1997: 21). It was responsible for maintaining contacts with the studios' international branches, thereby placing pressure on those foreign officials who dealt with film imports. The committee co-ordinated with the State Department to ensure that American diplomatic attachés understood the economic and ideological value of film.

Hays made his first trip to Europe in 1923 as a goodwill ambassador for US film in what he would describe as a 'quasi-government representative' capacity (Jarvie, 1992: 295). His overseas policy within foreign markets was defined by a commercial, rather than cultural, view of film. It had two main planks: the removal of any foreign impediments to US films abroad; and the removal of any impediments to foreign films within the US marketplace.

The MPPDA denounced foreign quotas and tariffs on the grounds of free trade. It sought to remove such barriers through a covert form of persuasion. The association endorsed a foreign country's right to establish a profitable film sector and would provide a percentage of the studios' overseas profits to support the indigenous industry. This form of cooperation often led to foreign ministries relaxing tariffs on US films to aid a perceived benefactor. Hays' tacit strategies invariably provided the MPPDA representatives with the leverage to push for the further removal of trade restrictions. However, when all else failed, he utilised his relations with the Congress, the presidential administration and the Departments of State and Commerce, to pressure the international governments to open their film markets.

With regard to the second plank, the free flow of foreign films within the domestic market, the case was less clear. Although the studios did not lobby for the imposition of high tariffs or quotas, the US film market was not open to competitors as few foreign films were

Hollywood's Movie Czar: Will Hays and the studio executives

distributed in America. The exclusionary policy resulted less from government intransigence than from the dynamics of supply-and-demand in the American film market which reflected the studios' control over the aggregated output of films.

Therefore, in creating the MPPDA, the US film industry's international development was as strong an imperative as the staving off of federal censorship. Moreover, a common thread existed between the association's establishment of the Production Code and its support for Hollywood's international interests:

> Just as the American industry had to persuade its domestic audience that its products were harm-less and morally sound, its domination of the markets of the world depended at least in part on its ability to convince its foreign customers that its output was inoffensive and ideologically neutral (Vasey, 1997: 5–8).

Over the following decade, Hays convinced government officials 'trade followed film' by claiming motion pictures could globally advertise American products. The MPPDA would often cite the statistic that, for every foot of film sent abroad, a dollar's worth of product would be exported (Segrave, 1997: 59). This understanding helped it to form a strong alliance with the federal government in seeking to remove restrictions. Thus the studios, by appointing Hays, had achieved their strategic goal in which: 'The interlock between government and the film industry became almost seamless. At times it would be hard to tell where one stopped and the other started' (ibid.: 23).

A MUTUAL RELATIONSHIP: THE MPPDA AND THE DEPARTMENT OF COMMERCE

For Hollywood, the US government's support in removing foreign tariffs allowed it to become an international industry. For Washington, Hollywood films would advertise US products and cultural values within the world marketplace. The MPPDA was aided by the Republican administrations' (1921 to 1932) decision to keep clear of any direct form of foreign intervention. Instead, these isolationists employed the US's industrial might, along-side its mass culture, to seek an international political consensus to maintain peace and formulate a new sphere of influence through economic power and cultural expression.

Throughout the 1920s, the Department of Commerce promoted US films abroad, most especially when Herbert Hoover led it from 1921 to 1928. His overarching goals were: waste elimination, the collection and distribution of statistical material, and the expansion of foreign trade (Jarvie, 1992: 282). Thus he increased the power of the Bureau of Foreign and Domestic Commerce (BFDC), headed by Julius Klein and responsible for film, by quadru-pling its staff and expanding the number of foreign offices from twenty-three in 1921 to fifty-eight in 1927. In a 1924 circular addressed to foreign commerce attachés, signed by Warren L. Hoagland, chief of the Specialties Division, the BFDC contended:

> Our services to [the film] industry should be effective and we should make a special point of keep-ing it posted on all developments affecting it throughout the world. This is desirable because of the great importance of the industry, as well as by reason of the high esteem and appreciation in which the Bureau and its efforts are held by this organisation (Jarvie, 1992: 309).

In 1924, Klein and Hoagland appointed Clarence Jackson North to direct the bureau's assistance to Hollywood. Although North was a career bureaucrat with no experience of film, he demonstrated an eagerness to promote the industry abroad. The agency provided the MPPDA with fact-gathering facilities from over 400 consular officials attached to the State Department. In turn the MPPDA reciprocated by providing statistical data for North's 1925 survey of the US film industry. From this review, North created an extensive system for disseminating trade figures within comprehensive commerce reports and foreign trade bulletins.

The relationship between the BFDC and the MPPDA became so strong that by 1926, North extolled the virtues of American films which, through their exportation of US ideals and cultural values, were contributing to a subtle 'Americanisation' of other countries (Bjork, 2000: 2). And 1926 proved to be a crucial year in extending the cosy relationship between Hollywood and Washington when Congress approved $15,000 for the BFDC to establish a small motion picture division on 1 July to be headed by North and Nathan D. Golden.

The division would remain in place over the following twenty years, although its position was often subject to budgetary cuts, sometimes leading to its amalgamation with other divisions, to be followed by its reappearance in healthier times. However, in its 1926 decision to appoint George Canty, who had been a congressional aide, a State Department employee and a journalist for the motion picture trade press, the division indicated how a shift had occurred in the BFDC's perception of its position *vis-à-vis* the US film industry.

On one level, Canty had the experience to secure detailed statistics concerning the industry. More importantly, he had been mandated to 'uncover the official source of agitation against American films and to do what he could to minimise its effects' (Klein, 1926) when the Austrian commerce ministry proposed quota legislation to protect its film industry. In appointing Canty to fulfil this agenda, the BFDC demonstrated its preoccupation with pressurising foreign chanceries to remove quotas or restrictions. Canty and North came to understand that they were no longer aides to Hollywood but had become industry leaders. To succeed, they believed, 'it was essential for the American film industry to present a united front in negotiations with European governments, acting in effect as a cartel' (Bjork, 2000: 5–6).

THE CREATION OF THE HOLLYWOOD CARTEL AND ITS INTERNATIONAL POWER

The BFDC's advocacy of a cartel coincided with Hays' belief that the studios must provide a united front to establish a coherent approach to film trade. However, the MPPDA faced many difficulties in achieving industry consensus as the studios saw themselves as competitors in their domestic and foreign markets (Gomery, 1986: 14). In attempting to forge a common position for Hollywood, the MPPDA not only battled with the studios, but incurred the wrath of the BFDC officials.

These differences in approach became conspicuous when the trade body and the government agency sought to create a unified response to the 1927 British Cinematographic Act which enforced quotas for UK film product (Jarvie, 1992: 312–18). The BFDC felt the MPPDA had failed to convince the studios to reform their commercial practices. Eventually, when other European states such as Germany and France pursued more restrictive forms of legislation and with sound films cutting off lucrative markets:

it hardly made sense for the industry to be divided against itself and for the trade organisation to stand in rivalry to government officials charged with assisting them . . . Government and the industry needed to work together in facing attempts to restructure the market (ibid.: 320).

In the late 1920s, the BFDC provided a tacit leadership to the Hollywood studios without appearing to do so. On several occasions, for example, it recommended that the Hollywood studios responded to quota legislation 'by ceasing to distribute any films in countries with restrictions, a threat that was often effective because of the wide popularity American films enjoyed with European audiences and cinema owners' (Bjork, 2000: 5–6). The BFDC also ensured that the MPPDA's calls for a united response to foreign trade would achieve universal acceptance and moulded the association so it would become the fulcrum for co-ordinating the studios' interests.

Consequently, Hays took a more active role in leading MPPDA delegations to national ministries. This began in 1928 when he successfully negotiated with the French government for the removal of internal legislation to enforce exports. Subsequently, the MPPDA sought the removal or reduction of those restrictions which had been applied within Germany, Canada and the UK.

Another contributor to the MPPDA's accession to industrial leadership was Horace Villard, an official in the State Department's Office of Economic Adviser. He drafted several trade memos in 1929 which commented on how the foreign governments' restrictions had been facilitated by the studios' incoherent response to international trading. To rectify this situation, Villard proposed:

- The formation of a foreign arm for the MPPDA to study world markets and regulate overseas distribution by means of internal agreements within the companies and external agreements with the foreign states.
- A review board to pass on the social, cultural and racial suitability of a film for export.
- The development of a common policy on overseas investment and on measures taken against unfair or arbitrary discrimination (Jarvie, 1997: 324).

Villard's recommendations indicated that he was not completely versed with the organisational structures governing the industry. For instance, the MPPDA already had a Foreign Relations Committee. Yet his memos provided a guideline to the association on how it could unify the industry to enhance foreign trade. His intervention demonstrated how Hollywood had secured another ally in the State Department. Subsequently, on 29 March 1929, it issued instructions to the US ambassadors to France, Germany, Italy, Austria, Czechoslovakia and Spain to distribute notes to these countries' chanceries stressing that the restrictions on US film exports were undermining a vital American resource.

THE MPPDA AND THE US GOVERNMENT IN THE 1930S AND 1940S
Despite a change from Hoover's corporatist values to Franklin D. Roosevelt's New Deal Keynesian economic policies in the 1930s, the Republican Hays, in a difficult decade for the

industry because of the Depression, forged successful relations with the Democrat administration. The federal government continued to support the MPPDA's calls for the removal of
trade restrictions on US film exports and gained a vocal supporter in the Secretary of
Commerce, Cordell Hull.

More crucially, the Roosevelt administration's state planning through the 1933 National
Industrial Recovery Act (NIRA) actually enhanced rather than diminished the majors'
monopolistic controls at the expense of small exhibitors and producers. In exchange for a
government-approved code, each industrial sector was exempted from prosecution under
anti-trust rulings, to boost the failing national economy. The MPPDA took advantage of the
NIRA ruling by reviving the studios' monopoly controls and the government approved the
motion picture code in November 1933:

> Instead of the informal collusion which had existed throughout the 1920s, open and explicit collu-
> sion and exploitation took place, free from any threat of anti-trust action. This was a strong action
> by the state which increased the profits of the movie monopolists and guaranteed strict barriers
> to entry, at a point of the most severe economic downturn of the 20th century. Moreover, this
> analysis of the NIRA hardly scratches the surface of state-film industry interaction. We know little,
> for example, about tax laws, or special tariffs imposed by the state (Gomery, 2005a: 170).

To gain support for the US's entrance into World War II, Roosevelt agreed to financial
control exemptions for the studios' accounts in return for the production of anti-German
movies. This led to the extra-legal peculiarities that still affect the majors' finances to this day
(Gems, 2005: 8).

THE REPLACEMENT OF HAYS BY ERIC JOHNSTON

In 1945 Eric Johnston replaced Hays as president of the MPPDA. Like Hays, Johnston, a
one-time door-to-door salesman of vacuum cleaners, came from traditional American stock
and had strong ties with the US government.[4] He was an ardent anti-Communist and supported the House Un-American Activities Committee (HUAC) investigations in the second
half of the decade. Johnston continued to pursue Hays' foreign policies in seeking to open
up international markets and maintained a close relationship with the power brokers in the
US government (Segrave, 1997: 144–5).

By the time of Johnston's appointment, the MPPDA's position within Washington was
secure. Its status had been enhanced by Hollywood's production of voluminous amounts of
propaganda and entertainment to raise morale in World War II (Koppes and Black, 1977:
87–105). It also became apparent to the MPPDA that the key institution to be cultivated in
the US government was no longer the Department of Commerce but the State Department:

> Economic intelligence was a far less problematic matter than orchestrating the full majesty of the
> newly powerful United States in behalf of its loyal and selfless motion picture industry. The industry
> felt that it cooperated with alacrity in government schemes . . . and through its War Activities
> Committee . . . had acted as good corporate citizens. The industry hoped to spend the credit thus
> built up on avoiding the restoration of the restrictive pre-war trading situation (Jarvie, 1992: 375).

The association's efforts led to A. A. Berle, Assistant Secretary of State, circulating a letter, 'American Motion Pictures in the Post-War World', to all diplomatic posts on 22 February 1944. This declared to US foreign staffers that they should ensure there would be an unrestricted distribution of US films within the defeated states in the post-war period (Guback, 1976: 249; Jarvie, 1998: 37). Simultaneously, the chief of the motion picture section of the US government's War Production Board urged the MPPDA to establish a permanent organisation to represent the industry's international interests after the war. Therefore on 5 June 1945, Johnston divided the association into two bodies, the Motion Picture Association of America (MPAA) for domestic concerns, and the Motion Pictures Export Association of America (MPEAA) for foreign affairs (Guback, 1976: 254; Jarvie, 1998: 227).

THE MOTION PICTURES EXPORT ASSOCIATION OF AMERICA (MPEAA)

As the studios' sole export agency, the MPEAA enforced the power of the cartel by coordinating the majors' commercial interests abroad. To this end, it received support from the Truman administration in the 1947 General Agreement on Tariffs and Trade (GATT) negotiations. In particular, the State Department took aboard Johnston's suggestions to play down the issues of national sovereignty relating to films and consider them like any other export. This remains official US policy for motion pictures in foreign markets (Gomery, 2005a: 181)

Simultaneously, the MPEAA was referred to as the 'little State Department' as its methods were so in line with the US government's propagandist aims in the Cold War (Segrave, 1997: 144). Truman viewed films as being a crucial weapon for re-educating the peoples of Germany, Italy and elsewhere about the virtues of democracy, and about American democracy in particular (Puttnam, 1997: 213). This offensive in creating 'a world-wide Marshall plan in the field of ideas' (ibid.: 213) was reflected in the MPEAA's choice of personnel, such as Frank McCarthy, its representative in Paris, who had been General George Marshall's aide and a former assistant to the Secretary of State (ibid.: 203).

These principles tied in with the aggressively expansionist mood which had taken root in the US film industry. The Allied victory had reopened markets that had been denied to US distributors since the 1930s (ibid.: 203). The interplay between politics and commerce not only encouraged the studios' profitability within foreign territories, but enabled them to become missionaries of American democracy and free enterprise. To Spyros Skouras, president of 20th Century-Fox:

> . . . it [was] a solemn responsibility of our industry to increase motion picture outlets throughout the free world because it has been shown that no medium can play a greater part than the motion picture in indoctrinating people into the free way of life and instilling in them a compelling desire for freedom and hope for a brighter future. Therefore, we as an industry can play an infinitely important part in the worldwide ideological struggle for the minds of men and confound the Communist propagandists (Skouras, 1953).

HOLLYWOOD SEEKS TO DOMINATE THE POST-WAR EUROPEAN FILM MARKETS

The MPEAA oversaw the dismantling of the Axis film industries and ensured the defeated countries became open to US film exports. Moreover, as the studios had granted it an exclusive licence to distribute their films in thirteen foreign areas, the MPEAA recaptured lost territories for the industry by releasing a huge backlog of pictures (Balio, 1976: 325; Guback, 1976: 255). For instance, in Germany, until mid-1946, the studios had only been able to release forty-three features. In the following years, the MPEAA increased the number of releases so the figure stood at 225 films per annum in 1951 (Guback, 1976: 266).

In Italy, it faced little resistance in the immediate aftermath of the war as the Italian government had dismantled the protectionist legislation that had kept Hollywood at bay. However, in 1949, after a major protest by industry workers in Rome, Guilio Andreotti, the minister responsible for the cinema trade, passed a new law restricting imports and providing loans for production. The Italian government had not only been concerned about the effects of US films on the home industry but also about their impact on cultural values. These difficulties became more conspicuous in Britain and France.

In the UK, a full-scale trade war occurred when the British cinema chain Rank boycotted American films in an attempt to allow its productions, such as Laurence Olivier's *Henry V* (1944), to seize control of the market. In March 1948, the boycott ended when Harold Wilson, the president of the Board of Trade, and the MPPDA president Johnston and Allen Dulles (later head of the CIA) hammered out a compromise to allow the studios to remit at least $17 million per annum back home (Puttnam, 1997: 209). In the wake of this acrimonious deal, the UK studios became wholly reliant on the US majors who employed their blocked currency to finance the production activity in Britain.

In France, an agreement was signed on 26 May 1946 between a special envoy of the French government, Leon Blum, and the US Secretary of State James F. Byrnes concerning American aid for post-war recovery. In this document, a brief set of paragraphs agreed to remove the restrictions governing US film imports to France. This section of the Blum–Byrnes negotiation angered many members of the French political and cultural establishment (Ulff-Moller, 2001: 146). It led to a major debate in parliament in which the 550 deputies voted to protect the fragile French cinema and restrict US film exports and interests in France's exhibition chains (Jeancolas, 1998: 47–50). The hostilities led to the partial nationalisation of French cinema under the Centre National de la Cinématographie (CNC) which was created in October 1946.

The successive mobilisation of the French political elites led to the government's introduction and rigid enforcement of quotas and subsidies by the early 1950s (Ulff-Moller, 2001: 150–3). These measures not only indicated the extent to which France saw the protection of film in terms of economic value, but also demonstrated how it viewed its cinema as being a vital contributor to the national culture. The authorities perceived Hollywood films as representing an encroaching form of 'Americanisation', which should be resisted.

Hollywood cartelism and US anti-trust rulings

The MPEAA was established under the 1918 Webb-Pomerene Act, which allowed American businesses to create export agencies whose activities, such as blind-bidding and block-booking, would normally violate US anti-trust laws.[5] However, while the government sup-

ported the US film cartel abroad, the studios' anti-competitive dominance in the home marketplace raised questions about their practices in the Justice Department and the Federal Trade
Commission (FTC). From the 1920s, in a contradictory trend that would also define Hollywood's relationship with the US government, the major studios were subject to investigation
because of their vertically integrated control over domestic production, distribution and exhibition of motion pictures. Ultimately, this led to Paramount, the mightiest vertically integrated
company, being taken to the Supreme Court in May 1948 (Puttnam, 1997: 186–7).

Anti-trust laws and the Hollywood cartel: The FTC investigations

US anti-trust rulings are contained in the 1890 Sherman Act, 1914 Clayton Act and the 1914
Federal Trade Commission Act. The Sherman Act was established to outlaw every contract
or combination that sought, in the form of a trust or conspiracy, to restrain trade or commerce among US states or with foreign nations. It is divided into two parts. In section one,
it proscribes all conspiracies and agreements that unreasonably stem trade. In section two, it
prohibits any form of monopolisation or attempts to monopolise, as well as conspiracies to
monopolise. The Clayton Act amended the Sherman Act by prohibiting price discrimination, exclusive contracts and anti-competitive mergers. In the Federal Trade Commission
Act, which may only be enforced by the FTC, all unfair methods of competition are declared
illegal.

Owing to their dominance in the production, distribution and exhibition of films, the
Justice Department and the FTC believed that the major Hollywood studios had violated the
anti-trust laws. In 1921, the FTC filed its first suit against the film companies concerning
the block-booking and blind-bidding distribution practices established by Zukor when he
formed a consortium under the umbrella of Paramount Studios. These methods for ensuring profit were followed by the other majors to '[make] it difficult for small and independent producers or distributors of films to enter into or remain in the moving picture industry
or market' (Borneman, 1976: 333).

Concurrently, Hollywood's control of the first-run movie chains came under the spotlight. During the trial the majors argued that, as they only owned a small fraction of the
nation's movie theatres, they could not enforce a monopoly. While this was strictly true, it
did not take into account their control of the distribution and licensing of motion pictures
across second-, third- or nth-run chains. However, it proved to be a strong enough defence
to undermine the prosecution as no monopoly or conspiracy to monopoly could be proven
(ibid.: 335). Following the 1921 trial, the FTC took the Hollywood studios to court in 1928
and in 1930, they were found guilty of monopolisation. However, the effects of the decision
were nullified by the imposition of the NIRA motion picture code between the majors, who
pleaded their poverty in the Depression, and the Roosevelt administration.

The US Justice Department versus Paramount 1938 to 1945

During the 1930s, the MPPDA fought the Justice Department and the FTC to preserve the
studios' dominance (Maltby, 1995: 66). The studios were aided by the Roosevelt administration's demand for economic stability and the NIRA-approved motion picture code pre-

served the oligopolistic interests of the major studios. However, New Deal attitudes to trusts and corporations swung 180 degrees when the Supreme Court declared the National Recovery Administration (NRA) to be unconstitutional on 27 May 1935, better known as 'Black Monday'. Previously, Roosevelt had seen the cartels as a necessary evil for economic recovery. Conversely, with the collapse of the NRA, the administration's attitude was transformed from acceptance to hostility.

Therefore, the pugnacious Thurman Arnold, head of the Justice Department anti-trust division, brought a further suit on 20 July 1938 against the studios in the US versus Paramount case. This included twenty-eight separate offences, paired with the principal objective to abolish all monopolistic practices in the film industry by divorcing the theatrical chains from the production and distribution of motion pictures. Arnold called for a permanent injunction, the appointment of trustees and a court order to cancel those contracts violating the principles of fair competition.

In March 1939, the studios tried to appease Arnold by establishing a new Trade Practice Code. However, this was declared illegal in June 1940 and the anti-trust trial began in earnest. Over the course of the following eight years, the case collapsed on several occasions, for instance when Roosevelt allowed the moguls to sign a consent decree in 1940 and then the Hollywood companies convinced the investigators to postpone the prosecution because of their perilous finances. When Arnold was appointed as an appeals judge in 1944, the studios even believed the suit might be forgotten.

Yet, in spite of these hopes, assistant Attorney-General Robert L. Wright reopened the case at the New York District Court on 8 October 1945 after the majors had enjoyed a huge box-office bonanza during the war. Owing to their enhanced profits, the studios could no longer argue that their finances were unstable to stave off investigation.

THE 1946 NEW YORK EQUITY RULING

The prosecution presented over 300 documents in the prima-facie case against the studios' monopoly in distribution and for the divorcement of Hollywood's theatrical chains from their production and distribution bases. The trial wrapped in January 1946. However, the New York equity ruling, which was handed down in June 1946, by the three District Court judges, Henry W. Goddard, Augustus N. Hand and John Bright, surprised both sides.

The Hollywood studios, including the Little Three (Universal, Columbia, United Artists), were judged guilty of conspiring to restrain trade. The court argued the combined copyright ownership of two or more films through block-booking threatened free trade and was illegal. However, it permitted the studios to retain control over their own theatre chains. Vertical integration was not illegal, rather the theatrical pooling of films, wherein two competing theatre chains combined for mutual advantage, was outlawed. So the court ordered the studios to dismantle their theatre pools, while allowing them to keep their interests in the large cinema circuits. The judgment concluded that by controlling a film's exhibition, as well as its production and distribution, 'none of the defendants [had] monopolised . . . to restrain trade or commerce in any part of the business of producing motion pictures' (Borneman, 1976: 340).

Instead, it contended the divorce of the theatres from the studios might lead to the Hollywood companies being replaced by new owners who would perpetuate even greater territorial monopolies. The court's solution was competitive bidding, whereby the studios would accept the auction price from 'the highest responsible bidder'. The distributors would be forbidden from discriminating against any theatre and were required to sell each film without the semblance of block-booking.

For the studios, the District Court's decision to find against the divorcement was met with some relief as the cinema chains accounted for 93 per cent of their investment in comparison to the 5 per cent in production. Yet they contended that, as the judgment had only named the main studios (the Big Five and the Little Three), rather than B-picture production companies such as Republic and Monograph, its applicability to the whole of the industry was disputable. More importantly, the majors had another reason to fear the implications of the ruling, as there remained the possibility that an independent theatre owner might pursue a private litigation over their conspiracy to restrict trade:

> The decree, therefore, did not merely threaten them with a possible loss of income in the distant future, but put them in imminent danger of millions of dollars of damage claims stretching back through the whole period prescribed by the Statutes of Limitation (ibid.: 341).

For the independent exhibitors, who had sided with the government, the judgment was unacceptable. They argued that the decision had enhanced, rather than restricted, the studios' control over the theatre chains. For instance, under the ruling, if the majors owned less than 95 per cent of a theatre, they were not required to divest their interests. Instead, they could use their partial ownership to petition for the rights to acquire the whole of the theatre. Also, with regard to the auction to buy rights to exhibit films, the independents feared the distributors might enforce a hike in the costs of the film rental price. As the decision had been unsatisfactory to all parties, the majors, the independent exhibitors and the Justice Department launched a series of appeals and counter-appeals which would be presented to the highest court in the land – the Supreme Court.

THE 1948 SUPREME COURT CASE AND THE PARAMOUNT DECREES

The Paramount case appeared before the Supreme Court on 9 February 1948. The US Attorney-General Tom C. Clark sought to prove the divorcement would halt the Big Five's monopoly of the film industry. He contended that, in the 92 US cities with a population of 100,000 or more, the studio-owned theatre chains held domination in all but four. Moreover, over one-third of all American cities had no independent theatres. Conversely, the majors could only argue that, by dismantling their trade practices, the court would undermine the service they provided in presenting the best pictures at the lowest prices to the largest number of customers (ibid.: 344).

When the Supreme Court's Chief Justice William O. Douglas handed down the ruling on 4 May 1948, the studios were found guilty of violating anti-trust laws. Instead of pursuing the New York ruling, the Court's 'Nine Old Men' interpreted the principle of trade restriction as referring to the *effect* on, rather than the *intent* to, output. Therefore, they threw out the six key issues of the District Court's ruling – theatre divestiture, joint ownership of the theatres, franchises, cross-licensing, auction bidding and arbitration. To this end, the Supreme Court ruled 'so far as the five majors are concerned . . . the conspiracy had monopoly on exhibition as one of its goals' (Puttnam, 1997: 216–17).

The Paramount Decrees prohibited the studios from owning exhibition as well production and distribution businesses. They also abolished the practice of block-booking, as all films would henceforth be sold on an individual basis. This occurred through the establishment of three rules, which were designed to ensure that competition in the exhibition sector was open and transparent:

- There should be no agreement on pricing among exhibitors or among distributors.
- Distributors should license films for exhibition on the merits of each individual cinema without regard to its affiliated cinemas.
- The right to show a film should not be conditional on agreement to show one or more other films.

In addition, the majors were ordered to terminate all their pooling arrangements and joint interests in the theatres which belonged to one another and to other exhibitors. Finally, the Supreme Court rejected the competitive bidding mandate as it felt this would play into the hands of the buyer with the 'longest purse' (Balio, 1976: 317).

THE IMPACT OF THE PARAMOUNT DECREES ON HOLLYWOOD

Almost immediately, Howard Hughes, the owner of RKO, announced the studio would comply with the Supreme Court's decision by divorcing its theatrical chain from its production base. The RKO consent decree was signed on 8 November 1948 and the company was split into RKO Pictures Corporation, in which Hughes retained a controlling interest, and the RKO Theatres Corporation, which was sold. For Hughes, his break with the rest of Hollywood made perfect sense. RKO was by far the weakest company among the majors and as the other companies would be forced to divest their interests, he believed his company could achieve parity with the more powerful motion picture studios.

With RKO providing the precedent for divorcement, the trial of the remaining theatre-owning studios was set for April 1949. In anticipation of an expensive and futile battle, the mighty Paramount was the next studio to submit to divorcement. It had felt the burden of the impending legislation looming over its profits and preferred to voluntarily divest its theatrical interests than submit to a court-directed liquidation. Paramount entered into its divorcement decree with the Justice Department on 25 February 1949.

Conversely, Warner Bros., MGM and 20th Century-Fox decided to fight on. Only a few hours after Paramount's capitulation, Harry Warner stated he would 'not give up [the] theatres without a court fight. We have taken years to accumulate the company assets we have, and we will fight to hold them' (Warner, 1948). The Loews cinema circuit similarly refused to sell off MGM and reminded the Justice Department that, while the Supreme Court outlawed block-booking, it had not made vertical integration illegal. Twentieth Century-Fox also protested disintegration and offered to eliminate its more notorious regional exhibition monopolies, if the Attorney-General would regulate rather than demand that the studio sell its entire chain.

The government rebuffed the calls for clemency and a decisive blow occurred when the Federal Statutory Court approved both decrees on 25 July 1949. This left the remaining majors with no choice but to gradually dismantle their interests in the theatre chains. By 1954, RKO, Paramount, Warners and 20th Century-Fox had distributed their stock to shareholders in new, separate exhibition subsidiaries. However, Loews failed to achieve divorcement until 1959, due to a $30 million debt, whose burden it was required to divide between MGM and the new theatre chain (Conant, 1976: 347).

The divestiture proved effective as the producer–distributors were kept at an arm's length from their former circuits. For instance, in 1951, the Paramount Theatre in New York started to book films from firms other than Paramount Pictures for extended first-run showings. The Paramount Decrees, therefore, marked a sea-change in business practices in the Hollywood studio system. In one moment, they removed a huge slice of income from the companies' coffers. Therefore the rulings contributed, along with the arrival of television, to a crisis in profitability which would irrecoverably change the US film industry in the 1950s and 1960s.

Conclusion

During the first fifty years of its history, the US film industry underwent a remarkable transition from being a sideshow attraction to becoming an internationally dominant business enterprise. The embryonic film production and exchange companies, run by immigrant risk-takers, had been transformed into vertically integrated studios which relentlessly sought profits through their control over the production, distribution and exhibition of motion pictures.

Although the studios remained resolutely private, the American government shaped their growth as Hollywood's financial sustainability was accommodated to suit contemporary political interests: 'For all its rhetoric of pure competition . . . the US government . . . devoted massive resources to generate and sustain its "private sector" film industry in the interests of ideology and money' (Miller et al., 2001: 25).

The MPPDA's president Will Hays brokered the relationship between Hollywood and Washington during the inter-war years. Hays realised the trade association provided a collective voice to represent the industry and gain the ear of government. He was in tune with the corporatist values which had predominated in the 1920s, and successfully forged links with the Department of Commerce. In turn, the Secretary of Commerce, Herbert Hoover, and the trade officials supported Hollywood by pursuing interventionist policies which were designed to remove foreign trade restrictions and increase overseas exports. The close affinity between the studios and the government was reflected by their adherence to the contradictory principles of free trade and protectionism to establish an international monopoly or film cartel. The affiliation between government and commerce was further institutionalised after World War II, when the MPEAA combined Hollywood's trading interests with a Cold Warrior's determination to promote US values abroad.

Hollywood was also the beneficiary of the two world wars, as US governments determined to enhance America's post-war dominance through business. This occurred despite foreign resistance, most prevalent in France, Italy and Germany, where rival cinema industries had been international competitors. Yet the disputes between the US and European film industries were not only to do with trade, but also do with culture. In particular, among European politicians and trade officials, fears abounded that Hollywood films would act as a Trojan horse for the Americanisation of indigenous cultural values.

Domestically, the US film industry faced a seismic upheaval in its domination of theatrical exhibition. The Justice Department's long-running battle with the majors eventually resulted in the Paramount Decrees and the divestiture of their interests in first-run cinema chains. This meant that, by the end of the 1940s, while it surged ahead abroad, Hollywood suffered a major setback at home. The Supreme Court's divorcement of production–distribution from exhibition and the outlawing of block-booking practices struck at the heart of the studio system. The ruling would have huge implications for the foundations of the industry and meant it would never be the same again.

Notes

1. United Artists was the only studio to exist outside the Hollywood mainstream. It was formed in 1919 by Mary Pickford, Douglas Fairbanks, Charlie Chaplin and D. W. Griffith to ensure their autonomy. The company was mainly responsible for the distribution of films made by independent producers.

2. Hoover enjoyed considerable support from the US film industry in his 1928 presidential campaign. He had close links with Louis B. Mayer who was the Chairman of the Southern California Republican Party. See Colin Shindler (1996), *Hollywood in Crisis: Cinema and American Society 1929–1939*, London and New York: Routledge: 60.

3. The MPPDA's headquarters were in New York (where the studio's financial holding companies operated) and Hays only visited Hollywood four times a year. It would later include offices in Washington and Hollywood. Its membership not only included the major studios, but the Eastman Kodak Company and the sound equipment firms, Western Electric and RCA. See Larry Ceplair and Steven Englund (2003), *The Inquisition in Hollywood: Politics in the Film Community, 1930–60*, Urbana and Chicago: University of Illinois Press.

4. Johnston would become President Eisenhower's special ambassadorial representative for the Middle East.

5. The 1918 Export Trade Act, better known as the Webb-Pomerene Act, was passed to enable US exporters to fight foreign cartels by permitting them to form export associations which contravened the Sherman Anti-trust Act. This legalisation of the film export cartel established the use of monopolistic practices abroad. See Jens Ulff-Moller (2001), *Hollywood's Film Wars with France: Film Trade Diplomacy and the Emergence of the French Film Quota Policy*, Rochester, NY: University of Rochester Press: 49.

2
The US Film Industry and Trade from 1950 to the Present Day

Introduction

The transformation of Hollywood into a global business occurred as multinational media conglomerates bought studios, agencies packaged films and high-concept movies became the norm. The industry has changed as it has engaged in the production of television shows for the syndicated networks and as new communication technologies have created ancillary markets for the theatrical distribution of films.

Washington has supported Hollywood because the copyright industries have a combined income of $400 billion per annum or 6 per cent of the US's total annual Gross Domestic Product (GDP). They are the largest exporters of American products and the surplus of profits produced by the international film trade has aided the US's $400 billion balance of payments deficit (Valenti, 2002). In 2001, the foreign sales and exports of the combined US copyright industries stood at an estimated $88.97 billion per annum (Richardson, 2003).[1] In turn, motion pictures advertise US goods and cultural values to an international audience. This understanding led to the Reagan administration of the 1980s removing the 1948 Paramount Decrees leading to a new phase of vertical integration between production, distribution and exhibition.

The Motion Picture Association of America (MPAA) has co-ordinated relations between Hollywood and Washington, and these links were cemented in 1966 when Jack Valenti, Lyndon Johnson's chief assistant, was appointed as the third president of the MPAA and its international arm, the MPEAA. The latter, renamed the Motion Picture Association (MPA) in 1994 to better represent its global ambitions, has offices in sixty nations, employing over 300 workers. It remains a 'little State Department' campaigning to remove foreign film quotas, subsidies and non-tariff barriers, with the support of the State Department and the Office of the United States Trade Representative. In response, international film associations have objected to Hollywood's dominance and this created a dispute with the European Union (EU) when the MPA pursued a course of liberalisation in the multilateral negotiations during the 1994 General Agreement on Tariffs and Trade (GATT) and the General Agreement on Trading Services (GATS/2000).

As communication technologies developed, the MPAA protected its members' intellectual property rights as technological reforms allow for the piracy of motion pictures. In particular, the association has positioned itself against Internet libertarians who, it believes, through the illegal downloading of feature films, will irrevocably harm the industry. The association called for controls on copyright infringements through the administration of harmonised Trade-related aspects of Intellectual Property Rights (TRIPs).

This chapter will outline the relationship between power, organisation and output in US film. It will consider how Hollywood's interests provide an entry point into debates about the impact of the US trade and cultural practices nationally and internationally. Finally, it will demonstrate the methods through which the MPAA has shaped the industry's political, social and economic interests.

Characteristics of the post-war Hollywood film business: 1950 to 1980

From 1950 to 1970, the studios declined, as they became an anachronism in America's post-war economic, political and social life. Hollywood's revival in the 1970s reflected the embracement of television, reforms in production, the rise of a new generation of filmmakers, agency packages, alternative types of marketing and distribution, the concept of the summer blockbuster and the support of American legislators through the introduction of tax breaks. These changes resulted in trends that continue to define US film:

> Film used to be an industry: its aim was to make films first, money second. . . . Though its object was to make profit . . . it was preoccupied by making as many films as possible. . . . [Subsequently] film [became] . . . a business. If studio land [was] more profitable as real estate than as back lot [it was sold]. If the accountants' analysis [showed] the profit margin [was] greater if . . . spent on one blockbuster . . . than it would be if spent on ten smaller films, then the blockbuster [would] be made (Monaco, 1979: 31).

THE DECLINE OF THE CLASSIC STUDIO SYSTEM

The divestment of the cinema chains meant revenues were removed from the industry. Yet the industry survived as the majors' distribution arms extracted extra rentals (the profits made by the distributors) from the independent exhibitors. Moreover, as distribution was a more reliable business than production, it made up for any shortfall in the studios' profits. This led to them pursuing monies from a film's release in home and overseas markets (Puttnam, 1997: 219). Further, the divorcement may have stemmed the studios' losses as they were spared from the collapse in exhibition which occurred when audiences were attracted away from cinemas by television.

However, television had a drastic effect on Hollywood production as there was an exponential decline in audiences from 1947 to 1957. The moguls tried to compete for audiences with innovations such as widescreen, CinemaScope spectacles, lavish costume dramas, musicals and the occasional novelty 3-D production. These attractions, however, failed to attract customers back to cinemas. In the resulting crisis of profitability, Howard Hughes sold RKO in 1955 and a short time later it was closed. The other majors, particularly MGM, Warners and 20th Century-Fox who had fought the Paramount Decrees, divested themselves of their backlots and their contracts with stars, character actors, writers, producers, directors and technicians.

For some, these changes were of great benefit. In the 1940s, Bette Davis had sued Jack Warner in the British courts to break out of the shackles of her contract. Similarly, in America, Olivia de Havilland's trial led to the abolition of the seven-year contract in 1944. Both had been advised by their agency, the Music Corporation of America (MCA), founded by optician Jules Stein, to pursue their rights. MCA's appearance in Hollywood affected the balance of power between the studios and the talent as it ruthlessly supported its clients' independence from the majors. Its top agent, Lew R. Wasserman, concluded a deal for James Stewart to appear in Universal's 1950 Western *Winchester '73*, in which the star gave up his fee to be paid a percentage of the film's box-office revenues. Stewart became a millionaire and others realised that by tying their earnings to a picture's profits they could increase their rewards.

The industry was hampered by the constraints of film content. While television provided audiences with groundbreaking dramas, Hollywood's movies remained lightweight. These restrictions occurred as films continued to be submitted to the Production Code Administration (PCA) for approval. Hollywood's reluctance to focus on political and adult subjects reflected the House Committee of UnAmerican Activities' (HUAC) attack upon it during the anti-Communist witch-hunts. The blacklist created an indirect form of censorship in which politically motivated or connected talents were removed from the industry (see Chapter 5).

FINANCIAL COLLAPSE

Hollywood remained under the control of the ageing generation of moguls whose choices proved disastrous. They were out of touch with a burgeoning youth market, which had expanded as baby-boomers reached maturity to embrace rock music, counter-cultural values, radical politics and a critical view of the establishment. Instead, Hollywood financed epics such as Fox's *Cleopatra* (1964), which cost $44 million and failed to recover its costs. It led to the sale of the backlot and when Darryl F. Zanuck returned as head of production, he realised the studio faced bankruptcy. In turning the studio around, he discovered it had the rights to *The Sound of Music* (1965) and the film was a spectacular success. This proved a double-edged sword, as the studios unwisely believed a market existed for family entertainments and they were left counting the costs of expensive, flop musicals including *Star* (1968), *Doctor Dolittle* (1967), *Hello Dolly* (1969), *Darling Lili* (1970) and *Paint Your Wagon* (1969).

Consequently, fewer films were produced, leading to fears that exploitation and pornographic films would become the staple product for US moviegoers. The studios were sold to transnational corporations. For example, Warners became a subsidiary of the Kinney Corporation, which had made its fortunes in car parks, Paramount was sold to the oil company Gulf and Western and United Artists became part of the insurance behemoth Transamerica. MGM, Hollywood's most glamorous studio, was bought by property magnate

Kirk Kerkorian, who used the brand for his casinos in Las Vegas, reducing film production and selling off the Culver City backlot.

From industry to business
LEW WASSERMAN, MCA AND TELEVISION PRODUCTION

Hollywood's rebirth occurred as new executives such as Lew Wasserman and Arthur Krim took control. They had one foot in the old system but realised the industry had to change. The studios had declined as they saw television as a competitor. MCA, led by Wasserman, embraced the medium as it realised Hollywood had the facilities to produce syndicated programmes for the television networks. Therefore, he transformed MCA from a talent agency to a television producer.

In 1952, he secured a blanket waiver from his client and Screen Actors Guild (SAG) president, Ronald Reagan, stating the SAG would not prohibit agents from simultaneously acting as producers. In return, Reagan secured residual rights for actors appearing in television programmes. He also resurrected his career, as the agreement allowed him to host MCA's weekly anthology, the *General Electric Theater*. The deal enabled MCA, known as the Star-Spangled Octopus, to become the leading supplier of prime-time programming for the National Broadcasting Company (NBC). From this success, MCA bought the 367-acre Universal Studios City backlot in the San Fernando Valley in 1958 for $12 million and bought Decca, Universal's parent, in 1962, thereby ensuring control of the studio.

As MCA's profits soared, the waiver reached the attention of the Justice Department who felt it had violated anti-trust rulings. MCA was taken to court in 1962 and Reagan was subjected to extensive questioning by prosecutors but no case could be proven due to his 'folksy, conversational answers [which] became convoluted, indecipherable and finally gibberish' (McDougal, 1998: 293). By this time, MCA had become a film and television producer as the SAG had rescinded the waiver in 1961 and its success continued with popular series such as *Columbo* and *Kojak*: 'Through a series of deft manoeuvres, Wasserman had transformed [MCA] into a new sort of studio, one that spoke the modern corporate language of diversifying its assets and rationalising the "manufacture" of its product' (Brownstein, 1990: 184).

ARTHUR KRIM, UNITED ARTISTS AND THE PACKAGE-UNIT SYSTEM

Krim, a former entertainment lawyer who, with his partner Bob Benjamin, took over United Artists (UA) in 1951, oversaw a changeover in film production from the producer-unit to the package-unit system. Previously, studios had fixed costs in which departments were established for writing, cinematography, art or costuming, and the talent was placed on contracts so that power rested with the front office.

Alternatively, Krim and Benjamin provided a 'package' for the talent through which they would appraise a film's potential, arrange its financing, provide the production facilities, distribute the picture and make an equitable participation deal for its box-office revenues. Whereas under the producer-unit system the studio controlled all aspects of the film's production, the package-unit system enabled independent producers to develop a property and assemble the talent. By 1970, the transition was complete as the majors functioned as bankers supplying finances and renting out studio space.

For Krim and Benjamin, once a film had been approved, the film-makers were given creative autonomy. Thus, UA became a byword for quality, financing risky projects such as *Midnight Cowboy* (1969), which became the only X-certificate film to win the Best Picture Oscar, and achieved a remarkable balance between critical and financial success.

NEW HOLLYWOOD

The independence achieved at UA, proved attractive to a new generation of film-makers who were drawn from the counter-culture, exploitation films and film schools. Throughout the 1960s and 1970s, these talents went from Hollywood's margins to become its leading figures. They were aided by the MPAA's decision to replace the Production Code with the Ratings system in 1968 enabling Hollywood to produce films with adult themes (see Chapter 3). Moreover, the studios' financial difficulties had created 'breaches in the defences [of the walled city], and occasionally you could get in through these breaches [to] see what was on the other side of the wall' (Milius, 2003).

Several writers, directors and actors served their apprenticeship as cheap labour for the B-picture magnate Roger Corman. They included Peter Bogdanovich, Dennis Hopper, Peter Fonda, Jack Nicholson, Jonathan Demme and Robert Towne. In poverty-row productions, they learnt how to work to budget and made exploitation films that tapped into new youth markets. From this experience, Hopper, Fonda and Nicholson, with the backing of Bert Schneider and Bob Rafelson (who had made their fortune from the television show of *The Monkees*), made *Easy Rider* (1969). This low-budget film connected with a new and lucrative youth market.

Two members of Corman's alumni, Francis Ford Coppola and Martin Scorsese, represented another dynamic: the cross-over of talent from film schools to mainstream movies. They were accompanied by other 'Movie Brats' including Brian DePalma, Paul Schrader, John Milius, George Lucas and Steven Spielberg. This group wanted independence and Coppola and Lucas attempted to forge a film collective, American Zoetrope, away from Hollywood in San Francisco.

Paradoxically, it was Coppola's bankruptcy in the wake of Zoetrope's financial collapse, which led to him directing a studio assignment, *The Godfather* (1972), whose success confirmed the power of 'auteur' film-makers in Hollywood. The film marked a turnaround in Paramount's fortunes which, led by Robert Evans, forged close relations with European directors such as Roman Polanski and produced hits like *Rosemary's Baby* (1968) and *Love Story* (1970). Other blockbusters, such as William Friedkin's *The Exorcist* (1973) and Universal's *The Sting* (1973), produced by Michael and Julia Philips, represented the ascendancy of Hollywood's younger film-makers.

They desperately guarded their freedoms and produced films as diverse as Scorsese's *Taxi Driver* (1976) and *Raging Bull* (1980), with actors/stars including Robert De Niro, Al Pacino and Dustin Hoffman as leads. As their films were packaged, their rise was paralleled by the rise of aggressive agents such as Sue Menges, Mike Medavoy and Mike Ovitz, and the growth of agencies including International Creative Management (ICM) and Creative Associates Agency (CAA).

AGENCY PACKAGES: OPTIONS, DEVELOPMENT AND 'PAY-OR-PLAY' DEALS

Historically, the agencies served as an intermediary between the talent and the studios. They were responsible for representing their clients in negotiating contracts, selling scripts and finding funds. For these services, they received a 10 per cent commission and were certified by the Californian Talent Agency Act. With the predominance of the package-unit system in Hollywood film production, their power was enhanced, as the agencies became the means through which the creative elements were brought together in a fragmented studio system. The powerful agencies, William Morris, Creative Management Agency and International Famous Agency merged in 1975 to form International Creative Management, and Creative Artist Agency also formed in 1975 by a group of agents led by Ovitz who had left William Morris, packaged some of the 1970s' most successful films, thereby ensuring the loyalty of a roster of stars, directors, writers and producers.

In the process the deals between agencies, producers, talent and movie executives became more complex. Rather than buy a property outright, studios and producers often took an 'option' on the material, usually for one or two years at 10 per cent of the purchase rights, to reduce their financial risk. This meant that, if the buyer failed to place the story into production, s/he would only lose the option money and the owner regained his or her full rights. Similarly, to reduce financial risks, producers entered into 'overall development deals' with studios, in which the studio agreed to finance a producer's projects in return for the producer making all his films at the studio, or at least giving it the first opportunity to fund his pictures (Litwack, 1987: 156–7).

A further complexity was the introduction of the 'pay-or-play' deal, which occurred once a script was completed and packaged with a star or director. Under this negotiation, a studio was required to pay the talent whether the film was made or not. Such fees were needed to hold the talent in place while the studio sought additional elements or oversaw rewrites (ibid.: 157). Alternatively, by the mid-1970s, this led to projects in which no agreement could be made being placed into 'turnaround', or studios rushing ill-prepared films into production (ibid.: 158).

THE BLOCKBUSTER PHENOMENON

Ironically, despite these changes, the film-makers who had contributed to Hollywood's financial rebirth lost many of their freedoms in the fallout from the industry's new phase of profitability. In part, this occurred due to their excesses, culminating in Michael Cimino's *Heaven's Gate* (1980), an epic Western whose $35 million budget and disastrous box-office returns brought about the sale of UA to MGM in 1981. However, this collapse in creative independence showed how the studios had realised their films could be mass marketed to ensure their profitability.

The success of the early 1970s' blockbusters demonstrated to the corporations that studios could be lucrative once more. As a consequence, they changed the releasing strategies of

'Shark Attack': Richard D. Zanuck and David Brown, producers of *Jaws* – the first high-concept Summer Blockbuster

event films from the traditional 'roadshow' openings, in which a picture would play in a few selected theatres in large cities and gradually be opened nationwide, to the wide release of movies with a higher built-in distribution cost to be paid by exhibitors leading to a massive increase in film rentals. This meant a smaller number of heavily marketed films were made to ensure the studios' profits. For a corporation like Gulf and Western, the financial rewards of these practices were evident when Paramount's box-office success increased its stock prices.

However, the revenues from the first set of blockbusters were dwarfed by the returns achieved by Steven Spielberg's *Jaws* (1975) and George Lucas's *Star Wars* (1977). These genre films provided B-picture thrills on A-picture budgets to a newly defined audience, ranging from sixteen to twenty-four years in age, and were released in the summer to maximise profits. Their success led to the development of high-concept features in which readily identifiable stories could be sold to the public. This led to an escalation in budgets for pictures, such as Spielberg's *Close Encounters of the Third Kind* (1977), as the majors realised an expensive blockbuster, rather than a series of smaller films, could ensure their profitability.

The summer blockbusters were accompanied by distribution techniques associated with exploitation film-making, as 'event' movies were blanket-released across hundreds of US screens (for example, in the case of *Jaws*, 464) and marketed through television-led advertising campaigns. As with exploitation films, the idea was to achieve as large an audience as possible within the film's first week, invariably before they had time to read the reviews. They were supported through a range of merchandising including book tie-ins, games, clothing, bubblegum and magazines. With regard to *Star Wars*, the profits from these associated products exceeded the $500 million in box-office revenues made by the film. The phenomena generated higher returns and screens became dominated by sequels, remakes and the culling of comic books and television shows to create lucrative franchises.

INVESTMENT TAX CREDITS

The revival of the film industry not only resulted from its internal reorganisation, but also from its intense lobbying, skilfully led by Wasserman, of the US government to reform the tax system. In 1962, the Inland Revenue Service (IRS) introduced investment tax credits to allow American firms to write off against tax 7 per cent of any investment they made in equipment and machinery located in America. Despite their elimination in 1969, they were reintroduced in the 1971 Revenue Act. Subsequently, the film industry pushed for investments in motion pictures to qualify for tax credit status, as long as features were produced in the US.

These measures led to a surge in Hollywood's fortunes and, as they required films be shot at home, they reduced the number of 'runaway' productions, thereby boosting employment. In 1972, as a result of the new rules MCA posted a 97 per cent increase in its profits. Consequently, Disney sued the government for retrospective credits and, with the other studios, won $400 million in the settlement. When the credit rate was raised to 10 per cent, film and television production escalated. This was not without a degree of irony: 'For years, the studios had fulminated against the preferential tax incentives offered by foreign governments. Now they had successfully lobbied their own legislature to introduce just such a programme' (Puttnam, 1997: 268).

Unsurprisingly, the French consul in Washington argued that tax credits were discriminatory and foreign governments were angered as a clause in the Revenue Act allowed the studios to establish subsidiaries called Domestic International Sales Corporations (DISCs) who could indefinitely defer tax on half the profits they achieved from exports. In effect, the legislation provided the studios with the direct impetus to expand further into international markets.

Characteristics of contemporary Hollywood

Hollywood studios have become film production entities within global media conglomerates. The repeal of the Paramount Decrees enabled the corporate behemoths to establish a vertical chain of supply in the US communications industries. Concurrently, Hollywood poured greater monies into the production, marketing and merchandising of blockbusters, leading to higher production costs, and looked beyond its shores to ensure the success of its films.

IDEOLOGICAL REFORM: FROM ANTI-TRUST TO NEO-LIBERALISM

In the early 1980s, the studios lobbied the Reagan administration to overhaul the Paramount Decrees, which they argued were of out of date as new technological and economic practices had entered the industry. They had the ear of the President who, as a former Hollywood player, advocated a return to the integrated system of movie production, distribution and exhibition. Reagan was opposed to anti-trust rulings, preferring supply-side economics and perceiving vertical integration as promoting corporate efficiency rather than restricting trade.[2]

Therefore, the Justice Department reviewed all those consent decrees in place for America's national industries. Consequently, if an affected company demonstrated a change in circumstances, it could be freed from the rulings. In 1983, the department concluded there might be other instances, which justified the termination of such decrees that failed to operate in the public interest. In 1985, it introduced more lenient rules over vertical restraints, which tolerated behaviour that had previously been understood as being anti-competitve.

In keeping with Reagan's *laissez-faire* approach to mergers and acquisitions, the Justice Department announced in February 1985 that it would support such developments in the film industry where the action was 'in the public interest'. Yet, although the anti-trust chief J. Paul McGrath considered the decrees irrelevant, he was unwilling to scrap them. However, the decrees' authority became non-existent when the department stated it was acquiescent to their eventual removal: 'As a result . . . the essence of Paramount [was] . . . transformed from an iron fist wielded by the federal government into a facade manipulated by the studios; this facade has effectively solidified their power and kept potential government scrutiny at bay' (Holt, 2001).

By reducing the anti-trust rulings, the Reagan presidency facilitated a period of sustained growth in the Hollywood studio system as cross-media conglomerates, such as Time-Warner, were formed, allowing films to be sold across a variety of distribution markets. Moreover, the majors invested in multiplex chains, cable-television subscription systems and videocassette sell-through markets as ancillary revenue streams were sought in the US and abroad. The industry's expansion was therefore founded on the vertical and horizontal reintegration of movie production, distribution and exhibition under the favourable investment climate promoted by Reaganomics and deregulation. This would be fostered further when the Hollywood studios were incorporated into global media conglomerates after the passage of the 1996 Federal Communication Commission's Telecommunications Act which removed the cross-media regulations which had stemmed the monopolies.

HOLLYWOOD IN THE GLOBAL MEDIA MARKETPLACE

In the latter half of the 1990s, a series of mergers in the US media turned the communications economy into an industry dominated by multinational conglomerates who diversified their interests across content and entertainment businesses, and Hollywood became subject to their control. A benefit of conglomeration has been that the costs and risks of producing a film may be spread over the whole company if required. It also allows for the cross-promotion of film and other entertainment properties across a range of audiovisual media.

The majors, Paramount, 20th Century-Fox, Warner Bros., Universal, Disney/Buena Vista and Columbia-Tri Star, remain at the forefront of the US film industry and are owned by a parent conglomerate. For instance, Warner is the profit-making constituent of the world's largest media company, AOL/Time-Warner, the first 'internet vertically integrated content provider' (Chapman, 2000: 13). Despite the profits associated with franchises such as the *Harry Potter* and *Lord of the Rings* movies, Warners' parent made substantial losses in its provision of broadband communication services.

Paramount was taken over by Viacom, which runs cable television companies and a range of television stations including Music Television (MTV). Twentieth Century-Fox was incorporated into Rupert Murdoch's News Corporation in 1985, and owns Fox 2000, a producer of big-budget films, and Fox Searchlight which commissions smaller, art-house productions. Sony bought Columbia-Tri Star in 1989 to effect a synergy between the hardware manufacturer and content provider.

A greater synergy was sought by Disney/Buena Vista, as the corporation has exploited Disney's cartoon characters and theme parks to ensure profitability. Disney is composed from Walt Disney Studio Entertainment, a production and distribution division; Buena Vista International, a distribution arm for live-action and animated titles; and production companies, Touchstone and Hollywood pictures. Disney's corporate expansion has not been without controversy, as former chairman and CEO Michael Eisner was taken to court in an infamous litigation by former head of production Jeffrey Katzenberg. More recently, Eisner faced a boardroom battle with Roy Disney for the hearts and minds of the company, and was forced by stockholders to step down as chair.[3]

A complex story emerged in the wake of developments at Vivendi-Universal. After Universal's Japanese owners Matsushita sold the company to Canadian brewers Seagrams in the 1990s, the French media conglomerate Vivendi bought the studio in 2000. This was heralded as a triumph for French business as Vivendi was the first European company to enter the top five worldwide media groups. On 3 October 2003, however, it was announced that owing to the financial difficulties facing the corporation, Vivendi-Universal had merged its US assets with the US media conglomerate General Electric (GE).

In the next tier, there are several smaller, less influential production and distribution companies, known as minor majors, which include MGM/UA, New Line Cinema, Miramax and the newest studio DreamWorks SKG (created in 1994 and led by the combined talents of Steven Spielberg, Jeffrey Katzenberg and record company entrepreneur David Geffen, with investment from Paul Allen, co-founder of Microsoft). The previously independent production companies of New Line and Miramax were taken over by AOL/Time-Warner and Buena Vista respectively, to act as autonomous production outfits which distribute their films through the majors' distribution divisions.[4] Alternatively, DreamWorks, whose initial success led to Academy Award-winning films, *American Beauty* (1999) and *Gladiator* (2000) and computer-animated blockbusters including *Shrek* (2001), has made distribution deals with Paramount and Universal.[5] Yet the collapse in profits from its live-action films led to the non-animated side of the studio being sold to Viacom in 2005. Finally, there are the smaller independent distributors and production companies (Wasko, 2003: 60).

DOMESTIC, INTERNATIONAL AND ANCILLARY MARKETS

The Hollywood studios invest in expensive blockbusters, so the average cost of a feature film stands at $75 million. This figure includes the expenditures incurred through star salaries, saturation release patterns, marketing and promotion campaigns, product ties-ins and brand placements (e.g. *The Untouchables* wearing Giorgio Armani suits or Charlie's Angels phoning one another on Motorola mobiles) which have become synonymous with a movie's launch. For example, a summer blockbuster like *Troy* (2004) was released on 3, 411 screens to gross $45.6 million in its opening weekend (Duncan, 2004: 28).

This strategy is targeted to attract the largest possible audience for the film in its first few days. A film opens on a Friday to draw the weekend audience which may account for 80 per cent of all its tickets sold in the first week. Distributors may open a film earlier in the week if they believe the film will benefit from word-of-mouth increasing the weekend audience. When a film receives a poor response from the audience in the first weekend, advance publicity may be enough to override bad word-of-mouth. In the subsequent weeks the distributors expect a decline in admissions so the film will be withdrawn from many theatres. The other form of domestic marketing is used for niche films which are aimed at minority audiences in art-house cinemas: 'The two-tier system in American cinema . . . in some ways resembles the old A-film and B-film system of the studio era. . . . It now makes business sense for the studios to spread their investment across many different niche markets (ibid.: 28).

As they have benefited from the size of their domestic market, the Hollywood studios have renewed their efforts through their international distribution arms such as United International Pictures (UIP) to sell their films in a wider foreign marketplace, most especially the burgeoning Asian states. This realisation led to the dubbing of blockbusters such as *Jurassic Park* (1993) and *Goldeneye* (1995) into Hindi to attract audiences away from the indigenous films produced by Bollywood. Hong Kong has also become an international competitor and the US film industry has successfully raided its directors and stars, including John Woo and Jackie Chan, martial arts expertise and filmic style in films such as *The Matrix* (1999) and *Kill Bill: Volumes One and Two* (2003–4), catering to home and foreign audiences.

According to the MPAA, the distribution of US film abroad constitutes 42 per cent of the industry's revenues (Wasko, 1994: 223). In the case of Hollywood's most profitable film, *Titanic* (1997), its international box office accounted for $1.234 billion of its income compared to $600 million in domestic returns. This film was also subject to a co-production/distribution deal in which Fox, to share the burdens of its investment in the $200–250-million budget, combined with Paramount to distribute the picture domestically, while retaining the rights to handle it abroad. As budgets escalate and profit margins decrease, the studios increasingly depend on profit from foreign markets.

Hollywood's films are marketed through a variety of 'windows' of distribution and are exhibited through theatre chains (owned by the parent companies), videocassettes, DVD, television packages including pay-per-view and video-on-demand, and sale to terrestrial broadcasting stations. To exploit these markets, the majors run their own ancillary divisions selling their library of film titles to the home video and television rights markets (Gomery, 2005a: 173). Thus, the major studios/distributors are structured through an integrated strategy which controls the value of filmed entertainment from production through to theatrical, video and television distribution.

Recently, the studios have tentatively employed information technologies, such as the Internet, as a means of distribution. However, these revenue streams have risks involved with them, including the protection of the studios' intellectual property rights. And piracy remains of great concern, as in countries like China and India, it has been impossible to stop the illegal selling of films, even before they have been previewed or shown theatrically, on video and DVD.

The MPAA/MPA

The MPAA/MPA is a trade association representing the seven Hollywood majors: Buena Vista International, Columbia-Tri Star, MGM, Universal International Pictures, Warner Bros., Paramount Pictures Corporation and 20th Century-Fox. It is responsible for the administration of the audience ratings system (see Chapter 3), lobbying against such legislation that contravenes its members' interests and the monitoring of piracy and other illegal practices such as product splitting (e.g. when regional exhibitors agree not to bid against each other to obtain more favourable distribution terms for a film). Its international counterpart, the MPA, serves the MPAA members' foreign interests and conducts its activities in Los Angeles, Washington DC, Brussels, Rome, New Delhi, Rio de Janeiro, Singapore, Mexico City, Toronto and Jakarta.

JACK VALENTI AND THE MPAA: APPOINTMENT, ORGANISATION AND POLITICAL CONNECTIONS

In 1966, President Johnson's chief assistant Jack Valenti was approached by Lew Wasserman, Arthur Krim and Ed Weisl (lawyer for Paramount and chairman of the New York State Democratic Party), who were some of Johnson's closest allies (see Chapter 7)[6] to become president of the MPAA and MPEAA. His appointment occurred in the wake of Eric Johnston's death in 1963, after which there had been a three-year interregnum when Ralph Hetzel and Louis Nizer led the association. It was noted for Wasserman's manoeuvring when he removed any support within the board for Nizer to the untested Valenti (Champlin, 5 February 1967).[7] Valenti agreed to operate in partnership with Wasserman to control the industry's political and labour relations, and the MCA president became the chairman of the MPAA and took over its labour arm, the Association of Motion Picture and Television Producers (AMPTP) from Y. Frank Freeman (see Chapter 6) (Bruck, 2004: 235–6).

For Hollywood, Valenti's influence and connections within Washington were vital as he had access to the White House and the respect of foreign diplomats (ibid.: 235). For Valenti, the position provided him with financial security, as he would be paid $150,000 per annum compared to his White House salary of $30,000 (ibid.: 236). It also allowed him to pursue his interests in US business and international affairs: 'To my knowledge, the motion picture is the only US enterprise that negotiates on its own with foreign governments' (Trumpbour, 2002: 114).

The MPAA/MPA benefited from Valenti's zeal as an astute lobbyist in Washington who often employed hyperbole to target the presidency as well as many cabinet officials during his

Hollywood's last Movie Czar?
Jack Valenti, President of the
MPAA from 1966–2004

thirty-eight-year reign.[8] He was shrewd enough to court both Democrat and Republican administrations, despite modern Hollywood's support of the Democrats (Brownstein, 1990: 176–7). An early example of this bipartisan cunning occurred when Valenti persuaded Lyndon Johnson to approve military cooperation for rightwing icon John Wayne's pro-Vietnam film, *The Green Berets* (1968). Valenti realised Hollywood had friends on both sides of the political divide and the US film industry received state support in its domestic and global affairs.

To promote Hollywood, the MPAA lobbies at local, state, and national level to ensure the industry does not have to rely solely on its own resources, but also benefits from the considerable backing of the US government. To affect these opportunities, the MPAA officials have specific duties and responsibilities, and it outsources some of its activities to public relations companies (Wasko, 2003: 212–13).

Valenti was also aided by several presidents who have had close affiliations with Hollywood including not only Ronald Reagan but also Bill Clinton, who courted support from leading members of the entertainment establishment. For his efforts, Valenti was paid $1.15 million and ranked as the fifth highest-paid head of a US trade association in 2000 (ibid.: 212). However, in recent years, his attempts to provide a unified front for the majors were complicated by the corporate ownership of the studios and the diversified interests of the parent organisations in rival mediums such as television and new areas of competition, such as information technology (Waxman, 2004). And on 1 July 2004, the MPAA announced that the eighty-two-year-old Valenti would be replaced by former Democrat Congressman and Agricultural Secretary Dan Glickman from 5 September 2004.[9]

TRADE LIBERALISATION

Throughout his stewardship, Valenti demanded the removal of trade barriers when entering into negotiations with foreign chanceries and film associations. In this capacity, he became a tireless advocate for the benefits of the Webb-Pomerene Act, which allows US companies to form export associations that would otherwise contravene the anti-trust rulings within the Sherman and Clayton Acts:

> Without [it] the American film industry would be an invalid . . . [as it] is peculiarly vulnerable to unfavourable action by foreign governments and by foreign private interests, by industry cartels, and by an avalanche of non-tariff barriers that are both endless and ingenious. . . . [Webb-Pomerene has enabled the MPA] to counter these restrictions . . . and preserve the freedom of the American film industry to compete fairly in the world entertainment marketplace (Valenti, 1980).

Under the auspices of the act, Valenti led the MPA in more than eighty negotiations to liberalise the international film and broadcasting markets on the lines of US business. This enabled the US film and television industries to return more than $3.5 billion per annum in surplus balance of payments to the US economy (Puttnam, 1997: 6). Furthermore, through the close relations he established with successive presidential administrations, Congress, the State Department and the Office of Trade Representative, Valenti secured the backing of the US government in his calls for the liberalisation of the international film trade: 'Valenti explains: "Our movies and TV programmes are hospitably received by citizens around the world." Perhaps. But it doesn't hurt to have a little help from friends in high places' (Wasko, 2003: 181).

BILATERAL TRADE NEGOTIATIONS

Valenti fulminated against those foreign chanceries that inflicted curbs on the US motion picture industry through the imposition of film quotas and subsidies (Valenti, 2000). He argued, somewhat disingenuously, that these controls undermined reciprocal relations in the international film trade as the US rights to foreign markets were stymied while foreign films had open access to the American market. This position actively ignored the cartel-like practices operated by MPA members and their market closure in distributing films from overseas (Jarvie, 1998: 41). However, it contended the limits on US film trade constitute a loss of $1 billion per annum for the industry and the MPA sought to remove such barriers in bilateral trade negotiations (Valenti, 2000).

In 1992, the association, under the North American Free Trade Agreement (NAFTA, the economic trade pact between the US, Canada and Mexico), argued that Canadian quotas and protections should be stripped away as it was eager to gain unlimited access to Canada's film and video distribution markets. However, the Canadian government held firm and the US trade representative Carla Hills exempted Canada's 'cultural industries' from the NAFTA pact. Yet, while the MPA had not extended Hollywood's interests, this was not a victory for the Canadian film and television industry as it reinforced the status quo in which there was almost complete US domination (Segrave, 1997: 266–7).

NAFTA was employed in the MPA's dealings with the Mexican film industry and its authorities were required to protect the US majors' intellectual property rights owing to the extent of piracy south of the border. This triggered a boom in US video sales in Mexico. Moreover, another NAFTA clause cut the percentage of home-produced films to be shown on Mexican screens from 50 to 30 per cent. Valenti hailed this reduction in the quota as a victory for free trade (ibid.: 267). However, it meant Mexico's audiovisual sector shrank by 80 per cent in the following five years (Sanchez-Ruiz, 2003).

As Hollywood's global reach expanded, the MPA pursued market reforms in Free Trade Agreements (FTA) with Oceanic, Latin American, Eastern European and Asian states. In 2003, the MPA vice-president for trade and federal affairs, Bonnie J. K. Richardson, provided testimony for the US Trade Policy Staff Committee on US–Australian FTA. She argued that there should be a free flow of all kinds of goods and services, along with the protection of intellectual property. Thus, the MPA contended its goals of free trade and cultural diversity in Australia could be realised by the removal of tariffs over filmed and electronic entertainment, the reduction of quotas for domestic productions and greater market access for US pictures (Richardson, 2003). Also, in 2003, the MPA with the Entertainment Industry Coalition for Free Trade (EIC) heralded the US–Chilean FTA as a means for securing robust market access and protecting intellectual property rights (Entertainment Industry Coalition for Free Trade, 6 June 2003).

For many years, the former Soviet Union and Eastern European Communist states were closed to US films. However, with the collapse of these Stalinist regimes in the late 1980s, the MPA negotiated several percentage deals concerning the provision of rentals to the majors so they could distribute pictures in Poland, Hungary and Russia. Yet these contracts were fraught with difficulties, partly owing to the extensive piracy of US films, the greed of local theatrical exhibitors who did not report their box-office returns and a sharp decline in admissions in the early 1990s (Segrave, 1997: 257–60).

During the 1990s, the MPA led several trade delegations to the Asian states to negotiate openings for American motion pictures. In 1993, the Indian government relaxed trade barriers and Hollywood distributed eighty-two Hindi-dubbed prints (plus thirty English language copies) of *Jurassic Park*. It became the most successful US film at the Indian box office and in Pakistan (where twenty-five prints were shipped in Urdu). In 1994, China announced it was prepared to buy US films on a percentage basis wherein the state kept 60 per cent of the profits with 40 per cent being given over to the majors' distribution arms.[10] Consequently, through the opening up of China, along with the removal of trade barriers in other Far East states, the MPA reported profits for Hollywood within these markets had grown from a combined total of $6.4 million in 1988 to $125.2 million in 2000 (Valenti, 2000).

Yet, American films faced many difficulties in achieving acceptance in the sub-continent and Far East whose governments remained conscious of cultural imperialism and developed protectionist measures for their indigenous film and audiovisual industries. These policies have led to boycotts, as in the case of Thailand in the late 1970s, and limits being placed on the number of US movies that can be exported to countries like India, in which domestically produced films continue to account for 95 per cent of all films shown.

These issues would become conspicuous in the European film and audiovisual market-places when *Jurassic Park* was released in France in 1993. Its outstanding success at the French box office brought to attention the paucity of funding in the European cinema and the US domination of the regional box office. Valenti's response was to accuse old-world financiers of being unprepared to invest in a high-risk industry and to argue 'a subsidised industry will never be a global industry because you have got to have a free marketplace and you've got to have private capital going in there' (Guttman, 1998: 25). Its release also coincided with a dispute between the US and the European Union (EU) which occurred during the 1994 GATT multilateral negotiations. This debate not only referred to the requirements of trade, but made evident two diametrically opposed views of culture and market society.

THE GATT MULTILATERAL NEGOTIATIONS: THE 1986–1994 URUGUAY ROUND

For the first time in its history, the GATT negotiators combined the liberalisation of services with the liberalisation of goods, and the audiovisual sector was included within its remit. Yet, because of their neoclassical ideological principles, the negotiators failed to realise that the inclusion of this sector would impact on the multilateral agreements (Miller, 1996: 73). Therefore, as it had paid scant attention to audiovisual services through its eight-year process, the omission led to a nearly disastrous set of consequences for the Uruguay Round of the GATT (Puttnam, 1997: 4–5).

In a protracted debate between the US and EU, led by France, difficulties emerged in defining the cultural dimensions of audiovisual services, most especially with regard to national film subsidies and quotas. For the US government and the MPA, with the global-isation of communication outlets, greater revenues could be attained for the American film industry through the removal of barriers on film exports. To this end, Valenti pursued, with his typical rhetorical flourish, a liberal view of market economics and their relationship with cultural products:

> Why this EC quota? Its defenders, those who would build the siege wall claim 'Our culture is at stake!' Can this be true? Is a thousand, two thousand years of an individual culture to collapse because of the exhibition of American TV programmes? Is this culture so flimsily anchored, so shakily rooted, that European viewers must be caged and blinded else their links with their honoured and distinguished past suddenly vanish like an exploding star in the heavens? (Jarvie, 1998: 42)

To mobilise support, the MPA approached several high-profile directors including Steven Spielberg and Martin Scorsese, who took out a full-page advertisement in the trade paper *Variety* attacking the imposition of trade barriers by European states. The importance of Hollywood to the US government also became apparent when President Clinton telephoned Helmut Kohl, the German Chancellor, and Édouard Balladur, the French Prime Minister, to tell them he would not back down over the audiovisual industry (Puttnam, 1997: 6–7).

Some European states, notably France, opposed the American position, arguing that the unique cultural nature of films made them quite unlike any other internationally traded goods and services. They insisted on their right to protect their film and television industries through the continuation of a complex series of subsidies and quotas. At the 1993 Venice Film Festival, then French Cultural Minister Jack Lang suggested the cinema and broadcasting sectors should be excluded from GATT, thereby protecting these vital national cultural industries from a flood of American films. Later, the French Prime Minister François Mitterrand expressed the official French position – in an unprecedented manner, since the French presidency had never engaged in a debate about trade before – in a speech at Gdansk on 21 September 1993:

> Creations of the spirit are not just commodities; the elements of culture are not pure business. Defending the pluralism of works of art and the freedom of the public to choose is a duty. What is at stake is the cultural identity of all our nations. . . . A society which abandons to others the way of showing itself . . . is a society enslaved (Jeancolas, 1998: 58–9).

Indeed, the MPA had inadvertently achieved a unique feat in French politics by binding together the left and the right in an anti-American consensus to protect France's culture. Franco-français unanimity also became apparent within the whole of the film industry which spoke with one voice ranging from left-wing director Bertrand Tavernier to Nicolas Seydoux, president of Gaumont, Buena Vista's French partner and a major distributor of US films in France.

The standoff created a critical debate between the American GATT negotiator Mickey Kantor (a Clintonian Democrat and Californian lawyer with close links to Hollywood), the French Cultural Minister Jacques Toubon (who had succeeded Lang) and the EU, led by the less than enthusiastic European Commissioner Leon Brittan. Eventually, these delegations were brought together for one final meeting in order that the GATT negotiations could be finalised by the self-imposed deadline of 15 December 1993. In this meeting, relations grew so tense that Kantor gave Clinton an ultimatum: either the US would have to back down or the whole GATT edifice would unravel with regard to the audiovisual sector. Finally Clinton, having sought advice from Wasserman, relented to stem a trade war. Therefore, the European audiovisual sector was exempted from thirty-three Most Favoured Nation (MFN) clauses, with an additional thirteen MFN exemptions applying to all service sectors allowing room for manoeuvre (European Commission, DGX, 1999: 1).

Despite an acrimonious response from the US negotiators and jubilation from the Europeans, and the French in particular, a compromise was reached in which neither side had achieved victory. The US had failed to 'liberalise' the European film and television industries, while the Europeans had not been able to win a lasting 'cultural exemption' from GATT (Puttnam, 1997: 343). Instead, the result was a draw and the battle had been put off for another day.

GATS 2000

The General Agreement on Trade and Services (GATS), which is administered by the World Trade Organisation (WTO), replaced the GATT in 1995. In this agreement, two disciplines are applied – market access and national treatment – on a voluntary basis. The market access principle obliges members to open their domestic markets to all service suppliers from all members. The national treatment principle obliges the members to grant all service suppliers, whatever their nationality, the same treatment accorded to domestic service suppliers. Therefore discrimination between national and foreign suppliers is forbidden.

In the light of these liberalising rules, the EU member states' margin for manoeuvre in the audiovisual sector has been questioned during the ongoing GATS 2000 Round. In particular, the technological convergence of broadcasting, telecommunication and new information and communication technologies (ICT) raises concerns over the interventionist regulation of the transport and content of audiovisual services. Virtual goods and online services have raised concerns about whether the GATS articles are appropriate for electronic trading and the extent to which these markets should be open to competition.

The MPA has confirmed to the EU that it would not try to reopen the status of the Television without Frontiers directive or reiterate its previous demand for national treatment in the field of audiovisual revenue or subsidy. However, it has challenged the European Commission's (EC) desire to be free to manoeuvre to regulate emerging services based on new technologies. The exponential growth of these forms of communication transfer has meant the US copyright industries surpassed the staples of automation, agriculture and aerospace to become America's number one export sector. By 1996, they had a combined worth of $60.18 billion (Siwek and Mosteller, 1998). Within this overall total, the US film and entertainment industry accounted for $12 billion in foreign revenues (Richardson, 1999).

The MPA has argued there should be no quotas or restrictions on the US entering the European market for new communication services. This view became apparent when Latvia applied to join the EU. The MPA was prepared to allow for the existing exemptions to be applied to Latvia's theatrical and analogue-based audiovisual services. However, it demanded there should be a full liberalisation of Latvia's emerging services like e-commerce and online goods. It also argued that no distinction should apply between services and goods under GATS, as services formed part of the sectorial extension of the multilateral liberalisation which had been limited to goods before the Uruguay Round of GATT.

Technological reforms in the distribution of the film and audiovisual sectors will impact on production and the EU trade associations maintain such developments have serious implications for the preservation of indigenous cultural industries. They have suggested their film and television industries have only made limited advances since 1993 and the US has remained the predominant supplier of content in their audiovisual economies. Therefore, it has been contended that GATS', inherently liberalising agenda, tied to the convergence of communication services, may enable the US to attain a more significant, if not dominant, foothold in the European audiovisual and information sectors.

INTELLECTUAL PROPERTY RIGHTS AND PIRACY

The MPAA/MPA's other major concern is the protection of its members' copyright over the distribution of their content, and the losses incurred by various forms of piracy (e.g. theatrical and signal theft, broadcast theft).[11] As far back as 1982, Valenti compared the introduction of the video cassette recorder (VCR) 'to the American film producer and the American public as the Boston strangler is to the woman home alone' (Valenti, 1982). Yet, despite the MPA's reluctance, Hollywood's majors realised the lucrative nature of the video rental and sell-through markets for licensed tapes.

However, with the growth of the new, domestic technologies (digital versatile discs [DVDs], recordable DVD hardware, CD writers and the Internet) and the phenomenal success enjoyed by US films internationally, the piracy of audiovisual product has led to losses of in excess of $3 billion per annum. The MPA argues the illegal copying of films undermines the studios' release schedules across international markets and within different distribution windows. For example, in 1999, pirate copies of *Star Wars: Episode 1 – The Phantom Menace*, created by camcorder recordings of the film in US cinemas, flooded Asia while it was playing in US theatres. So when it opened in Asia, attendances were considerably lower than expected. The MPA claimed rental chains lost business during the home video window release of the film because of the widespread distribution of pirated copies. Therefore, piracy affected legitimate theatrical distributors, exhibitors and local businesses.

Moreover, the MPA contends this activity is dominated by organised crime and operates on an industrial scale so that in 2002, 7 million illegal DVD copies of US films had been seized worldwide (Valenti, 2003). Previously in 2000, to combat these infringements on its members' product, the MPA launched over 60,000 investigations into suspected activities, and co-ordinated with local authorities 18,000 raids on internationally pirated material. To achieve these results, the association spent over $40 million per annum reminding the US federal authorities of the dangers associated with the violation of the studios' copyrighted features.

In tandem, the association lobbied the US government to advance more sophisticated forms of copyright legislation (the 1976 US Copyright law was amended in 1982, and there are amendments in the 1984 Communications Act) and combine with foreign chanceries over the implementation of the TRIPs agreements, the World Intellectual Property Organisation (WIPO) treaties, the Universal Copyright Convention (UCC) and the Berne Convention. Since 1976, it has also directed a comprehensive international anti-piracy programme:

• To strengthen existing copyright protection legislation;
• To assist local governments and law enforcement authorities in the investigation and prosecution of piracy cases;
• To initiate civil litigation on behalf of its' member companies against copyright infringers; and
• To conduct education outreach programmes detailing the harmful effects of piracy.

In recent years, the MPA focused its attention on the Internet as it provides a perfect, electronic copying medium for downloaded films. Primarily, the association sought to prosecute file swappers and Valenti has testified in numerous House and Senate hearings about the pernicious nature of what he called 'a virtual pirate shopping mall' (Valenti, 1997). To this end, Hollywood benefited from the 1996 Telecommunications Act which gave it complete control over the distribution of its copyrighted product (Mikulan, 2001: 29).

Valenti also argued that Internet search engines should be responsible for the policing of such illegal traffic. Ironically, his vehemence led to an embarrassing dispute between the MPAA and the Hollywood industry, when he outlawed the distribution of videotapes and DVDs to Academy members watching nominated films to vote for the 2003 Oscars. Valenti had to tried clamp down on piracy but ended up being rebuked by the Screen Actors Guild (SAG), art-house distributors and the courts.

In April 2004, the divisions between the copyright industries and the tech companies responsible for manufacturing the hardware necessary to produce pirate copies became conspicuous. This occurred when a Californian District Court dismissed a suit pursued by the studios against a file-swapping network called 'Grokster'. Subsequently, this network proclaimed its practices had been deemed legal and the Hollywood companies and Microsoft pressed the Senate Judiciary Committee to pursue legislation which would make it a crime to 'induce' the public to violate copyright. This action induced the wrath of forty-three tech companies and trade groups, including Intel, eBay and Google, who maintained the bill would allow content owners to kill off any nascent technology which they found threatening. It perhaps remains appropriate to give the retired Valenti Hollywood's final word on the subject. In his signing-off speech, Valenti warned the film industry about an Internet-based video content technology produced by the Californian Institute of Technology called FAST TCP:

> I visited the labs at Cal Tech, and they're running an experiment called FAST where they can bring down a DVD-quality movie in five seconds. The director told me it could be operative in the market in 18 months. Well, my face blanched (Valenti, 2004a).

Conclusion

In the modern era, the Hollywood film industry has become part of the global media economy because worldwide media conglomerates own the studios and they have expanded their interests across a range of content-driven communication services. This diversification has meant the studios maintain a close control over the value chain of their films from their production to their distribution to their exhibition. Consequently, Hollywood has been reformed from operating as a movie 'industry' to becoming a film 'business' modelled on modern corporate practices.

As the costs of production exponentially increase, the returns need to be higher and different market practices have become the norm. The studios continue to produce and market expensive blockbusters aimed at a youth audience in the summer months. The profitability of these 'event' films is enhanced as they are subsequently sold through a variety of distribution windows and tie-in markets. The financial imperatives associated with these projects have led to the majors seeking overseas' revenues to ensure their dominance abroad. The MPAA/MPA has been an assiduous representative of Hollywood's interests. Under the stewardship of Valenti, aided and abetted for many years by Wasserman, the association provided a unified front for the studios and remained a vocal presence within the circles of power and influence in Washington. It has advocated the liberalisation of US trade in foreign markets and employed bilateral and multilateral trade agreements to advance its case. This has led to a number of trade disputes, most notably the standoff between US and EU negotiators during the 1994 Uruguay Round of the GATT. Presently, the MPA's position in the GATS 2000 negotiations is one in which a clear vision of the free market, due to the interests of global market pressure, 'radically challenges the cultural viability and social value of local identities' (de Grazia, 1998: 30).

The other major concern has been the MPAA's protection of its members' intellectual property rights. The new communication technologies have provided the Hollywood studios with both the opportunities to extract profits from new revenue streams and raised anxieties about their ability to retain control over their distributed product. The massive increase in the illegal copying or piracy of motion pictures has coincided with the ascendancy of the Internet as *the* perfect copying medium in which (unlike video) there is no deterioration in second-, third- or nth-copied material. As a result, the MPAA has pursued a battle against piracy at home and abroad, and Hollywood is faced with a dangerous enemy in the high-tech Silicon Valley companies which have manufactured the hard and software packages responsible for making illegal copies. These problems remain Valenti's legacy to his successor Glickman, and it will be interesting to see how the latter copes with such complex predicaments.

Therefore, for all its apparent strengths, the Hollywood film industry continues to be dependent on the studios' ability to dominate foreign markets and to retain control over the distribution of their product. In both cases, the introduction of new forms of technology and the companies' willingness to adapt will prove crucial in shaping the destiny of an industry which stands on the cusp of extraordinary change as it enters the new millennium.

Notes

1. Copyright industries include motion pictures (television, theatrical and home video entertainment), recording, music publishing, books, journals and newspapers, computer software, legitimate theatre, advertising and radio, television and cable broadcasting.

2. Reagan's benevolence to Hollywood was evident as Governor of California when he supported a tax break for the studios' film libraries which was worth a minimum of $3 million per studio.

3. Michael Eisner announced on 10 September 2004, the eve of his twentieth anniversary with Disney, that he intended to retire as CEO when his contract finished on 30 September 2006.

4. The 1990s saw the growth of the independent film sector. Miramax, formed by Harvey and Bob Weinstein, supported Quentin Tarantino, whose second feature *Pulp Fiction* (1994) scored over $100 million at the US box office. The film gave Miramax respectability and it was incorporated into Buena Vista (owned by Disney). In 2004, Harvey Weinstein feuded with Disney CEO Eisner when Disney refused to distribute Michael Moore's *Fahrenheit 9/11*. On 5 July 2004, Harvey Weinstein announced he would establish another independent production company under a plan negotiated with Disney, in which Miramax was controlled by Bob Weinstein and would continue to distribute his films. See Peter Biskind (2004), *Down and Dirty Pictures: Miramax, Sundance and the Rise of Independent Film*, New York: Simon and Schuster.

5. In 2004, DreamWorks' lucrative animation division was split from the business and floated on Wall Street, while DreamWorks sold its music division in 2002, disposed of a video-games unit and scaled back its television-production business. Hollywood watchers cite the failure as evidence of the difficulty of competing as an independent studio.

6. Valenti was a partner in a top advertising agency in Houston, Texas, before working as Johnson's publicist and closest aide. Wasserman and Krim were fundraisers for Johnson, who became frequent visitors to the White House. See Ronald Brownstein (1990), *The Power and the Glitter: The Hollywood–Washington Connection*, New York: Pantheon Books: 194–200. For further details on Valenti, see Douglas Gomery (2005b), *The Hollywood Studio System: A History*, London: British Film Institute: 288–98.

7. Nizer was appointed as MPAA General Counsel.

8. Despite Hollywood's reluctance to his appointment, Valenti won over his constituency with a mixture of guile, charm and enthusiasm. He unified the diverse elements within the film trade and linked the East and West Coast branches of the industry more effectively than his predecessors, Hays and Johnston, who worked out of New York. See Charles Champlin (1967) 'Movie Chief Jack Valenti – Seal of Approval, So Far', *LA Times*, 5 February.

9. Glickman's appointment was somewhat unexpected as Valenti's anointed successor had been Louisiana Congressman Republican Billy Tauzin, chair of the House Telecoms Committee. However, when Tauzin shifted his interests to represent the US pharmaceutical industry, Glickman, with his experience of negotiating international trade agreements in the agricultural sector and a film producer son John, was headhunted. See Leonard Klady (2005) 'Switching Food Chains', *Screen International*, 18 March. In his semi-retirement, Valenti will co-ordinate with the theatre owners to administer the ratings system.

10. To pressure Congress to establish permanent US–China trade relations, Valenti organised a Hollywood committee including Lew Wasserman, Sumner Redstone, Rupert Murdoch and Michael Eisner to ensure 'America's "glittering trade prize" could take a gibbon-like plunge into the cinematic swamp of protectionism' (Bromley, 2003: 40).

11. For further details, see Chapter 4 on copyright, piracy and information communication technologies in Toby Miller *et al.* (2005), *Global Hollywood 2*, London: British Film Institute (2nd edn).

3
The MPPDA, the Production Code and the Ratings System

Introduction

From Hollywood's earliest days, US films were considered to have a profound influence on the public. In 1922 the Jewish studio bosses, responding to pressures from state censors, anti-Semites and Christian groups, established the MPPDA led by the Presbyterian Will H. Hays. Hays attempted to develop a 'formula' to ensure the moral content of films. And by 1930 he presided over the Production Code, which had been drawn up by the Catholic publisher of the *Exhibitors Herald-World* Martin Quigley and Jesuit priest Father Daniel Lord.

However, while a successful publicist, Hays' role as Hollywood's 'movie czar' was undermined when the studios used sex to sell films during the Depression. As pressures built up to censor pictures, Hays, backed by the Catholic Legion of Decency, Hearst newspapers and Quigley, campaigned to enforce the Production Code. He reasoned with the moguls that if they did not agree to a self-enforced code, Washington would establish federal censorship in accordance with the Supreme Court's 1915 decision stating that films did not enjoy the First Amendment privileges of freedom of speech.

Hays appointed the staunchly Catholic and anti-Semitic Joseph I. Breen to head the Production Code Administration (PCA) offices in Los Angeles from 1934. Breen applied the Hays Code in which all studio pictures were vetted for sex, violence, crime and language, and had to carry the PCA Seal of Approval. Hays and Breen also had a secondary agenda – to root out those films dealing with social and political issues.

While the Code remained in place for thirty years, several directors circumvented its controls, and its purpose to withstand government censorship was undermined when the Supreme Court granted free-speech protections to movies under the First Amendment in 1952. This led to the collapse of state censors and to film-makers becoming more courageous in their battles against the PCA. For instance, Otto Preminger's *The Moon Is Blue* and *The Man with the Golden Arm* were released without the Seal of Approval in 1953 and 1956 respectively. By the 1960s, films such as *Who's Afraid of Virginia Woolf?* (1966), *Alfie* (1966) and *The Pawnbroker* (1964) received PCA exemptions and demonstrated the idiosyncrasies of the Code.

When Jack Valenti became President of the MPAA he replaced the Code with the Ratings system which has been applied since the late 1960s. Consequently, in the last forty years, mainstream movies have dealt graphically with the issues of sex and violence. Such representations have led to renewed calls for censorship. In the 1990s, films such as *Reservoir Dogs* (1992), *Pulp Fiction* (1994) and *Natural Born Killers* (1994) provoked fears about copycat violence. Alternatively, liberals argued that all forms of censorship were retrogressive. This debate has grown incrementally as moviegoers' viewing habits have changed in the advent of home video, DVD, pay-per-view, video-on-demand and the Internet.

This chapter considers the social, cultural and religious imperatives which led to the introduction of the Hays Code and the contradictions that occurred when it was applied. It will address how the MPAA replaced the Code with the Ratings system and the extent to which this liberalisation affected US films in the 1960s and 1970s. Finally, the study outlines the recent debates on US film as new voices and actors have dominated the agenda of censorship since the 1980s.

The establishment of the Hays Code

Hays' appointment was determined by his political connections (see Chapter 1), but more importantly by his Presbyterian background which offset the anti-Semitic attacks aimed at Hollywood in the early 1920s. Initially, Hays was more of an industry mouthpiece than a censor, as the studios' priorities lay in their profits rather than their films' virtues. This disregard led to Hays allying with Protestant and Catholic groups to establish the Production Code. And the divisions between Hollywood and its critics were exacerbated in the Depression when provocative films were produced to attract audiences. Hays warned the moguls that, if they did not abide by his Code, Washington would intervene and by 1934 every studio picture carried the PCA Seal of Approval.

HOLLYWOOD BABYLON: MORALITY, SIN AND CENSORSHIP

In the 1920s, over 40 million Americans watched films every week and the wealthy moguls remained oblivious to concerns about freedom of expression or censorship. However, their pictures attracted the wrath of Christian organisations, temperance associations, anti-Semitic groups and local censors who believed the studio's Jewish entrepreneurs were corrupting the nation's morals.

These attitudes belied America's image of a nation built on tolerance. Instead, the 'Hollywood question' concerning the participation of Jews in public life came to the fore with regard to the moral content of the films. In particular, the anti-Semitic Henry Ford considered the Jewish control of films an insidious means to dictate tastes and to erode decency: 'The movies are of Jewish production. If you fight filth, the fight carries you straight into the Jewish camp because the majority of the producers are there. And then you are "attacking the Jews"' (Ford, 1921).

Hollywood's independence was further undermined by the political elite's contempt for the film industry when the Supreme Court decided in the case of the *Mutual Film Corporation versus the Industrial Commission of Ohio* that films were a form of commerce whose content should not be protected by the First Amendment. This ruling led to state and city censors being established to ensure public propriety and to stop America being scandalised by films with blatant sexual imagery (Carr, 2001: 63).

The ire of these censors was intensified by the scandals surrounding the film community in the late 1910s and the early 1920s. In 1919, 'America's sweetheart' Mary Pickford shocked the nation when she filed for a 'quickie' divorce from Owen Moore, to marry her co-star Douglas Fairbanks. However, worse was to come when matinee idol Wallace Reid died from a drugs overdose and director William Desmond Taylor was murdered in a love tryst that implicated Mary Miles Minter and Mabel Normand.

Yet these events were nothing compared to the controversy in 1921 when Fatty Arbuckle, the industry's leading comic star after Charlie Chaplin, was accused of raping starlet Virginia Rappe at a wild party in San Francisco. Sensing a high circulation, William Randolph Hearst's newspaper, *The San Francisco Enquirer*, contended that the overweight Arbuckle had sexually assaulted the 'virginal' Rappe with a bottle. When Rappe died from her injuries, the monstrous vision of Arbuckle forcing himself on her was too much for the public to bear. However, in the subsequent trial for manslaughter, the District Attorney failed to make a case because the prosecutions' witnesses were unreliable and Rappe's reputation as a 'party girl' with a drink problem was revealed. Despite his acquittal, Arbuckle's career was finished as public opinion had turned against him.

The combined effect of these scandals, alongside the calls for censorship, forced the moguls to address the industry's image problems. They hired Hays to bolster Hollywood's tainted reputation and to convince the public the film community would clean up its act.

WILL HAYS AND THE MPPDA

For Hays, the film industrialists' offer to become 'movie czar' was well timed, allowing him to extricate himself from the Tea Dome scandal that overtook the 1920s' Republican administration. For the moguls, Hays, as a conservative Republican, teetotaller, Presbyterian elder, Rotarian and Mason, represented Middle America in a Jewish industry and was 'the visible sign of invisible grace' (Black, 1994: 33).

In the light of 100 censorship bills in thirty-seven states, Hays had a free hand in shaping the MPPDA to enforce self-censorship and to effect better public relations. In 1924, Hays introduced a voluntary scheme called the 'Formula' requiring the studios to put forward each play, novel and story synopsis to the MPPDA to determine the suitability of the material. However, this was a failure as the association only rejected 125 projects.

To develop further controls over content, Hays established the Studio Relations Department (SRD) in Los Angeles, successively headed by Jason Joy, James Wingate and Catholic activist Joseph Breen. The SRD developed a voluntary code consisting of the most common complaints from the local censors. This included 'Don'ts and Be Carefuls' prohibiting nudity, profanity, drug trafficking and white slavery. It also required the studios to show sensitivity in representations of sexuality, violence and criminal behaviour.

Despite the SRD's liaisons with the studios, they ignored its recommendations and Hays, located in New York, had few powers to effect self-censorship. He became a more effective spokesman for Hollywood and saw off further state censorship when he won the 1922 Massachusetts' referendum concerning controls over film content. In this campaign, he argued that such regulations were unAmerican and the mandate declared a three-to-one victory. This success stemmed the momentum for other state censorship initiatives and stymied the passage of the bills appearing in Congress.

Hays' impotence on the self-regulation issue angered the anti-movie Protestant lobby including the Women's Christian Temperance Union, the Motion Picture Research Council, the Federal Motion Picture Council and the Hearst press which called for federal intervention. Their criticisms of Hollywood were exacerbated when the moguls introduced sound into their films and the state censors worked furiously to regulate the 'talkies'. With the advent of sound, Catholic leaders demanded Hollywood should abide by stricter stand-ards or the church would organise a boycott. The influential Jesuit priest Father Daniel Lord complained, 'Silent smut had been bad, vocal smut cried to the censors for vengeance' (Vaughn, 1990: 51).

Yet it was Lord and Catholic publisher Martin Quigley, as authors of the Production Code, who provided Hays with the blueprint through which he could control the industry. Although US films outraged Quigley, as the proprietor of the exhibitors' trade paper he sought to protect the interests of the theatre owners. Thus, he opposed federal censorship as it might undermine the industry's fragile financial structure. Instead, he argued for a motion picture code to ensure censurable material could be removed before a film hit the nation's screens. This would quell further forms of state censorship, stem the boycott and render unnecessary the Protestant groups' calls to restrict the block-booking of films.

From this position, Hays convinced the moguls to accept the voluntary Code to ward off governmental intervention. In turn, the studios were aware of the damage that might be caused by a Catholic–Protestant boycott as a 'major interruption in the cash flow from the box office or from the bankers could bring the movie house of cards tumbling down' (Black, 1994: 43). Hays informed the studios that by policing themselves they could affect savings as the Code could be adhered to when a film was produced thus removing the expense associated with revising prints after the censors had made their cuts. These argu-ments fell on fertile ground as the majors had lost fortunes in the Wall Street crash and with the introduction of sound (ibid.: 57). Hays could therefore sell the Code to Holly-wood as the money-saving measure it had been looking for and it was adopted on 31 March 1930.

THE 1930 PRODUCTION CODE

Quigley and Lord's Production Code instigated restrictions on representations of sex and violence, regulated screen kisses and banned proscribed words and phrases. The sanctity of marriage and the home were upheld, and adultery or illicit sex, though sometimes necessi-tated by the plot, could not be made explicit. The Code prohibited nudity, suggestive dances and the ridicule of religion, while forbidding depictions of drug use, venereal disease, child-birth and miscegenation. The criminals were not to inspire sympathy, murders had to avoid imitation and brutal slayings should not be shown.

To publicise the Code, Hays' and Quigley's diplomatic skills were tested as the Catholic Legion of Decency and the Protestants called for further censorship. Only the first half of the Code was published and the second part detailing 'The Reasons' was not made public. Hays' reluctance reflected his desire to placate the moguls who objected to Lord's declaration that a film's subject matter should be qualified as it was made to attract a mass audience (Vaughn, 1990: 53–4). He did not want to make conspicuous to Protestant groups that the Code had been drawn up by a Jesuit Priest and a Catholic layman. Similarly, Quigley sought anonymity due to the dangers of associating the rules with the Catholic Church. He omitted any reference to his own role in the process and declared the Code:

> . . . was formulated after intensive study by members of the industry and, according to Will H. Hays, by church-leaders, leaders in the field of education, representatives of women's clubs, educators, psychologists, dramatists and other students of our moral, social and family problems (Black, 1994: 241).

The public and the presses' reaction was mixed. Some newspapers argued the Code had gone too far, while others maintained it would ensure a higher calibre of entertainment. Several groups suggested it was no more than an extended version of the 'Don'ts and Be Carefuls' which had been employed by the SRD since the mid-1920s.

Many sceptics doubted the producers would abide by the Code and when Quigley surveyed the studio executives after its adoption, he discovered most believed it was a public relations exercise designed to curb excesses. Moreover, as they appreciated the bottom line, Hollywood's industrialists realised their chances to compete with the lurid tales available in the press could be undermined if 'we are obliged to . . . drive with our brakes on' (Walsh, 1996: 62). This attitude placed them on a collision course with the moralists when US films' content was foregrounded by the decline in audiences brought about by the Depression.

SEX AND VIOLENCE SELLS THE MOVIES: HOLLYWOOD, THE DEPRESSION AND THE PRODUCTION CODE

As their financial woes increased, the studios slacked off in their adherence to the Code. Instead, from 1930 to 1934, they produced tales of wanton women employing their sexuality to get ahead. These 'bad girl' movies included *Red Headed Woman* (1932), *Possessed* (1931), *Baby Face* (1933), *Blonde Venus* (1932) and *Susan Lennox* (1931) with stars like Jean Harlow, Barbara Stanwyck, Marlene Dietrich and Greta Garbo. As they were hits, executives sought more explicit material to keep the public returning to the cinemas.

Thus, Cecil B. De Mille included scenes of sexual debauchery to sell Victorian morality tales such as *The Sign of the Cross* (1932) and Merian C. Cooper's *King Kong* (1933) included references to bestiality between the giant ape and his human paramour Ann (Doherty, 1999: 289–93). Even cartoons like Max Fleischer's 'Betty Boop' demonstrated a liberalised attitude to sex. Paramount was saved by the returns associated with the comedies it made with the sexually voracious Mae West including *She Done Him Wrong* (1933). On the back of West's success, the studio bought William Faulkner's tale of rape, perversion, impotence and homicide, *Sanctuary*, and produced a sanitised version of the novel called *The Story of Temple*

Drake (1933). However, this film and *Ann Vickers* (1933), based on a book by Sinclair Lewis, were cited as being dangerous by Hays as they challenged his authority and demonstrated the Code could not easily be implemented.

With this realisation, the independent producer/mogul Howard Hughes made *Hell's Angels* (1930) which, while being noted for it aerial dogfights, concerned a two-timing female schemer using her sexuality to bed the male leads. In his next production, *Scarface* (1932), Hughes encouraged director Howard Hawks to stage violent gun battles and to portray the anti-hero Tony Camonte as an attractive figure, in violation of the Code. Hays demanded revisions which toned down the gunfights so the film passed through the state censors. With favourable reviews and large returns, along with Warner Bros.' classics such as *Little Caesar* (1930) and *The Public Enemy* (1931) with vibrant performances by Edward G. Robinson and James Cagney, it paved the way for the gangster movie genre in the 1930s. It also demonstrated the dual function of the MPPDA as both a self-censor and a protector of the industry's financial interests (Black, 1994: 131).

Hollywood producers demonstrated a social and political conscience in films which challenged US legal structures, penal systems and government affairs such as *I Am a Fugitive from a Chain Gang* (1932) and *Gabriel over the White House* (1933). The latter favoured a fascist dictatorship in America and was co-written by William Randolph Hearst. Again, Hays was worried by the film's content, as it was taken as a direct insult by Washington, and demanded cuts to tone down its political implications:

> . . . Films that questioned basic values, as did the gangster genre, illustrated the corruption and unfairness, as did prison dramas, or challenged the view that government was dedicated to the general welfare of the public . . . were worrisome to Hays. . . . The lesson Hays learned . . . was no amount of postproduction cutting . . . could change a film's basic flavour. Controlling content would require strong, firm, preproduction control at the studio level (ibid.: 144–5).

Hays found it impossible to balance the interests of the moralists with the financial inclinations of the producers. Although the SRD reviewed 1,391 scripts between 1931 and 1933 and declined to recommend 20 per cent of them, ecumenical conservatives lobbied Washington to express their displeasure (Vaughn, 1990: 62). In 'the Storm of '34' these forces were harnessed by the National Legion of Decency, the Motion Picture Research Council and New Deal reformers who were open to federal censorship. The confluence of these religious and political interests meant Hollywood had to clean itself up as Congress was readying itself to pass a range of censorship bills backed by President Roosevelt (Doherty, 1999: 320).

When federal rulings became a distinct possibility, the moguls relented to Hays' reorganisation of the MPPDA. First, they abolished the Producers Appeal Board which had reversed decisions made by the SRD. Second, a more powerful body, the PCA, whose decisions could only be reversed by the MPPDA's directors in New York, replaced the SRD. By taking the power away from the moguls and returning it to the holding companies, Hays ensured the PCA's autonomy. This was further cemented by the Bank of America's president A. P. Giannini (one of the industry's must powerful backers) who informed the producers that no film would receive funding without a PCA Seal of Approval.

By confirming the PCA's authority, Hays demonstrated to the religious associations that the Code had sufficient teeth. In return, Quigley was able to call off the Catholic boycott and the federal government retreated. To enforce the Code, Hays appointed the SRD head and Catholic layman Breen as the PCA director and his authority was assured as from 'henceforth . . . [his power] . . . flowed not from a council of Hollywood-based executives but from the MPPDA board back in New York, the same men the studio moguls served' (ibid.: 327). Moreover, Breen's Catholicism would offset further boycotts and provide him with access to the Wall Street hierarchy which held the paper assets on the studios.

The Hays Office

The PCA, known colloquially as the 'Hays Office',[1] had the authority to review every Hollywood movie from its inception to its completion. It could demand changes in the script, on the set and once a film had been made. And from 1935 to 1948 the PCA considered 7,071 features and a further 4,553 original screen stories. The producers acquiesced to this process, as each film was required to carry the PCA Seal of Approval to be shown in the first-run theatres owned by the majors. Hays and Breen employed the PCA to vet those newsreels and films that showed any sympathy to the principles of organised labour. However, the PCA faced innumerable battles with film-makers who found ways to circumvent the Code or chose to challenge it outright.

'If I were Will Hays': The Hays Code tries to outlaw sin in Tinseltown

THE HAYS OFFICE UNDER JOSEPH BREEN

Each studio picture was reviewed by the Hays Office, whose power was instituted by the MPPDA's decision to administer a $25,000 fine to any theatre that showed a film without a PCA Seal of Approval. Through its enforcement of the Code, Breen pledged that the PCA would root out cheap, vulgar and tawdry films which offended common decency. A forceful figure, Breen opened the PCA in a blaze of publicity with a series of radio interviews and newsreels. He would remain in charge of the PCA, with a brief interregnum at RKO from 1941 to 1943, until his retirement in 1954.

The Hays Office was located in a Spartan, four-storey building on the corner of Hollywood Boulevard and Western Avenue. In contrast to the moguls' palatial offices, the PCA's atmosphere was defined by austere bare floors and steel desks. An enlarged staff supported Breen so the voluminous number of scripts and films could be reviewed. To this end, he was assisted by former SRD head James Wingate, linguist Karl Lischka, screenwriter Iselin Auster, theatre manager Arthur Houghton and a former studio employee, Douglas Mackinnon.

To effect the PCA's new powers, Breen demonstrated his intransigence in dealing with Hollywood's producers. This was apparent in the Hays Office's first showdown with MGM over a comedy entitled *Forsaking All Others* (1934) starring Clark Gable, Joan Crawford and Robert Montgomery. Breen believed the feature, in its depiction of a love triangle, undermined the sanctity of marriage by including a potentially adulterous relationship between the single Crawford and the married Montgomery. In a seven-page memo, he demanded dialogue rewrites to underscore the heroine's virtue and the director W. S. Van Dyke was mandated to shoot retakes. Similarly, Breen refused to pass films from the old epoch unless they were re-cut to conform to the strictures of the Code. Through these interventions, Breen showed Hollywood that the balance of power between the PCA and the studios had shifted (Doherty, 1999: 329–30).

In becoming the industry's enforcer, Breen also demonstrated his political, ideological and anti-Semitic biases:

> These Jews seem to think of nothing but moneymaking and sexual indulgence. . . . [and] decide what the film fare of the nation is to be. They and they alone make the decision. 95 per cent of these folks are Jews of an Eastern European lineage. They are, probably, the scum of the earth (Breen, 1934).

Additionally, he not only sought to remove representations of sexual congress or violent behaviour, but kept back images of class-consciousness from US screens. He censored strike footage from newsreels, condemned movies advancing labour rights and removed scenes that placed an emphasis on the antagonistic relations between capital and labour. In 1934, Hays communicated his concern to Breen that riots between the police and the public had been included in the film *Manhattan Melodrama* (1934), and matters of community order were from then on treated with circumspection.

Conversely, films promoting a distorted view of workers acting as a lawless mob were allowed on the screen (Ross, 1999). Further, Breen's conservative tendencies led to him tacitly supporting fascists and he made his displeasure known over films such as *Confessions of a Nazi Spy* (1939), *The Great Dictator* (1940) and *I Married a Nazi* (1940). His opposition to these pictures was partly dictated by his own personal views and by his belief that such movies would cut Hollywood off from the world market (Vasey, 1997; Lewis, 2000: 23). For Breen and Hays:

> Films were not vehicles for social and political criticism; rather . . . they were opportunities to promote the 'social spirit of patriotism.'. . . Promoting a conservative political agenda, [they] felt [they] had to protect audiences [by adhering] . . . to accepted conservative moral standards and were not to challenge, attack or embarrass the government; they were, in fact, to support the government (Black, 1994: 246).

To effect Hays and Breen's social engineering, more saccharine films such as *Stand Up and Cheer* (1934) with child superstar Shirley Temple emerged and, in the fallout, several stars survived while others were not so fortunate. Jean Harlow swapped her seductive image as a platinum blonde to become an all-American, girl-next-door and her career flourished. Conversely, Mae West's career was ruined when Breen refused to countenance her trademark sexual innuendos and double entendres. Her first Code-approved film, *It Ain't No Sin* (1934), was retitled *Belle of the Nineties* after the Catholic church threatened to boycott the production, and proved a tepid version of her earlier successes. An exhibitor complained, ' "Mae West is through, I'm afraid . . . The 'kick' audiences expected wasn't there nor were the expected cracks . . . The Decency Campaign took the edge off Mae" ' (Doherty, 1999: 338).

Although there were protests, the majority of Hollywood's scriptwriters, film-makers and producers acquiesced to the PCA. This occurred because of the costs they saved, as their films no longer had to be altered in post-production. These family entertainments, most especially the films of Temple and a cycle of movies based on literary classics such as *Little Women* (1933), accorded with the conservative visions of moguls like Louis B. Mayer and were successful at the box office. As there was an upturn in the industry's finances in 1934, whether or not because of the Code, its supporters pointed to the link between the new morality and the studios' prosperity:

> Why quibble? The Code kept the Catholics happy, restored Hollywood to the public respectability, greased the production machinery, and pumped up the profits in the midst of the crippling Depression. . . . censorship was a basic assumption of moviemaking, a necessary item on the balance sheet, factored into the cost of doing business. As such it had best be done in a businesslike manner, and the Production Code Administration under Joseph I. Breen was nothing if not businesslike (ibid.: 336).

THE HAYS OFFICE VERSUS HOLLYWOOD

Throughout the second half of the 1930s, the Hays Office passed those films which showed sufficient decorum, restraint and conformity. Consequently, Breen ensured Maureen O'Sullivan's jungle outfit in *Tarzan Escapes* (1936) was extended to her knees, Betty Boop wore a longer hemline without her garter belt, Clark Gable kept his shirt on and Cecil B. De Mille's epics became more chaste. Gangster movies were toned down and James Cagney switched allegiances to become a government agent in *G-Men* (1935). Hoodlums saw the errors of their ways and Cagney's character in *Angels with Dirty Faces* (1938), in a final sacrifice to his boyhood pal Father Connolly, gave up his courageous reputation to 'die yellow' so the parish boys would not follow his career path.

Although Breen's powers grew, the PCA's interventions led to conflicts with Hollywood on several notable occasions. MGM's version of the light operetta *The Merry Widow* (1934), directed by Ernst Lubitsch and starring Jeanette MacDonald and Maurice Chevalier, became subject to a debate between Breen, Hays and Quigley. While the PCA had called for a few script changes, it passed the film without further cuts in September 1934. However, on seeing the picture, Hays and Quigley were outraged by the principal male characters' preoccupation with sex. Therefore, they required thirteen cuts from MGM head of production Irving Thalberg, who reluctantly cabled his distributors to change the prints. While Breen believed he knew 'immorality' when he saw it, this experience chastened the enforcer who had seen the picture as nothing more than a farce (Black, 1994: 201–2).

On the back of this dispute, the PCA entered into conflicts on such films as *Nana* (1934), *Anna Karenina* (1935), *The Barbary Coast* (1935) and Mae West's *Klondike Annie* (1936). Breen objected to the movies of the Austrian sex symbol Hedy Lamarr, most especially her European debut *Ecstasy* (1933), and to the tight sweaters worn by Lana Turner to emphasise her breasts.

The Hays Office also compiled a long list of restricted words including 'alley cats', 'broads' and 'nuts'. And it was in this context that David O. Selznick came into conflict with the PCA during his production of Margaret Mitchell's epic novel *Gone With the Wind* (1939). Under the Code, a number of the story's elements were taboo including scenes of Melanie Wilkes' giving birth, Belle Watley's whorehouse and Rhett Butler's husbandly rape of Scarlett O'Hara. However, Breen most vehemently objected to the inclusion of the obscenity 'damn' which appeared in the book's most famous line 'Frankly, my dear, I don't give a damn'. He refused to allow Selznick to include the line in the film if the producer wanted it to receive the PCA Seal. Ultimately, Selznick with the backing of Loews chief Nicholas Schenck took the fight to Hays who, realising where the power laid, granted the expensive picture a special dispensation (Gomery, 2005b: 176).

Films with social commentaries attracted the Hays Office's attention. German émigré Fritz Lang's first American film *Fury* (1936) was produced by MGM and starred Spencer Tracy whose character, after being unjustly accused of kidnapping, appears to be killed in a lynching. While the character survives, he uses the resulting trial of the small-town mob to exact his revenge. Although there was a requisite happy ending in which Tracy grants clemency to the townsfolk, the studio took the film away from Lang to ensure a cut which adhered to the Code (Black, 1994: 264–8).

Similarly, the independent producer Samuel Goldwyn had to deal with the Hays Office on such films as *These Three* (1936) and *Dead End* (1937), both directed by William Wyler. The former was a bowdlerised adaptation by Lillian Hellman of her play *The Children's Hour*, whose lesbianism was dropped in favour of an emphasis on gossip and betrayal. The latter dealt with the lawlessness in America's slums owing to the deprivations of the Depression. Realising the original play would have to be toned down, Goldwyn informed Hellman to drop the vulgar language, adultery, venereal disease and violence. In turn, he told Wyler to reduce the emphasis on the poverty and disease that dominated the film's representation of New York's slums. Goldwyn shrewdly included the PCA in the decision-making process and the film was praised as an outstanding condemnation of the urban decay affecting US cities (ibid.: 274–81).

In these cases, the PCA combined its efforts with the Legion of Decency's reviewers and local censorship boards to enforce order, and its position became more dominant in the Hollywood hierarchy. However, over the years, Breen remained mindful of the strategies screenwriters and directors employed to circumvent the Code, while several film-makers openly challenged his authority.

CIRCUMVENTING AND CHALLENGING THE CODE
Throughout the 1940s, a number of films brought into question the PCA's effectiveness and a depressed Breen left the Hays Office in 1941 to become the general manager of RKO. However, he returned in 1943 to recommence his battle with Hollywood's producers and the various techniques they employed to evade the Code.

One of the industry's greatest satirists, Preston Sturges, directed several films including *Hail the Conquering Hero* (1944), *Sullivan's Travels* (1941) and *The Lady Eve* (1941) which attacked the Codes' sacred cows. Most especially, his comedy *The Miracle of Morgan's Creek* (1944) lampooned the military, virgin birth and the nativity in its tale of a single woman who discovers she is pregnant after a night out on the town. It led to critic James Agee commenting, 'The Hays Office has either been hypnotised into a liberality for which it should be thanked or it has been raped in its sleep – *The Miracle of Morgan's Creek* is a bit like talking to a nun on a roller coaster!' (Erickson, 2005) Yet, Sturges, in dealing with the PCA, provided Breen with such an outrageous script that once the offending passages were removed he got through what he had wanted to include in the first place.

In film noirs such as *Double Indemnity* (1944) and *Sunset Boulevard* (1950), Billy Wilder provided representations of murder, lust and adultery. With regard to the latter film, Wilder and co-writer/producer Charles Brackett played a game of cat-and-mouse by releasing selective portions of the script to Breen to read. This allowed them to introduce the more controversial elements of the plot, such as the affair between hack screenwriter Joe Gillis and the older, silent cinema legend Norma Desmond, when they saw fit and to Breen only passing the entire script on 20 July 1949, a month after principal photography had been completed. Years later Wilder wistfully commented, 'There are times when I wish we had censorship, because the fun has gone out of it, the game you played with them' (Staggs, 2002: 34).

Others, including Otto Preminger, Tay Garnett, Robert Aldrich and Alfred Hitchcock, used noirs to circumvent the principles of the Code. In *Laura* (1944), Preminger provided the audiences with coded meanings to indicate the homosexuality of the characters played by Clifton Webb and Vincent Price. Garnett retained the seedy imagery of the underbelly of US society in *The Postman Always Rings Twice* (1946), while Aldrich demonstrated the immorality of private eye Mike Hammer in *Kiss Me Deadly* (1955) in using his secretary/girlfriend Maxine to entrap his clients. In *Notorious* (1946), Hitchcock got around the PCA's regulations concerning the length of a screen kiss by having Ingrid Bergman and Cary Grant repeatedly peck one another for just long enough to cumulatively effect Hollywood's longest smooch.

'Mean, moody and magnificent': Jane Russell in Howard Hughes' *The Outlaw*

While these film-makers found ingenious methods to outwit Breen, others challenged the Hays Office outright. The most spectacular conflagration concerned Howard Hughes' 1941 Western *The Outlaw* in which the size of Jane Russell's bust stirred an intense debate between the PCA and the multimillionaire. During the production, Hughes employed his airplane designers to create a bra which increased Russell's cleavage and Breen declared the film to be unreleasable. Yet in removing the sequences the PCA demanded, Hughes realised the production was a disaster. Therefore he withdrew the film until 1944 claiming it was too shocking to be shown to the public.

After three years on the shelf, Hughes reinstated the shots of Russell's breasts and reopened the movie in a publicity blitz which focused on the starlet's cleavage under the tagline 'Mean, Moody, Magnificent'. In response, Breen removed the Seal of Approval and Hughes exhibited the film in those cinema circuits which showed exploitation features. This strategy encouraged public interest and the poorly conceived feature was a massive hit.

Another Western which caused the PCA consternation was David O. Selznick's *Duel in the Sun* (1946) which earned the sobriquet 'lust in the dust'. However, by the late 1940s, with the changes in post-war attitudes affecting American audiences it was Italian neo-realist films such as *The Bicycle Thieves* (1948) and *Bitter Rice* (1940) with their focus on poverty, criminality and raw sexuality which caused offence. A major controversy surrounded the extramarital affair portrayed in *Stromboli* (1950) and the one which occurred during its filming between director Roberto Rossellini and his leading lady Ingrid Bergman. The latter was attacked by the Papacy and withdrawn from Hollywood. Further, the adult nature of these films coincided with new developments in the US theatre as playwrights like Tennessee Williams, directors such as Elia Kazan and actors including Marlon Brando delved into more difficult subject areas.

This trio had a tremendous Broadway success with *A Streetcar Named Desire* and were employed by Warner Bros. to make a film version of the play in 1951. The PCA was shocked by the pictures' representation of the brute sexuality of Brando's Stanley Kowalski, the rape of Blanche DuBois and the jazz score from Alex North. While the film-makers agreed to tone down the material, they remained adamant that the rape of DuBois by Kowalski was integral to the film which, due to its origins as a play, was treated by the PCA as an exceptional case and was not subject to the general application of the Code. This decision resulted in more adult-orientated movies, such as *Born Yesterday* (1949), *A Place in the Sun* (1951), *The African Queen* (1951), *The Red Badge of Courage* (1951) and *From Here to Eternity* (1953), being made. To this end, Breen believed the studios were conspiring to undermine the Code and the Association of Motion Picture Producers Inc. (AMPP)'s Arch Reeve complained:

> Our [offices] are disturbed . . . over the bad publicity continually going out of Hollywood on the Production Code Administration. Many of the worst blasts against our system of self-regulation stem from persons in Hollywood . . . I need not tell you that the Production Code Administration is the protector of the entire industry. It means just as much to you and your studio as it does to me and our associations. It stands for the fine and decent, it is our defence against censorship and against attacks from quarters that have proven so menacing (Reeve, 1945).

THE COLLAPSE OF THE CODE

For many years, the PCA justified self-regulation as the means through which the US industry had offset the proliferation of state censors and had stemmed federal censorship. This was necessitated because of the Supreme Court's decision to consider films as being a form of commerce which should not receive First Amendment privileges.

However, in 1952, the Supreme Court overruled its 1915 decision due to the state of New York's release of Rossellini's *The Miracle*. In this forty-minute short, a simple-minded peasant girl tells her village she has conceived a child by immaculate conception when in fact a bearded stranger claiming to be St Joseph has seduced her. The film was denounced as sacrilegious by the Catholic Archdeacon of New York Cardinal Francis Spellman who lobbied the State Board of Regents to revoke the film's licence. This decision was contested by the distributor Joseph Burstyn who went to the state's Courts of Appeal to have it overturned. When this failed, he took the case to the Supreme Court in February 1952 and three months later it upheld Burstyn's appeal when Justice Clark declared: '. . . it cannot be doubted that motion pictures are a significant medium for the communication of ideas . . . And, as such, they [are] within the free speech and free press guarantees of the First and Fourteenth Amendments' (Randall, 1970: 29).

Consequently, although the PCA had not been involved in the case, the justification for its existence was undermined. This difficulty was compounded by Breen's retirement and replacement by Geoffrey Shurlock in 1954. With the powerhouse enforcer gone, the Code looked anachronistic in the Cold War era. Preminger challenged the PCA's authority when his 1953 sex comedy *The Moon Is Blue* and his 1956 drama on drug addiction *The Man with the Golden Arm* were released without the Seal of Approval. In response to these and others films, such as *The Wild One* (1954), *East of Eden* (1955) and *Baby Doll* (1956), Shurlock made a few amendments to the Code which, in reality, demonstrated its obsolescence (Lewis, 2000: 114). By providing these films with its Seal of Approval, the PCA fell foul of its most ardent backers including the Legion of Decency and lost support from the moral organisations who had backed its establishment in the first place.

At the same time, Hollywood was facing greater competition from television which enabled American audiences to view adult plays and news programmes. The PCA, along with the House Committee of UnAmerican Activities' (HUAC) political censorship of films (see Chapter 5), restricted film-makers from mature explorations of different facets of human behaviour. For instance, when filming Vladimir Nabokov's novel, *Lolita*, in 1962, Stanley Kubrick had to remove overt references to Humbert Humbert's sexual desire for the under-age teenager. With the financial collapse of the studio system, many predicted US cinema-goers would only go to theatres to watch pornography.

Matters came to a head in the mid-1960s when three studios pictures, *The Pawnbroker*, *Alfie* and *Who's Afraid of Virginia Woolf?*, were granted exemptions by the PCA to include pro-scribed subject matter such as nudity, abortion, adultery and marital breakdown. Then in 1966, MGM circumvented the PCA when it released *Blow Up* (1960), with its scenes of naked models, without a Seal of Approval through its foreign distribution arm. Thus, the studios were not only challenging the PCA but had begun to actively ignore it.

Simultaneously, the Supreme Court ended prior censorship and licensing in the 1965 case of *Freedman versus Maryland*, in which it judged the state of Maryland's censorship board did not have the right to ban a motion picture unless it violated federal obscenity laws. Subsequently, the Maryland board, along with several remaining censors in Kansas, Virginia and Memphis, closed its doors within a year.

However, in a last hurrah for local censorship, the still powerful Chicago board banned three non-MPAA films – *Ulysses*, *Rent-a-Girl* and *Body of a Female* – for being obscene, in 1967. While the latter two films were no more than softcore pornography, Joseph Strick's adaptation of James Joyce's *Ulysses* received favourable treatment when theatre owner Walter Reade obtained a temporary injunction to allow him to show the film for three days without a city permit. As a result, the Chicago distributor of the exploitation films, Chuck Teitel filed a counterclaim stating his films should receive the same rights. While this skirmish did not directly impact on the PCA, it demonstrated the absurdity of a rigid code which equated a literary adaptation with softcore features (ibid.: 149).

With the decline of the Code and the removal of state censors, Hollywood needed to establish a national system of review consistent with the evolving federal legal standards on obscenity. Therefore when Jack Valenti was appointed as the MPAA president in 1966 he replaced the discredited Code with a new set of voluntary laws in the Ratings system.

The Ratings system

The introduction of the Ratings system was necessitated by the changes in legal rulings on obscenity, reforms in American society and the decline in studios' profits in the 1960s. In the era of the Vietnam War, the counterculture and civil unrest, Hollywood's films remained largely oblivious to contemporary trends owing to the Code's constraints. This was disastrous as it undermined the studios' survival by keeping a huge youth market away from the nation's theatres. Valenti appreciated these difficulties when he mobilised support for his classification system. Subsequently, US films dealt explicitly with matters of sex and violence. However, in recent years, both fundamentalists and libertarians have attacked the system. In response, Valenti declared the Ratings system had protected freedoms for movie producers and US society alike.

On 7 October 1968, Valenti unveiled the Ratings system, signalling the demise of the PCA. He claimed that by scrapping the Code, US films could reflect changing social mores and enjoy the rights of free speech, as film-makers would be provided with a set of voluntary guidelines rather than a mandatory set of rules to follow. He argued no set of censors should determine what the public might view and parental choice would effect the requisite degree of self-regulation over films seen by children (Valenti, 2004b).

Yet Valenti's pronouncement was driven as much by business considerations as by free speech. In 1966, he attended a meeting convened by Jack Warner to appeal against the PCA's refusal to provide a Seal for *Who's Afraid of Virginia Woolf?* The MPAA president used this and subsequent gatherings with the industry's leaders to mobilise support for the classification system which allowed them to make adult films to reconnect with American audiences. Concurrently, the Ratings system created a national film censorship standard and:

> More importantly [they] gave the studios control over the entry into the entertainment marketplace. You can't make much money on a film without an MPAA rating. And you can't get an MPAA rating without first paying a deed to the studio-run organisation (Lewis, 2000: 150).

Therefore, by ensuring a cartel in production, distribution and exhibition, the system not only received the producers' backing but that of the National Association of Theatre Owners (NATO) and the International Film Importers and Distributors of America (IFIDA). It also removed the need for the majors to make their films abroad and release them through foreign distribution arms to get around the PCA. This appealed to the guilds as it meant there would be an increase in local film production.

To sustain wider support, Valenti cultivated the friendship of leading film artists such as Robert Wise, Norman Jewison, John Forsyth, Burt Lancaster and Kirk Douglas who collectively wrote to the American Civil Liberties Union:

> We applaud the beginning of this voluntary film ratings system if it continues to be a programme of integrity, operating within the bounds it has set for itself, then we believe it will be a boom to the creative freedoms of the screen, our defence against the intrusion of the government and our declared pledge to the parents of this nation (Wise *et al.*, 1969).

Having achieved industrial and public backing, Valenti replaced the PCA with the MPAA's Rating Board of the Classification and Rating Administration (CARA). Although it has no legal standing, CARA reviews every studio film and its members vote on the classification of the picture under consideration. Classifications are:

- G – *General Audiences – All ages admitted*. This signifies that a film contains no material that parents would find offensive including representations of sex, violence and language.
- PG – *Parent Guidance Suggested*. This means a film may include material parents might deem unsuitable for their children. Explicit sex or scenes of drug abuse are absent, but moderate levels of nudity, horror and violence may be evident.
- PG-13 – *Parents strongly cautioned*. This indicates a film could contain images, languages and scenes which parents may deem inadvisable for pre-teens to see.
- R – *Restricted*. This rating demonstrates a film will include sequences of sexual, adult or violent nature. As scenes may contain drug use and expletives, an adult should accompany under-17s to the cinema.
- NC-17 – *No one under 17 to be admitted*. This classification tells parents a film contains strong sexual content, bad language or violence which means it cannot be shown to teenagers. It does not, however, rate the film as being pornographic or obscene.
- X – *Adults only*. This certificate is reserved for adult films and is designed to stop minors attending cinemas showing such content.

While the G, PG, R and X classifications were launched in 1968, the PG-13 certificate was added in 1984 to allow Steven Spielberg's *Indiana Jones and the Temple of Doom* to receive a rating, and the NC-17 grade was introduced in 1990 to take over from the X certificate so that Philip Kaufman's erotic *Henry and June* could be shown on NATO screens. The Ratings are MPAA trademarked (with the exception of the defunct X certificate), so producers cannot use them without submitting their films to the classification process, and have been diligently enforced by US cinema chains. And since the 1980s, they have been used by the Video Software Dealers' Association (VSDA) to classify videocassettes and DVDs.

The Ratings system has significant implications for a motion picture's box-office chances as the size of a film's audience will be determined by how it is classified. Thus there are appeals procedures through which producers can re-edit or resubmit a picture so the original rating may be overturned. The system allowed for a greater openness in the content of Hollywood's films. This liberalisation paved the way for the 'New Hollywood' of auteur directors such as Francis Ford Coppola, Robert Altman, Stanley Kubrick and Sam Peckinpah to explore more complex themes in mainstream films and led to a reinvigoration of the industry's finances.

THE EFFECT OF THE RATINGS SYSTEM

In the immediate aftermath of the introduction of the Ratings system, John Schlesinger's 1969 film *Midnight Cowboy* marked a sea change in its study of the seedy world of male hustlers and low lifes in New York's Times Square. When United Artists' released the film, they provided it with a self-imposed X certificate for ethical and commercial reasons. On one

Midnight Cowboy: Hollywood's first and only X-rated film to win the Best Picture Oscar

hand, it made apparent to audiences that the film was of an adult nature and enabled it to gain a strong reputation, leading to Academy Awards including Best Picture. It heightened its box-office takings by attracting an adults-only demographic and because Valenti had decided against obtaining an MPAA copyright for the X designation.

Superficially, Valenti made this decision so that Hollywood would not produce exploitative or pornographic movies. Yet his judgment had a hidden purpose – to undermine the competition against Hollywood from independent productions and the burgeoning porn industry. The independent distributors protested against CARA claiming it had unfairly employed classifications over non-MPAA films such as *Greetings* (1968) and UK imports *If . . .* (1969) and *The Killing of Sister George* (1968). Robert Aldrich, the director of *Sister George*, argued that there had been collusion between NATO and the MPAA to keep his film out of showcase cinemas and away from national newspaper campaigns, thereby undermining its box-office revenues. It demonstrated that the Ratings system had been established to service the needs of the MPAA's members and no one else.

For the majors, the classification process proved an outstanding success, by stymying the opposition, and enabling them to produce adult-orientated pictures which appealed to vast audiences. In 1969, CARA passed *Easy Rider, Goodbye Columbus, Bob and Ted and Carol and Alice* and *M*A*S*H* whose success signalled a shift from Old to New Hollywood. Sexually orientated pictures such as *Carnal Knowledge* (1971) and *Shampoo* (1975), along with films containing explicit violence including *The Wild Bunch* (1969), *The French Connection* (1971) and *Dirty Harry* (1971) dominated the studios' schedules. Furthermore, in Roman Polanski's *Chinatown* (1974) a central element of the plot concerned the incestuous rape of his daughter by the villainous water baron Noah Cross.

Such graphic representations of sex and violence provoked controversy, particularly in Peckinpah's *Straw Dogs* (1971) and Kubrick's *A Clockwork Orange* (1971) which included sequences of rape, siege and gang violence. In 1972, the R-rated version of Mario Puzo's *The Godfather* (1972), directed by Coppola, incorporated mafia slayings to complement the compelling story. At the time, it became the most successful film in Hollywood's history and ushered in the era of the blockbuster (see Chapter 2). Similarly, William Friedkin exploited the new freedoms to take horror to a new level in *The Exorcist* (1973). His frank realisation of a young girl's possession by the Devil, including the child's levitation, projectile vomiting and masturbation with a cross, could not have been made under the Code. The same could be said of Peter Bogdanovich's exploration of teenage sexuality and adultery in *The Last Picture Show* (1971).

While films such as *Taxi Driver, The Deer Hunter* (1978) and *Apocalypse Now* (1979) fruitfully mined darker territories, Hollywood became subject to several obscenity rulings, growing concerns about its content and the reintroduction of local censor boards. The 1972 release of Bernardo Bertolucci's *Last Tango in Paris*, with its inclusion of simulated buggery, brought about a division between the moral majority and liberalisers. It also led to feminists' concerns about Hollywood's representation of women and its objectification of females for male gratification.

Throughout the 1980s and 1990s, films such as Brian DePalma's sex thrillers *Dressed to Kill* (1980) and *The Body Double* (1984) attracted the wrath of the moral reformers, the Women's Movement and anti-porn groups in equal measure. Similar protests were organised by Mexican groups over the depiction of LA gangs in *Colors* (1988) and by the gay rights' lobby of *Basic Instinct* (1992) for its portrayal of homicidal lesbians. Moreover, with the ascent of the Republican right, a coalition of rightwing and Christian fundamentalist organisations achieved a powerful voice in US politics and on its airwaves. They have once again blamed the predominantly liberal and Jewish Hollywood for the nation's ills.

HOLLYWOOD VERSUS THE MORAL MAJORITY

In 1988, Universal produced Martin Scorsese's adaptation of Nikos Kazantkasis's *The Last Temptation of Christ*. The film detailed the Devil's temptation of Christ by offering Jesus a married life with Mary Magdalene and showed the couple consummating the relationship. For fundamentalist groups, this was blasphemous and it led to demonstrations from rightwing, religious figures including Pat Buchanan, Pat Robertson and Donald Wildmon. In attacking the picture, these zealots vented their spleen less at the Catholic Scorsese than at the Jewish studio executives who had allowed it to be made. In particular, anti-Semitic caricatures of MCA/Universal Chairman Lew Wasserman were paraded outside his house in

Beverly Hills. In response, Valenti stated the MPAA supported the film as no self-appointed group should decide what the public might watch. However, to defuse the controversy and to appease their own ethics, several NATO exhibitors refused to book the film and it died at the US box office.

Concurrently, the New Right formed itself into a range of groups which sought to monitor Hollywood output. These include Wildmon's American Family Association, Ted Baehr's Christian Film and Television Commission and Bob de Moss's Focus on the Family. While claiming to protect the nation's morals, Wildmon's association has catalogued 'unacceptable' incidences of fornication, religious mockery and tolerance of homosexuals in the media. It has also encouraged bigotry by publishing lists of Jews working in Hollywood. Similarly, Baehr circulated materials depicting South African anti-apartheid activists as bloody terrorists. De Moss's group has endorsed the corporal punishment of children. Yet these organisations have been legitimatised by rightwing radio shock jocks who have mobilised public outrage over the escalation of sex and violence on American screens.

It has been instructive to see the types of films which have caused offence. While the cartoonish antics of Arnold Schwarzenegger or the patriotic heroics of Sylvester Stallone's *Rambo* movies have raised few eyebrows, films such as *Scarface* (1983), *Reservoir Dogs* (1992), *Pulp Fiction* (1994) and most especially *Natural Born Killers* (1994) have been accused of inciting copycat violence. These movies attracted the wrath of Hollywood's pre-eminent rightwing critic, Michael Medved, who wrote a pseudo-scientific study based on figures garnered from Wildmon and de Moss's organisations. This was published in 1993 under the title *Hollywood versus America* and opened:

> This book will undoubtedly outrage a heavy majority of show-business professionals. I am painfully aware that one of the consequences of its publication will be my potentially permanent estrangement from some of the thoughtful and well-intentioned people in Hollywood I have been proud to call my friends. In their view, I am a traitor . . . and the criticisms I raise here are misguided, offensive, even dangerßous (Medved, 1993: 1).

As a self-styled prophet, Medved claimed he was subverting the perceived wisdoms of the 'loony left' who ran Hollywood, which had refused to allow the American public to enjoy family-orientated movies. He argued that, as G and PG films outperformed R features, US audiences were clamouring for tales of moral worth and he called for a boycott of offending films as a new Hays Code was an impossibility in the corporate era (Medved, 1996: 112). Medved's rather dubious statistics (for instance, a PG film is likely to make more money than an R because it can attract a much wider demographic of the audience) served to crystallise the right's attitude against Hollywood (see Chapter 7).

More recently, CARA has been criticised for passing films with strong amounts of sexual content under the NC-17 or R classifications such as David Cronenberg's *Crash* (1996), Adrian Lyne's remake of *Lolita* (1997) and Kubrick's final picture *Eyes Wide Shut* (1999). However, the furore over these films was nothing compared to CARA's battle with Trey Parker and Matt Stone when they produced *South Park: Bigger, Louder and Uncut* in 1999. In its parody of censorship, this film version of the animated television show satirised the groups who lined up to attack it. It also demonstrated that a sizeable number of younger Americans felt that the MPAA classifications were outmoded: 'The memos were like *Alice in Wonderland*, it was so crazy. I realise they're good people trying to do their job, but the MPAA's not meant to be some moral arbiter for the entire culture' (Lewis, 2000: 298).

LIBERTARIANS' CRITICISMS OF RATINGS SYSTEM

Libertarians have accused the MPAA of being a censor as an NC-17 classification signifies a film's commercial death, thereby forcing film-makers to remove offending sequences if they want to receive an R certificate. In the last decade, award-winning independent features such as *Kids* (1995), *Requiem for a Dream, L.I.E., Monster's Ball* (all 2003) and *Spun* (2002) were re-cut to conform to the MPAA's requirements. In effect, these pictures were placed in the same category as previously banned horror films because they dealt with taboo topics including teenage sex and drug addiction.

In regard to foreign features, the Ratings system has affected internationally acclaimed films such as Pedro Almodóvar's *Tie Me Up! Tie Me Down!* (1990). When the distributor of Almodóvar's film Miramax took CARA's NC-17 classification to the California State Supreme Court to sue for an R certificate, Judge Charles Ramos argued that the MPAA had encouraged the censorship of films through 'prior restraint' or from within the industry itself. He commented this meant movies were required to fit the ratings, rather than the other way round. The MPAA had used the difference between prior restraint and 'subsequent punishment' to pursue a backhanded form of censorship which enabled Valenti to present himself as an advisor rather than as a censor. In the fallout, Miramax lost its case.

Some distributors have challenged the NC-17 classification by releasing their films ratings-free. This occurred when Good Machine disagreed with the MPAA's decision to give Todd Solondz's *Happiness* (1998) an NC-17 and the film earned back almost its entire $3 million budget, even though audiences had to actively seek out those theatres where it played. Thus, civil libertarians have argued that the MPAA is out of touch and suggested that Valenti was working for his studio paymasters:

> Why is it okay for Steven Spielberg to show a guy getting his head ripped off by a dinosaur in a PG-13 studio movie, while a single second of semen hitting a wall in an independent film is smacked with an NC-17? And why is it that all of those films mentioned above are independent films, while studio films get away with an R rating or less? Perhaps the answer lies not in our definition of obscenity, but in the definition of who Jack Valenti works for (Parry, 2003).

Finally, the Ratings system's effectiveness has been questioned by the technological changes affecting the distribution and exhibition of film content. As many-to-many forms of interactive communication have become available in cyberspace, there are greater difficulties in determining who will see a film and whether parental responsibility can remain effective. This has led to calls for the complete declassification of films to accord with the First Amendment.

Conclusion

The introduction of the Production Code reflected Hollywood's outsider status among American elites in the first half of the 20th century. It demonstrated how the film industry was subject to tacit and overt forms of anti-Semitism as Hollywood occupied a central position with regard to the Jewish question in US life. And these developments would further impact on the industry's political ideologies and divisions which emerged throughout the 1930s and 1940s (see Chapters 4 and 5).

Through the appointment of the Protestant Hays and the Catholic Breen to run the PCA, the moguls withstood the criticisms aimed at them and sought to increase the industry's profitability by factoring self-censorship into their business planning. The genesis of the Code was long-standing and it was only fully implemented due to the alliance of pressures which coalesced in the early 1930s. The fear of federal regulation finally forced the studios' hands and Hays was able to appoint Breen as the industry's enforcer. In pursuing this role, Breen demonstrated a rigid sense of purpose and made evident his own anti-Semitism. Under his auspices, the PCA grew in its authority as hundreds of man-hours were spent so that every studio film would receive the PCA Seal of Approval. The studios and cinema chains were forced into line by the financial penalties associated with producing, distributing and exhibiting a picture without the PCA Seal.

Despite the PCA's powerful status, it worked to protect the industry's interests and allowed Hollywood to export its films. It became involved in a series of disputes with moviemakers about its application of the Code. Several directors found ingenious ways of circumventing the Code's spirit and employed indirect references to provide audiences with clues to determine their characters' motivations, desires and sexuality. In the case of *The Outlaw*, Howard Hughes used the PCA's retraction of its Seal as a means to market the film to gain healthy box-office returns.

The Code collapsed in the 1950s and 1960s. First, the 1952 Supreme Court decision meant that US films finally enjoyed First Amendment privileges. Second, with the decline in audiences and changes in the industry's structure, the Code became a financial restraint on the industry as it excluded new forms of subject matter which could attract audiences away from rival mediums such as television. Therefore in 1968 Valenti introduced the Ratings system with its range of parental classifications to allow films to explore more adult forms of content. The trademarking of the Ratings secured the status of the MPAA members' films and served to undermine competition from independent productions.

The Ratings system has proven to be successful as it catered to the interests of the industry and provided a clear set of classifications to the public. However, since the 1980s, the system has courted greater degrees of controversy as rightwing Christian fundamentalists have once again accused Hollywood of being the purveyor of forms of moral degradation. With the growth of the independent sector and the wider number of foreign films, it has been posited that the MPAA classifications have undermined those movies which are not studio-based. In particular, the introduction of the NC-17 rating to replace the X certificate has led to filmmakers arguing that they have been subject a new, more invidious form of censorship.

Throughout Hollywood's history, its position in influencing public opinion has been perceived to be vital. The industry, through the Code and then the Ratings system, has successfully withstood attacks from reformers, religious groups and politicians. The MPAA remains committed to the mechanisms of self-regulation through which it has offset external pressures and ensured the finances of major studios. Further questions concerning the dissemination of film content through new forms of distribution technology will clearly impact on these mechanisms of control. However, despite such reforms, it remains apparent that the debate over film content will continue to occupy a controversial position in US society well into the third millennium.

Note

1. The PCA would later be known as the 'Johnston Office' when Will Hays retired and was replaced by Eric Johnston as the MPPDA president in 1945. For the purposes of this chapter it is referred to as the Hays Office.

4
The Political History of Classical Hollywood: Moguls, Liberals and Radicals

Introduction

Hollywood's relationship with the political elite in the 1920s and 1930s reflected the trends which defined US affairs in the inter-war years. For the moguls, mixing with the politically powerful indicated their acceptance by America's elites who had scorned them as vulgar hucksters, responsible for the nation's moral degradation, due to their Jewish and show-business backgrounds. They felt that to achieve social recognition they should demonstrate a commitment to conservative principles and supported the Republican Party.

MGM's Louis B. Mayer held deep rightwing convictions and became the vice-chairman of the Southern Californian Republican Party. He used the position to form alliances with President Herbert Hoover and the rightwing press magnate William Randolph Hearst. Along with Hearst, Will Hays and an array of Californian business forces, 'Louie Be' and MGM's production chief Irving Thalberg led a propaganda campaign against Upton Sinclair's End Poverty in California (EPIC) gubernatorial election crusade in 1934. This form of 'mogul politics' was characterised by the instincts of its authors: hardness, shrewdness, autocracy and coercion.

In response to the moguls' mercurial values, the Hollywood community pursued a significant degree of liberal and populist political activism, along with a growing leftwing radicalism among writers, directors, actors and other artists. For instance, James Cagney and Charlie Chaplin supported Sinclair's EPIC campaign by attending meetings and collecting monies. Others campaigned to release unjustly imprisoned figures including Tom Mooney, the Scottsboro Boys and the Sleepy Lagoon defendants. Their actions reflected the economic, social and political conditions of the era, notably the collapse of US capitalism with the Depression, the New Deal, the establishment of trade unions and the emigration of European political refugees fleeing Nazism.

President Franklin D. Roosevelt courted Warner Bros. to make films supporting New Deal values and appointed Jack L. Warner as the Los Angeles Chairman of the National Recovery Administration (NRA). Stars and writers such as Edward G. Robinson, and Dudley Nichols lent themselves to liberal, international causes. Some activists became attracted to the Hollywood Communist Party, which was a small but potent force in the 1930s. This tide of Hollywood liberalism and radicalism was enhanced by the migration of previously New York-based writers and artists who, in the wake of sound films, had resettled on the West Coast.

This chapter will outline the development of the moguls' politics and consider how Mayer manoeuvred himself into a role in which he could court the 'great and good' in American civic and business life. It will demonstrate how the changes instituted by the New Deal in US political and social affairs provided the context in which the Hollywood workforce became politically conscious throughout the decade. Finally, it will discuss how the techniques employed by the moguls in the EPIC campaign reflected and defined the political divide which had emerged in Hollywood in the 1930s and into the 1940s.

The moguls' politics

The movie moguls (the Warner Brothers, Louis B. Mayer, Joseph and Nicholas Schenck, Adolph Zukor, Harry Cohn, Carl Laemmle, Samuel Goldwyn), with two exceptions (Darryl Zanuck, Walt Disney), shared a common Jewish immigrant working-class heritage. They embodied the American Dream, rising from immigrant ghettos to make their fortunes in the new medium of the cinema. As they had sampled the extremes of poverty and wealth, they preserved their fortunes, downplayed their Jewish heritage and assimilated themselves into mainstream American society.

THE MOGULS: STATUS AND INTEGRATION

The secular moguls were the unlikely offspring of a first generation of religious Jews who had 'somehow [seen] [their] seed [from] the Old World . . . produce [a breed] of brash, amoral, on the make Americans' (Schulberg, 1981: 191). They took a paternalistic pride in their accumulation of riches, which was measured in a limitless supply of limousines, houses on the beach and pliant young actresses (Brownstein, 1990: 24). However, they retained memories of the pogroms that had forced their families to emigrate and remained aware of the anti-Semitism which prevailed from ingrained WASP prejudice (Shindler, 1996: 61–2).

This manifested itself in several ways. Hollywood's Jewish complexion was attacked in vicious pamphlets and newspapers, backed by anti-Semites such as Henry Ford. The moguls were barred from Los Angeles' most exclusive country clubs and oldest business groups, and their children were excluded from the city's finest schools. In spite of their battles with one another, their real enemies were 'the New York boardrooms and *goyim* of Wall Street who were constantly plotting to take over their studios' (ibid.: 63). Despite their wealth, they remained conscious of their need to achieve respectability in America's circles of power:

> It was this nagging urge for status, more than a clearly defined political agenda, that . . . attracted . . .
> the . . . moguls to politics. Most . . . lacked abiding political convictions of any sort. . . . As [they]
> had scrambled up the hard way, their vague political views were anchored in an apostolic belief in
> hard work . . . that translated into the right of those who scrambled so fiercely to keep what they
> earned without much government intrusion (Brownstein, 1990: 26).

Therefore, the moguls remained apolitical. They were Republican not because of any deeply held conviction but because most wealthy Americans voted for the Grand Old Party (GOP) and because, by showing their attachment to 'sound' conservative principles, they could withstand any potential anti-Semitic attack. Their values were determined by self-interest and, as in the case of Jack Warner, if they acquired the requisite status from supporting the Democrats, they would vote Democrat (Shindler, 1996: 63). The exception was the vice-president and general manager of MGM – Louis B. Mayer.

LOUIS B. MAYER: THE 'PROUD PIGEON' MEETS HIS POLITICAL MATES

Mayer launched his career in 1907 when he rented a burlesque house to exhibit films in the working-class town of Haverhill, Massachusetts. In 1924 he combined his production company with Metro and Goldwyn to form MGM whose Culver City studios opened in a blaze of publicity (including visitations by local dignitaries and congratulatory telegrams from Calvin Coolidge and Herbert Hoover). An imperious, pompous man known for his feisty temper, Mayer had a propensity to fits of rage, bathos, cunning and outrageous flattery.

A tremendous egoist, he not only ran the industry's most glamorous studio, but wanted acceptance from the powerful elite who owned the country. If visiting notables, such as Winston Churchill or H. G. Wells, came to town, Mayer would invite them to star-studded

The Hollywood–Washington nexus: Will Hays, President Calvin Coolidge, Mrs Coolidge and Louis B. Mayer

luncheons. As an outsider, he embraced the respectable classes and spent as little time as possible with his fellow film-makers. Mayer championed conservative values based on the sanctity of order, authority, patriotism, clean living, small-town solidarity and family.

To realise his political ambitions Mayer served in Republican Calvin Coolidge's 1924
presidential campaign as an enthusiastic, but lowly, neophyte. During this campaign he met
Ida Koverman, Herbert Hoover's chief political operative in California, and established a
strong link with the formidable widow (who would become Mayer's personal secretary). She
had a network of connections and instructed Mayer on how to work his way up through the
state party. She gave him access to Hoover and Mayer wooed the Secretary of Commerce to
support the studio's financial interests. Moreover, he enjoyed the reflected glory of a close
personal attachment with a rising political star.[1]

To provide financial support for Hoover's presidential ambitions, Mayer required MGM's
studio workers to contribute to the candidate's campaign funds. To the annoyance of production chief Irving Thalberg, who was struggling to introduce sound into movies, Mayer
spent the summer and fall of 1928 absorbed in the political machinations necessary to secure
Hoover's nomination. He was the Californian delegate to the Republican Convention where
he persuaded the newspaper baron William Randolph Hearst to transfer his votes to Hoover,
despite the magnate's support for Treasury Secretary Andrew Mellon.

In his role as kingmaker, Mayer drew upon a relationship with Hearst which was founded
on mutual self-interest. As the syndicator of gossip columnist Louella Parsons, Hearst shaped
the country's view of Hollywood and Mayer realised that he needed him as an ally. To endear
himself to the press baron, Mayer supported the film career of Hearst's mistress Marion
Davies in spite of the public's indifference to the former chorus girl. This meant they engaged
in a friendship defined by a shared lust for power and glory wherein Mayer called Hearst
'chief' and Hearst named him 'son'.

Mayer's affiliation with Hoover's White House enabled him to expand his business
interests, especially after the death of Marcus Loew (the owner of MGM's holding company,
Loews) in 1927 when he outmanoeuvred industry pioneer William Fox and Loews' chief
Nicholas Schenck in a battle for stock and control of the studio. In this respect, he had
the ear of the Justice Department which forced Fox to sell his stock due to the anti-
competitive nature of his attempted merger with Schenck. Remaining loyal to Hearst,
Mayer lobbied Hoover to allow the magnate to obtain the wavelengths required for a new
radio station.

Mayer's personal ambitions were as strong as his professional interests. After Hoover's
presidential inauguration he swelled with pride when he was asked to be the first overnight
guest to stay at the White House and as Koverman noted to Lawrence Rigby, an aide to the
president-elect:

Re: Louis B Mayer. Do you remember our talk about making a gesture? Why could we not include
a trip to Florida [where Hoover was vacationing] for a couple of days? This is another small boy –
new at the game and used to a great deal of attention. I know he would strut around like a proud
pigeon (Brownstein, 1990: 21).

THE COLLAPSE OF THE HOOVER ADMINISTRATION AND THE 1932 PRESIDENTIAL ELECTION

Unfortunately for Mayer, the Hoover administration presided over the worst collapse of the US economy in history. The President's inability to act over the 1929 Wall Street Crash and the Depression led to severe criticism and mass unpopularity. Throughout, Mayer remained a committed supporter and in 1931 presented Hoover with a national survey of business leaders' ideas for reinvigorating the economy.

However, his political influence was limited when he tried to rally a disillusioned Hearst to the Republican cause in the 1932 presidential election. The press magnate was disappointed with Hoover and transferred his support to Texan Democratic House Speaker John Nance Garner, an uninspiring isolationist. Eventually Hearst, sensing the change in national mood, supported Roosevelt and cut his ties with Mayer. Similarly, despite Mayer's overtures, Hoover had little interest in meeting Hearst and the mogul became the unwitting instrument in the breakdown of relations between the pair.

Nonetheless, Mayer made radio broadcasts supporting the moribund Hoover, who spent his time locked away in the White House. He tried to lift the prevailing tide of gloom hanging over the 1932 GOP Convention by stage-managing a half-hour pro-Hoover rally on its final day, but could not remove the sense of foreboding. Undeterred, Mayer informed the press that the economy was about to turn that the Convention's anti-prohibition compromise would see voters flock back to the Republicans and that Hoover would win a triumphant re-election. To provide a higher profile for Hoover, he recruited MGM stars Ethel Barrymore and Wallace Beery to the campaign. For his efforts, Mayer was appointed as the chairman of the Republican State Central Committee in September 1932:

> That position cemented his pre-eminent political role in Hollywood and made him an even more visible public figure. Mayer increasingly was used as a party ambassador, though his speeches, presumably ghost-written, were most often smarmy and ponderous. An energetic speaker, he made up with force what he lacked in elegance (ibid.: 39).

Yet, while Mayer accused Franklin D. Roosevelt of providing meaningless promises in a series of statewide radio addresses, he watched helplessly as his friend was swept out of the White House. Although he remained Hollywood's most politically visible mogul, he never recovered from Hoover's defeat. In 1933, he accepted an invitation to meet Roosevelt in the Oval Office. Upon his arrival Mayer surprised the President when he produced a clock from his coat and placed it on the Chief Executive's desk. Roosevelt inquired, 'What's that for, Mr Mayer?' Mayer replied, 'Pardon me Mr. President. I heard you have the ability to have a man in your hip pocket after eighteen minutes.' Brandishing his cigarette holder, Roosevelt laughed and began chatting to the mogul. However, after seventeen minutes he was surprised to see Mayer get up, grab his clock and exit the room!

FDR AND JACK WARNER: GOOD CITIZENSHIP AND GOOD PICTURES

Despite Mayer's antipathy for Roosevelt, a large section of Hollywood was enamoured by 'the tribune of the people'. Roosevelt's flamboyant presentation of his New Deal policies, together with his Keynesian economic planning, found immediate favour in Tinseltown. Throughout the 1932 campaign he received the backing of film stars including Will Rogers, Gloria Stuart and Katharine Hepburn. Roosevelt also reached out to the rest of Hollywood because he understood the power of cinema and sought to make alliances in the motion picture industry.[2]

For Warner Bros. (a studio that prided itself on 'Good Citizenship and Good Pictures'), such an alliance provided the company with the status it felt it deserved as an industry leader. Its 1930s' films included political and social issues which reflected both the strengths (reform, social welfare) and the weaknesses of the New Deal: confusion, compromise and vagueness (Shindler, 1996: 157). Warners produced musicals such as *42nd Street* and *Gold Diggers of 1933* (both 1933), which portrayed recognisable struggles among Busby Berkeley's glamorously choreographed numbers.

Otherwise, Warners was best known for producing gangster pictures. In terms of content and characters these genre movies changed throughout the decade. For instance, the vibrant immorality of Edward G. Robinson and James Cagney in *Little Caesar* (1930) and *Public Enemy* (1931) was transformed into an advocacy of law and order, when these actors were cast as G–Men or as gangland figures who saw the errors of their ways. Most especially, the studio backed social-conscience movies including *I Am a Fugitive from a Chain Gang* and *Black Legion* (1937).

'We're in the money': prosperity is just around the corner in *Gold Diggers of 1933*

The relationship between the studio and the administration reflected the changing political convictions of the head of production, Jack Warner, who had transferred his allegiance from Hoover to Roosevelt during the 1932 presidential campaign. In this respect, Hearst was instrumental as he sought a film executive, in preference to Mayer, to be induced into supporting FDR. To complete his conversion, Warner was summoned to New York by his brother Harry to be presented to Democrat leaders Jim Farley, Joseph P. Kennedy, Al Smith, and J. J. Raskob who argued, 'There is revolution in the air and we need a change' (Warner, 1964: 215–16).

Assured of Roosevelt's undying gratitude, Warner organised campaign rallies and raised monies for the Democratic cause. One of the most spectacular of these rallies occurred at the Hollywood Bowl to which Warner and production chief Darryl F. Zanuck invited almost every major star in the industry except those who Mayer barred from attending. As a reward, Roosevelt appointed Warner as the Los Angeles Chairman of the National Recovery Administration (NRA).

Roosevelt and the moguls: Political interest and expediency

Roosevelt, however, was in no way star-struck by Hollywood. He used the studios to enhance his campaign and political image. He was shrewd enough to keep friendly relations with Will Hays, despite the movie czar's background as a Republican politician. He kept in with Zanuck, who was a constant visitor to the White House, and when Thalberg died sent condolences to his widow Norma Shearer.

The moguls' relationship with the presidency was tested when the Justice Department pursued anti-trust investigations into the vertically integrated structure of the industry (see Chapter 1) and the 1935 Wagner Act legitimised the fledgling guilds and unions operating among the workforce (see Chapter 5). Even Warner vacillated between sending the Commander-in-Chief fawning letters and describing him to writer Philip Dunne as a 'horse's ass' (Brownstein, 1990: 78).

Roosevelt called off the full forces of the Justice Department in the late 1930s, allowing the studios to sign a consent decree, when it suited his purposes to garner their support in the 1940 presidential campaign. And, if anything, it remained the case that Hollywood continued to be in awe of the President. He understood how much the moguls sought social acceptance and happily provided them with an autographed photo or an invitation to dinner at the White House. For example, Warner was won over not only by his desire to be close to the political centre but by Roosevelt's charm: 'I found him a vital and enormously magnetic man and . . . we began a friendship that endured to the day he died (ibid.: 93).

Hollywood liberals and radicals

While Roosevelt was not the first president to associate with entertainers, he was the first to understand the worth of mixing with Hollywood celebrities. Film stars were invited to luncheons and birthday balls to enhance FDR's standing with the electorate. An avid movie fan, Roosevelt used his charisma to bond with favoured actors and actresses. In this manner he sustained relationships with stars who, feeling suitably honoured, would lend themselves to election campaigns and public works schemes (Schroeder, 2004: 10–16). Even Republicans were won over, as in the case of comedian Bob Hope who described himself as a 'Republocrat' on being received by FDR in 1944 (ibid.: 65). Hollywood's liberals, in particular, were welcomed to the White House and the President formed close relations with Melvyn Douglas and his wife Helen Gahagan Douglas, Orson Welles and Frank Sinatra.

THE HOLLYWOOD DEMOCRATIC COMMITTEE AND CAMPAIGN SUPPORT

Douglas was especially keen to take the film community's burgeoning political values into the mainstream. To this end, he campaigned for Roosevelt, became a leader in the state Democratic Party and was the first actor to serve as a delegate to the national Democratic Convention. Under his tutelage Gahagan transferred her acting skills into political ambitions and became an advocate for the rural poor in California. She forged a close relationship with Eleanor Roosevelt and would outdo her husband in seeking electoral office (she would later become a Democratic Congresswoman and candidate in the 1950 California Senatorial contest against Republican Richard Nixon) (Mitchell, 1998: 21–2).

Roosevelt's liberalism appealed to the political elements in Hollywood who were seeking to mobilise public opinion about injustice at home and the encroachment of fascism abroad. As a consequence, a more strategic form of politicisation occurred when the Hollywood Democratic Committee (HDC) was formed to mobilise support for the President through-out his election campaigns in 1936, 1940 and 1944. Film stars, such as Humphrey Bogart, Edward G. Robinson, John Garfield and Judy Garland, accompanied the President on campaign rallies and whistle-stop tours across the country.

In 1944, Frank Sinatra entered the political fray when he extricated himself from crowds of bobbysoxers to preach street-corner populism and racial tolerance. He was invited to the White House to meet Roosevelt despite being criticised by Republican opponents as a mere 'crooner'. In a riposte he dropped a new lyric into his popular favourite, 'Everything Happens to Me':

> They asked me down to Washington
> To have a cup of tea.
> The Republicans started squawking
> They're as mad as they can be,
> And all I did was say 'hello' to a
> Man named Franklin D.
> Everything happens to me (Brownstein, 1990: 94).

Sinatra made a large donation to the Democratic cause and also upstaged the Republican candidate Thomas Dewey when he appeared at the Waldorf-Astoria hotel in New York at the same time as the GOP front-runner. His fans, who were mainly too young to vote, wore buttons which read, 'Frankie's for FDR and so are we'.

Another energetic supporter of Roosevelt's cause was Orson Welles. A legendary child prodigy, Welles became a celebrated figure on New York stages and the radio in the 1930s.

His success led to him coming to Hollywood with his Mercury Theatre group to star in, direct, produce and co-write with Herman J. Mankiewicz, *Citizen Kane* (1941).[3] Although the film would be admired as one of the greatest ever made, its thinly veiled critique of William Randolph Hearst led to it being blackened by the moguls and damned by his press thereby eliminating its chances at the box office. From then on Welles' film career wobbled precariously between outlandish brilliance and recurrent frustration.

Welles had been a member of the Popular Front, a movement formed from a coalition of parties, including American Communists against Fascism, in the 1930s. He supported numerous liberal causes and raised his level of political participation when he joined the Free World Association in 1943. As a man who did nothing by halves, he plunged himself into the political maelstrom of the HDC in 1944. In this capacity, he went on a barnstorming tour of the US, spoke on NBC, CBS and the Mutual Broadcasting network, addressed a luncheon honouring Eleanor Roosevelt, and introduced vice-presidential candidate Henry Wallace to a huge crowd at Madison Square Gardens. Indeed, he worked so hard for Roosevelt that he collapsed with a fever in the final days of the campaign. For Welles, this experience had been so entrancing that he considered standing for the junior senatorial seat in Wisconsin in 1946. However, on reflection, he believed an actor could never achieve political office. He later berated himself for not standing not only for his naivety, but because his Republican opponent would have been Joseph R. McCarthy!

THE GOTHAMISATION OF TINSELTOWN

This tide of liberalism reflected the migration of many New York-based writers and artists who in the wake of sound had resettled on the West Coast. As sound films required good dialogue, the studios sought out Broadway based-playwrights, novelists and short-story writers. This cohort included: George S. Kaufman, F. Scott Fitzgerald, Nathaniel West, Donald Ogden Stewart, Sidney Buchman, Edna Ferber, Moss Hart, Marc Connelly, Sidney Howard and Lillian Hellman. Such writers had risen from New York literary, liberal and socialist backgrounds, often being raised in the vernacular of Jewish street debates. They sought to challenge Hollywood by including politics in their scripts and, in contrast to the previous generation of scenarists, they had a greater sense of their worth in the industry:

> The Depression simply could not be ignored. Its impact on film people's lives and minds extended far beyond the salaries or staff cuts among artistic personnel in the major studios. . . . Political awareness existed [in Hollywood], but it was largely confined to a small handful of screenwriters who had garnered the rudiments of political education before coming to Hollywood (Ceplair and Englund, 2003: 85).

However, their experiences in Hollywood were mixed. Some readily worked within the system, took the money, lived in the luxury of the hills and concentrated their artistic endeavours on their plays or novels. Others found the studio experience nullifying and complained about the philistine-like tendencies of production heads like Thalberg, who believed writers occupied the lowest rungs of the studio food chain. For the studio executives the writer was a factory employee who clocked in, worked for five and a half days, and produced eleven pages of script per week:

> The art of screenwriting was prized but the office of the screenwriter wasn't. This was something that most playwrights and novelists took an agonisingly long time to comprehend. . . . Two writers were working for . . . producer David Susskind when the door to their poky office opened and couple of B'nai B'rith ladies peered in, shepherded by Mrs Susskind who said, 'And this is where my son David the Producer keeps his writers' (Shindler, 1996: 54).

Such conditions led to the formation of the Screen Writers Guild (SWG) in 1933 (see Chapter 5) and the politicisation of many writers. Initially, their education occurred in a Southern Californian landscape unencumbered by political machines, strong forms of partisanship or trade unions (which had been suppressed by reactionary business forces). They sought to mobilise public opinion around the abuse of migrant workers, unjustly arrested figures (Tom Mooney, the Scottsboro Boys, the Sleepy Lagoon Defendants and the Zoot Suiters) and anti-fascism. However, when they became more politically experienced, they were cannier operators who adopted clearly drawn ideological positions.

A number of activists were attracted to the Hollywood Communist Party, which was a small, but potent, force in 1930s. The enlistment of a cohort of talented writers, actors and directors to the Party, led by screenwriter John Howard Lawson, would have lasting consequences for the left in Hollywood as many would later be subject to anti-Communist witch-hunts. This radicalism was also evident in the struggles to gain recognition for the screen guilds and in the taking-up of various causes during the decade.

The case of Donald Ogden Stewart, a noted wit from the Algonquin Round Table, is instructive. In 1932, Stewart moved to Hollywood where he scripted classic comedies including *Holiday* (1938) and *The Philadelphia Story* (1940). For several years he thrived as one of MGM's highest paid writers and had little interest in politics, apart from contributing to Mayer's funds to stop Upton Sinclair. However, the Depression and the rise of fascism led to him joining the Hollywood Communist Party. As an obsessive convert to Marxism, Stewart used anti-fascism as the vehicle through which he could disseminate the principles of Communism and he subsequently became the president of the Hollywood Anti-Nazi League.

THE ANTI-NAZI LEAGUE, MPAC AND THE POPULAR FRONT

The Anti-Nazi League for Defence of American Democracy included many liberals. Within their number, there were writers and directors such as Philip Dunne and John Cromwell, and film stars and actors including Gloria Stuart, Fredric March, his wife Florence Eldridge, and Melvyn and Helen Gahagan Douglas. As more Jewish refugees from Europe came to Hollywood, with tales of the nationalists' atrocities in the Spanish Civil War and the Nazis' anti-Semitism, the League was joined by other anti-fascist movements. These included the Motion Picture Artists Committee to Aid a Republican Spain (MPAC), whose membership peaked at 15,000, and the left-dominated Popular Front groups.

Blockade: Hollywood's take on the Spanish Civil War

The refugees were welcomed into the Hollywood community and the industry became 'awash with "experts" in the nature, forms and evils of fascism' (Ceplair and Englund, 2003: 97). Indeed, many liberals who had visited Europe were appalled by the rise of Mussolini, Hitler and Franco, and the complicity of moderate and conservative states. In particular, they mobilised to support the Republican cause in Spain:

> The thinking people in the movie community were extremely caught up in the Spanish move-ment. They felt most strenuously that now was the time to take a stand to stop fascism. It was thrilling to see the understanding which motivated the most creative and successful people in the film industry to take time out from their busy careers (ibid.: 113)

Similarly, they were concerned by the extremists at home and decided to fight back through the Popular Front against the Ku Klux Klan, the American Nazi Party and the growing support for such rightwing hate figures as Father Coughlin, Gerald L. K. Smith and Dudley Pelley.

The recruitment of celebrities allowed the Front's leaders to transmit an anti-fascist agenda via the nation's media. Concurrently, the Anti-Nazi League mounted petitions, held public meetings, broadcast a weekly radio programme, published a biweekly paper and picketed the German embassy. In 1939 it sponsored several labour and Quarantine Hitler rallies while co-ordinating with the MPAC a 'Save Spain' rally at the Hollywood Legion stadium.

The MPAC proved to be equally active. To raise funds for the Republican cause, it staged a successful political cabaret called 'Sticks and Stones' which attacked those 'domestic gnats' that mobilised against the Popular Front and 'foreign soldier ants' who swarmed against the world's democracies. The skits, written by some of Hollywood's top writers, criticised reactionaries like Martin Dies (the first Chairman of the House Committee of UnAmerican Activities) and appeasers such as British Prime Minister Neville Chamberlain. An offshoot of the MPAC, the Freedom of the Screen Committee, sponsored the Communist writer John Howard Lawson's 1938 film about the Spanish Civil War, *Blockade*. And Lawson and other Hollywood Party members would grow in importance in the circles of anti-fascist activism.

THE HOLLYWOOD COMMUNIST PARTY AND THE POPULAR FRONT

In the 1930s the Hollywood Communist Party had become a lightning rod for those 'tender comrades' who believed Communism could answer the ills of American capitalism and fascism (McGilligan and Buhle, 1997: xv). Its membership included John Howard Lawson, Dalton Trumbo, Ring Lardner Jr, Alvah Bessie, Abraham Polonsky, Marsha Hunt, Lionel Stander, Budd Schulberg, Paul and Sylvia Jarrico and Jules Dassin. On being asked by Zanuck how he became a Communist, Dassin replied:

> It happened immediately after the opening night of *Waiting for Lefty*. I was tremendously moved, but embarrassed that I was not a member of the Communist Party. . . . It was one of the most unforgettable nights of my life. It was so moving, so irresistible . . . that you said to yourself, 'I must do something. I must behave like those guys, who are showing so much concern and love.' That's what did it for me. (ibid.: 206)

The Communist Party appealed to liberals and radicals who perceived it as providing the most effective organisation through which to achieve societal reform. Hollywood Communists were primarily committed, with the exception of some radicals who were in the thrall of Stalinism, to the Party's stands rather than to its ideology, structure or hierarchy. Subsequently, the US Communist Party (CPUSA) articulated the concerns of many in Hollywood regarding rights, decency, justice and equality. For instance, the actor Lionel Stander, who had supported farm workers in the Salinas Valley lettuce strike and campaigned against the imprisonment of militant labour organiser Tom Mooney for the 1916 anarchist bombing in San Francisco, believed the Party provided the forum for Spanish Loyalists, the revolution in China and the removal of Jewish refugees from Germany (McGilligan and Buhle, 1997: 609).

In turn, Hollywood's Popular Front organisations comprised a growing number of Communists. Although liberals actively contributed to the anti-fascist causes, Party members became responsible for their day-to-day business. As they were tactically astute, Party activists would caucus in fraction meetings to delay votes and wrestle control from liberal leaders. Later, anti-Communists would cite such infiltration as evidence that the Front had been duped by Communism.

The cadres' ascent to power made conspicuous the enmities which existed between liberals and Party members. For a while, the bonds between them remained reasonably strong, as revolutionary rhetoric was played down and replaced by demands for the establishment of a third party consisting of labourers and farm workers. Although liberals like Douglas and Welles agreed with anti-fascist sentiments, they did not intend to bring down capitalism. Conversely, Hollywood Communists advocated revolutionary change and uncritically supported Stalin's Russia. They also saw the Front as a means through which to open liberals' eyes to the benefits of socialism and to recruit them to the party (Brownstein, 1990: 67). The final break occurred in 1939 when Stalin signed the non-aggression pact with Hitler. It led to the collapse of the Anti-Nazi League, MPAC and the affiliated groups within the Popular Front (Ceplair and Englund, 2003: 135). The pact would lead to significant divisions within the Motion Picture Democratic Committee (MPDC).

THE MOTION PICTURE DEMOCRATIC COMMITTEE: THE STALIN–HITLER PACT AND THE COLLAPSE OF LIBERAL AND COMMUNIST RELATIONS

Philip Dunne and Melvyn Douglas had formed the MPDC and remained the unofficial leaders of its liberal faction. Although they had been subject to Communist recruitment, both remained staunch Democrats. However, as pragmatic liberals they had worked with the Communists as the Party had tied itself to the causes of social justice and anti-fascism.

This opinion changed overnight with the signing of the pact and the Nazi invasion of Poland. The unity in the MPDC was shattered as it became apparent that the liberal and Communist factions in the executive board stood against each other. Dunne and Douglas believed the Soviet Union's withdrawal from anti-fascism would lead to the disintegration of the cause across Europe. Conversely, Hollywood Communists who had previously dismissed rumours concerning the pact as 'fascist propaganda', pursued the CPUSA's line which maintained that World War II was nothing more than an imperialist exercise between fascists and illegitimate 'democracies'. They loyally supported the Soviet Union and argued that Stalin, by suing for peace with Hitler, had saved Russia from entering into a fruitless war:

> It was a practical manoeuvre. I was never amazed or startled by the flip-flops of international diplomacy. Like everything in this life, international politics is highly complicated. . . . I never had an idealistic view of Stalin. I respected him as the leader of the Soviet Union, but always felt my main problem was as an American, and that the government of the Soviet Union, like the government of any other country, was its own business (McGilligan and Buhle, 1997: 617–18).

Unsurprisingly, the MPDC's liberals had no patience for this volte-face and were indignant when the Communist members of the board rigged a vote of ten votes to seven to ensure the committee would reverse its anti-fascist stance. Dunne and Douglas, feeling the Communist organisers had been permanently discredited, forced the issue in the autumn of 1939 when they drafted a resolution to be presented to the MPDC executive to align it with Roosevelt's stance on international diplomacy.

However, the resolution was poorly received by the board at a meeting on 19 December 1939 as several Communists argued that an alliance with Roosevelt would push the MPDC

into the hands of the far right. To counter this position, the Dunne–Douglas faction maintained the CPUSA had already 'objectively aligned' the MPDC to the right by taking on
Stalin's isolationist position. In the event, the board's members were swayed by the
Communists and rejected the resolution. Despite Dunne and Douglas's submission of a
revised resolution, the MPDC continued to reject any affiliation with the Democrats.
Eventually, this led to a showdown meeting with Dunne which was attended by 300 people
at the Hollywood Women's Club wherein the resolution was thrown out. By then Douglas
had already resigned from the MPDC and the Anti-Nazi League, in which he had been
subject to personal abuse.

In the light of Dunne's defeat, the disillusioned liberals resigned *en masse* from the MPDC
and the fragile unity between them and the Communists completely disintegrated. Throughout 1940, Douglas publicly shamed Communist leaders in several speeches about the collapse of the Popular Front. He concluded Communists should be barred from any future
liberal organisation:

> It was a problem of trustworthiness . . . not of their being Communists *per se*. Their long-term
> goals were not mine, and they were using my goals as expedients to achieve goals in which I did
> not believe. They were obstructionists (Ceplair and Englund, 2003: 149).

THE CONSERVATIVE BACKLASH AND THE DIES COMMITTEE

It would be a mistake to believe everyone in the film industry supported the liberals' position
on social and international affairs or Roosevelt's New Deal vision. For instance, there were
several prominent Hollywood Republicans and rightwingers including W. C. Fields, Robert
Montgomery, Gary Cooper, Walt Disney, Hedda Hopper, Dick Powell, Ginger Rogers and
Fred Astaire. In particular, PCA head Joseph Breen held deeply anti-Semitic beliefs, embrac-
ing Nazism. He used his influence to undermine the Hollywood Anti-Nazi League, which
he believed was 'a conspiracy of left-leaning screenwriters . . . that strove to capture the
screen of the United States for Communistic propaganda purposes' (Hoberman and Shandler,
2003: 61–2).

Even while Douglas was attacking Communists, rightwing forces in Hollywood accused
him of being a fellow traveller of Communism. As conservatives sought to exploit the breach
between the two sides, Hollywood's liberals were forced to exaggerate the distance between
themselves and the Party members they had worked with in the Popular Front. For instance,
Douglas suffered the indignity of a *Photoplay* interview entitled 'Is Melvyn Douglas a
Communist?' in which he refuted all the links he had made with the Communists.

The right targeted Douglas because he had been appointed by Eleanor Roosevelt to head
the Arts Council of the Office Civilian Defence's Voluntary Participation Branch. He was
accused of enjoying the 'frills' of the post (a sinecure of $8,000), displaying Communist ten-
dencies and conforming to his Jewish heritage (ibid.: 150). For anti–New Dealer reactionaries the fact that the House Un-American Activities Committee (HUAC), chaired by a
rightwing Congressman, Martin Dies, had cleared Douglas was irrelevant.

The Dies Committee had been established in 1938 to root out anti-Americanism in civil society, but it was mainly noted for the anti-Communist, anti-labour and anti-New Deal bias of its chairman and membership which included J. Parnell Thomas. Dies believed it was his duty to root out Communist subversion and propaganda. His latent anti-Semitism meant that he conflated Jewishness with Communism in his vocal attacks on the Hollywood Anti-Nazi League.

In the first year of his investigation Dies brought about the closure of the Roosevelt-backed Federal Theatre and Writers' Project, along with a vehement attack against other public work schemes including the Works Progress Administration, the National Labour Relations Board, the Department of Labour and liberal organisations such as the American Civil Liberties Union. In his second year, he decided to place Hollywood's trade unions and its anti-fascist organisations under the microscope. Yet the Committee fell into disrepute between 1938 to 1940 when the Hollywood left refuted its blunt attacks on Communism.

Dies was ridiculed when he subpoenaed child star Shirley Temple to ask her whether she had been a stooge for Communism in films such as *Wee Willie Winkie* (1937). So, while the head of Paramount Studios Y. Frank Freeman (later President of the AMPP) informed Dies that Hollywood would fully cooperate with him, he also told him the industry's 32,000 workers would not 'yield to anyone in their true Americanism' (Carr, 2001: 172). Subsequently, Dies withdrew his attack on Hollywood and, on meeting liberals such as Douglas, March, Dunne, Cagney and Bogart, pronounced them to be good American citizens. After he met Dies, Cagney outlined his 'two-shirt' theory concerning capitalism and Communism: 'It wouldn't be economically sound for me to endorse a programme [Communism] which would give me just one shirt when I now have two' (Cagney, 1940). However, as a forewarning of what was to come the Dies Committee indicated how Hollywood would have to demonstrate its 'American' values to the US political elite. On each side of the political divide there was the realisation that the industry's tremendous popularity, tied together with its Jewish complexion, opened it up to White Anglo-Saxon Protestants' (WASP) suspicion. For the moguls, who viewed the liberalism and Communism within the industry with disdain, such anti-Semitism was a contributory factor to their reactionary defence of 'American' values against Upton Sinclair's 1934 campaign to become the Democratic Governor of California.

Upton Sinclair: Reformer, Democratic candidate and the EPIC crusade

Sinclair's End Poverty in California (EPIC) campaign made conspicuous the divisions in Hollywood's political affairs. For the moguls, he was a dangerous radical who could undermine their business interests by raising taxes. For Hollywood liberals and radicals, the EPIC campaign provided an opportunity through which they could demonstrate their opposition to their bosses and their support for social reform.

Sinclair was best known as the muck-raking author of *The Jungle* (1906), an exposé of Chicago's meatpacking industry. He also wrote several other reports outlining the vested interests that had corrupted US business and political affairs. A native Californian, he was an active socialist who supported the release of Tom Mooney and many other social causes.

In June 1934, Will Rogers announced that Sinclair, who had previously stood as a socialist for the Governor of California, intended to be elected as the Democratic candidate for the governorship. Six weeks later, he swept the Party's primary on 28 August 1934 to run on a platform to End Poverty in California (EPIC). His victory upset the state's business interests who feared Sinclair would raise taxes and redistribute wealth in the Californian economy. EPIC promised to radicalise Californian and American politics and it marked the closest attempt by a socialist activist to achieve high office. As there were over 700,000 unemployed workers in the state, Sinclair gained the approval of the disenfranchised population in California.

However, while Sinclair's platform promised redistribution and social justice, there would have been limitations on his powers, if he had achieved office, as the governor could only raise corporation taxes. Furthermore, Sinclair had problematic relations with Roosevelt who privately promised to, but never publicly endorsed his candidacy. For the state's businesses, however, which had moved to outlaw Communism, the perception of having a socialist as governor elected by the poor, angry and dispossessed was tantamount to a social revolution. In these circles, it was the bosses of the communications industries – the press barons and the movie moguls – who exercised their greatest disapproval of Sinclair (Ceplair and Englund, 2003: 90).

SINCLAIR AND THE MOVIE MOGULS

Sinclair's problematic relations with Hollywood dated back to the early 1930s. He had fallen foul of Irving Thalberg when the MGM production chief offered him the chance to write a script entitled *The Star-Spangled Banner*. However, after four meetings, in which Sinclair altered the title to *The Gold-Spangled Banner* to demonstrate his contempt for Thalberg, the studio terminated his contract. Subsequently, Sinclair offended the moguls when he tried to secure independent funding for the Soviet film-maker Sergei Eisenstein's *Que Viva Mexico* (1932), because they wanted the flamboyant director to return to Russia in defeat. Although the project ended in disaster the studio bosses' wrath could not be assuaged (Mitchell, 1992: 63).[4]

Worse was to come when Sinclair was offered $25,000 by the industry pioneer William Fox in 1933 to write an exposé of how he had been fleeced by his fellow moguls. While Fox had envisaged the resulting manuscript – *Upton Sinclair Presents William Fox* – could be used to regain control of his studio, Sinclair published the book in order to reveal and criticise the industry's business practices:

> So far as the motion picture industry is concerned, they have their directors or their boards of every one of the big concerns, and not one of these concerns would be running today, were it not for the money furnished by the Wall Street Banks and investment houses. This is the new stage to which America has come, and the story of how the wires are pulled and strings set – you will never see it more plainly and in greater detail than in this 'inside' story of Fox Film and Fox Theatre (Sinclair, 1933: xvi–xvii).

Sinclair proposed that the film industry be nationalised and strict federal regulations imposed upon it in order to put an end to its dubious business practices.

A year later on the campaign trail, Sinclair commented that those film workers who had been laid off owing to the economic downturn should be re-employed by the same companies which had let them go. He also suggested unemployed actors and technicians might be given the opportunity to rent out idle studio space to produce pictures of their own. For the moguls, this was a declaration of war and the call went out to 'stop Sinclair' (Sinclair, 1936: 190). Moreover, the Hollywood chiefs' intervention in the Sinclair campaign indicated a pivotal shift in their interest in political affairs:

> It was the first campaign in which . . . [the moguls] . . . participated primarily to protect their economic interests. . . . [Initially] the social attractions of politics – the desire to be embraced by powerful men . . . overshadowed the economic ones. After the Sinclair campaign the two came into closer balance. For the moguls, the social rewards always remained strong. But from 1934 on, these needs were reinforced by economic necessity (Brownstein, 1990: 42–3).

THE PROPAGANDA CAMPAIGN TO STOP SINCLAIR

The moguls claimed that if Sinclair was elected they would relocate their studios to Florida. For example, Columbia's Harry Cohn declared 'we will close our studios in a minute if [Sinclair] is elected' (Mitchell, 1992: 199). While this proved an idle threat,[5] led by Louis Mayer and Irving Thalberg with the backing of the Hearst press, they propagated an anti-Sinclair line in fake newsreels and supported the staid Republican candidate Frank F. Merriam. In many respects, the 'dirty' tactics employed by the moguls to smear Sinclair would give rise to the mass media campaign techniques which became commonplace in US politics after World War II:

> Media experts, making unprecedented use of film, radio, direct mail, opinion polls, and national fund-raising, devised the most astonishing (and visually clever) smear campaign ever directed against a major candidate. . . . The political innovation that produced the strongest impact, both in the 1934 race and long afterward, was the manipulation of moving pictures. Alarmed by the Sinclair threat, MGM's Irving Thalberg produced outrageously partisan film shorts. For the first time, the screen was used to demolish a candidate – a precursor of political advertising on television (ibid.: xii).

To mobilise public opinion against Sinclair, the moguls and the Hearst-controlled newspapers used anti-Communism as their principal weapon. The Hearst papers declared Sinclair to be a 'most dangerous Bolshevik beast' who was trying to 'Russianise' California. They staged a week-by-week attack on the campaign and in the first week instituted a news blackout on all EPIC activities. This was followed by a 'ridicule Sinclair week', a 'distort EPIC week', a 'sidetrack Sinclair week', a 'minimise Sinclair week' and a 'discredit Sinclair' week. Throughout, EPIC's message would be undermined and misrepresented (ibid.: 118).

In tandem, MGM and Fox produced a series of *California Election News* newsreels to be shown in cinemas two weeks before the election. In these shorts, actors pretending to be members of the public were employed to raise concerns about the EPIC platform. In this way, Merriam's supporters were presented as respectable members of the community or decent blue-collar workers who articulated the close relationship between business opportunity, economic prosperity and happiness. Conversely, Sinclair's supporters were made up from the state's riff-raff, gap-toothed bums, ethnic minorities and untrustworthy foreigners. They included itinerant low-lifes who declared they would flood California when the social-ist paradise was realised. For instance, in *California Election News No. 3* trainloads of hoboes and criminals were shown to be migrating to the state in search of the easy life promised to them by Sinclair.[6]

The moguls skilfully played on Californians' fears of outsiders and state intervention over their freedoms. They employed normal-looking people to compare and contrast the 'differ-ences' in the support between Merriam and Sinclair. It was obvious to whom middle-class Californians would direct their sympathies. Some scriptwriters and EPIC supporters found these shorts to be so blatantly biased that they were comical in their distortions:

> . . . they missed the point. They were judging the short too much on what it said, not on what it showed. The opinion expressed by the Merriamites might not, by itself, swing votes. But this was a new political medium – a visual medium. The spoken word might rule the radio, but in the darkened theatre moviegoers identified with the images projected on the big screen. . . . Forget the line of dialogue. It was the face – the visual evidence – that was important (ibid.: 371).

THE MERRIAM TAX

Along with these propagandist newsreels, the moguls pressurised their employees to support Merriam. At first studio executives made their rank-and-file workforce listen to anti-Sinclair speeches made by prominent Republicans. Then they insisted every worker who made over $90 a week should provide a contribution of one day's pay from their wages to stop Sinclair. In some studios employees were politely told that they would be required to donate a day's pay to the Merriam campaign funds. In other studios, they simply received a smaller pay-check at the end of the week.

At Columbia the set department installed an enormous thermometer on the patio of the executive dining room. As the studio workers were forced to contribute to Merriam, the bar rose inexorably to the 100 per cent mark. Even the studio's top writing and directing team of Robert Riskin and Frank Capra, whose films celebrated idealism, courage and integrity, were made to contribute by Harry Cohn. Cohn, however, could not get two writers, the first president of the SWG John Howard Lawson and John Wexley (who were both Communists) to pay up. In the event, both refused to budge and Lawson, who was on a weekly contract, was fired. Wexley was more difficult to remove because he was on a long-term contract. He was suspended and lasted for six weeks when Cohn decided not to renew his option (McGilligan and Buhle, 1997: 708).

At MGM, studio workers received vouchers made out to Louis Mayer in place of their day's pay. Yet, the 'Merriam' tax led to a mini-mutiny among a group of solid MGM creative personnel. Instead of contributing to Merriam, Sam Marx, the studio's story editor, immedi-ately sent monies to Sinclair. Others writers, such as Frances Goodrich and Albert Hackett, resisted the executive's pressure, and Allen Rivkin, on being told that if he worked for Sin-clair he would be in trouble, promptly raised money at the studio to support EPIC. Similarly at Warners, James Cagney wouldn't sign the studio's check to Merriam, despite his alleged involvement in Hollywood's Communist uprising in 1933.

The moguls' authoritarianism proved counter-productive as they inadvertently galvanised conservatives such as Morrie Ryskind, moderates like Nunnally Johnson and left wingers including Dorothy Parker to oppose their 'pleas' for money. They provided the fledgling SWG with a renewed sense of purpose when it passed a resolution condemning the threats the moguls had used to canvass for monies. For instance, the young Billy Wilder, an émigré from Nazism, found out he had no choice but to contribute $50 to Merriam and was left with two conflicting thoughts:

'One was: *It may not be democratic, but it's a brilliant idea. Maybe if businessmen in Germany had deducted fifty marks from their workers to stop Hitler, Europe would be a safer place today.* The other was: *I fled fascism for THIS?*' (Mitchell, 1992: 360).

HOLLYWOOD SUPPORTS EPIC

The moguls' coercion led to outrage in the Hollywood community. The liberal actor Fredric March, on discovering that Thalberg had produced the fake newsreels, castigated him at a cocktail party and the production head replied 'Nothing is unfair in politics' (Thomas, 1969: 269). Thalberg, who had been brought up as a socialist orator in the shadows of Tammany Hall, believed 'Fairness in an election is a contradiction in terms. It just doesn't exist' (Mitchell, 1992: 561). The moguls' condescending attitude led to many workers deciding to support Sinclair.

They particularly opposed Mayer's perception of himself as a wise shepherd leading his flock. Instead, they argued this flock was composed of wilful adults who no longer wanted to be treated as children and should speak out on public issues. Therefore, stars such as Will Rogers, Jean Harlow, Chaplin and Cagney campaigned for EPIC, and writers including Parker and Ryskind formed the Authors League for Sinclair. For many in Hollywood the Sinclair campaign marked a sea change in their political thinking and liberals such as Philip Dunne vowed revenge. Subsequently, Dunne and Melvyn Douglas established the MPDC and lined up to support the Democratic candidate Culbert Olson in the 1938 Californian gubernatorial election. To this end, the activists produced radio shows and film shorts and, displaying a keen wit, demanded that Merriam should contribute one day of his salary to Olson's campaign funds. For politicians and newspaper editors, the film industry's activism betrayed its role as the purveyor of American fantasies and they produced headlines to smear 'red herrings across the gossamer gowns of Hollywood' (Rosten, 1941: 134).

MERRIAM WINS THE ELECTION

On the day before the election, the Hollywood trade papers informed their readers to be certain to cast their vote and to: 'VOTE AGAINST UPTON SINCLAIR CAST A VOTE TO SAVE YOUR JOB VOTE TO SAVE THE MOTION PICTURE INDUSTRY' (Shindler, 1996: 65).

The power of the moguls and the Hearst press proved decisive as Sinclair only received 888,000 votes in comparison to the lacklustre Merriam's tally of 1,139,000. The new gov-

ernor praised his Hollywood supporters, especially Louis Mayer, and the moguls congratu-
lated themselves on securing Merriam's victory over Sinclair through their machinations.
Mayer declared that California had correctly chosen the route of patriotism over the evils
associated with radicalism. Through their vilification of EPIC, they had shaped the media's
coverage of the campaign and enforced their will on the Hollywood workforce. The moguls,
with the Hearst papers, introduced many of the trends (polls, political advertising and public
relation strategies) which would become commonplace in subsequent American elections.
A bitter Sinclair complained:

> They [the moguls] have made propaganda and they have won a great victory with it, and are
> tremendously swelled up about it. You may be sure that never again will there be an election in
> California in which the great 'Louis Be' will not make his power felt . . . California should stand
> up and sing hosannas for the greatest state industry, MOTION PICTURES, and the same industry
> should, for itself, point to its work whenever some . . . scary legislation comes up in the various
> State Legislatures during the next few months (Sinclair, 1936: 194–5).

Yet, in an ironic twist, the studios and the Hearst press were confronted by an increase in
corporation taxes by the Merriam administration. For Hearst this was disastrous and he was
forced to close down several papers. Concurrently, the loyal moguls announced they would
be leaving the state and Mayer went to see the Governor of North Carolina to negotiate a
relocation of his studio. Once again they mobilised their forces to stem the tide of 'socialism' associated with such taxes and lobbied to introduce a residency requirement for all those
Californians applying for welfare. Despite such pressure, they failed to convince Merriam to
reduce taxes or to find more favourable conditions elsewhere. As far as the moguls were concerned, the Bolsheviks had managed to inveigle themselves into the Republican Party! Their
politicisation of the Hollywood workforce would lead to the growth of liberal and
Communist activism in the industry for the rest of the decade.

Conclusion

Hollywood's politicisation in the 1920s and the 1930s reflected many of the trends which
affected America in the inter-war year period. Initially, the studio chiefs aligned themselves
with the Republican Party. In part, this was due to its ideology as the party of business and
because they wanted a minimal amount of governmental interference in their financial affairs.
For Mayer, however, his affiliation with the GOP was driven by innate conservative ideologies and a desire to be accepted by the US elites.

This understanding reflected Hollywood's outsider status in mainstream US business and
political affairs. For many WASPs, the film industry was treated with suspicion because of its
Jewish complexion and the vulgarities associated with its origins as a funfair sideshow. Thus,
the moguls sought to overcome such latent forms of anti-Semitism by assimilating themselves
into the elites who ran the country. This yearning for status, along with the preservation of
their businesses, was a significant factor in determining their entry into politics and it went
as far as Mayer perceiving himself to be a kingmaker for Hoover.

However, with the changes inaugurated by the New Deal, Hollywood was characterised by a growing liberal sensibility. In contrast to their bosses, the industry's writers, directors and actors associated themselves with FDR's progressive reforms of the welfare and economic systems. They actively campaigned for Roosevelt, who understood the benefits of such celebrity endorsement. Many of these liberals were alarmed about the growth of fascism and Nazism in Europe and formed groups within the Popular Front. For a number of Hollywood activists, this growing political consciousness led them to the Communist Party.

The division between the liberal and Communist factions of the Hollywood workforce became conspicuous in the fallout surrounding the Stalin–Hitler pact. This created a degree of acrimony which was profitably ploughed by the industry's reactionary forces. The 1938 Dies Committee marked the first major intervention of Congress in Hollywood's political affairs and, in spite of its almost farcical failings, served as a warning to the industry. For many in Washington, Tinseltown was the purveyor of moral degradation and a cover for godless Communism. The HUAC's anti-union stance would also establish divisions in Hollywood which were to reverberate in the anti-Communist witch-hunts that dominated the industry in the 1940s and 1950s.

Similarly, the differences between the management and workforce would simmer under the surface throughout the 1920s and 1930s. These reached a head in Upton Sinclair's 1934 EPIC campaign when the moguls manipulated the medias' messages through bogus newsreels and demanded that their employees pay the 'Merriam' tax. The hardness of such 'mogul politics' was both effective and counterproductive. On the one hand, Mayer and Thalberg led a successful campaign to determine the outcome of the election. On the other, their coercive actions galvanised the workforce into action and made apparent the divisions within the industry.

Hollywood's status in political affairs demonstrated its growing importance as a purveyor of popular dreams throughout the inter-war years. The moguls, liberals and radicals were united in their desire to represent their contradictory values in the films they produced. Consequently, as there were reforms and retractions across US civic and social spheres, Hollywood became a significant force in reflecting and informing the societal debates which existed throughout American life.

Notes

1. Mayer's growing role indicated a shift from Broadway to Hollywood during the 1920s as the voice for the entertainment industry in US politics. In 1920 and 1924, Al Jolson had led delegations of stage stars to serenade Republican presidential candidates Warren Harding and Calvin Coolidge respectively.

2. During the 1920s, Roosevelt had sought out the moguls to make a film of the life of revolutionary hero John Paul Jones. However, despite some initial interest nothing came of the project.

3. Mayer would lead the moguls in an attempt to buy the negative from RKO of Welles' *Citizen Kane* so the film could be destroyed because of its critical portrayal of Hearst.

4. Eisenstein wrote two scenarios for Paramount entitled *The Glass House* and *Sutter's Gold*. However, the studio showed no interest in producing either project and its option on the Soviet director was quickly dropped.

5. Industry insiders knew the studios had invested heavily in Hollywood and enjoyed outstanding profitability in California. The moguls themselves did not want to return east to New York after enjoying the bounteous pleasures of the 'promised land'.

6. Fake photographs were published to discredit the EPIC crusade in the *Los Angeles Times*. It showed a photo of a freight car full of tramps arriving in California on 26 October 1934. Eventually it was made clear that the still was not a news photo but a shot from the Warner Bros.' feature, *Wild Boys of the Road* (1933).

5
The Politics of Hollywood Labour

Introduction

The establishment of the Screen Writers Guild (SWG), Screen Actors Guild (SAG) and Screen Directors Guild (SDG) coincided with the evolution of collective bargaining in America's labour relations during the 1930s. The 1935 National Labour Relations (Wagner) Act provided recognition to American trade unions and Hollywood's guilds grew exponentially. The moguls opposed them because studio costs had been minimised through the maintenance of a disparate workforce. Consequently, they formed a company union in 1927, the Academy of Motion Pictures Arts and Sciences, to promote 'industrial harmony'. However, as Hollywood's workers could not be deterred, the moguls pursued aggressive practices to stem the growth of the craft guilds and technicians' unions.

Throughout the 1930s, Hollywood's industrial relations were characterised by conflicts and these difficulties came to a head when the SWG sought to amalgamate with other writers' guilds. In response, the producers promoted the Screen Playwrights Inc. (SP) composed of rightwing screenwriters, creating an open wound in the SWG. Similarly, divisions were visible in the 1940s when the International Alliance of Theatrical and Stage Employees (IATSE), which had ties with organised crime, faced a jurisdictional battle for its membership with the leftwing Conference of Studio Unions (CSU). The resulting strikes and lock-outs left a bitter legacy.

These conflicts provided the conditions for the rightwing Motion Picture Alliance for the Preservation of American Ideals (Motion Picture Alliance) to call for the HUAC to investigate the Communist infiltration of the industry's labour force in 1946. In contrast to its discredited predecessor (see Chapter 4), the new committee, chaired by Republican Congressman J. Parnell Thomas, benefited from the post-war climate of anti-Communism.[1] The trial of the Hollywood Ten, the prominent Communist writers, directors and producers who refused to cooperate with the HUAC, led to them being blacklisted and imprisoned. An extensive blacklisting of Communists and fellow travellers occurred during the 1950s as friendly witnesses revealed names to the HUAC. The blacklist fuelled an ideological debate between those who testified in front of the committee and those who refused to name names.

This chapter considers how the Hollywood workforce achieved its labour rights through the collective organisation of the craft guilds and technical unions. It outlines the disputes which accompanied their development and the links between trade unionism, political radicalism and the anti-Communist witch-hunts. As John Howard Lawson commented, 'the case of the Hollywood Ten goes back to the formation of the Screen Writers Guild in 1933' (Ceplair and Englund, 2003: 16).[2]

The formation of the Screen Writers Guild

During Hollywood's infancy, the moguls controlled the industry's working conditions through a form of benevolent despotism wherein they increased wages in line with their company's profitability. They had been attracted to Los Angeles due to the open-shop rulings established by *Los Angeles Times*' publisher Harrison Gray Otis in 1888 (Buhle and Wagner, 2002: 43). In 1924, in response to the actors' demands to establish a basic contract, the studios, with the exception of United Artists, formed a labour arm within the MPPDA, called the Association of Motion Picture Producers Inc. (AMPP). This body was located in Hollywood and was almost exclusively responsible for industrial relations. It drew up 'yellow dog' contracts with the workforce (e.g., join the company union or lose your job) and became an active member of the national open-shop movement (Nielsen and Mailes, 1995: 6–7). However, in 1933, these practices provoked a crisis when the studios' stability was undermined by the Depression, forcing the moguls to cut staff, reduce wages and demand greater productivity. Consequently, writers, actors and directors sought representation through the craft guilds. The most active of these was the SWG, which the bosses refused to recognise (Muscio, 1997: 129).

The genesis of the SWG occurred in 1912 when the Authors' Guild was set up to protect the rights of writers of books, short stories and articles. Subsequently, the Authors' and the Dramatists' Guilds combined to become the Authors' League and in 1921 the SWG was formed as a branch of the Authors' League. Neither the League nor the SWG could win a contract from the studios and the screenwriters became affiliated to the Academy.

Despite the concessions the Academy received from the producers, the writers realised it did not represent their interests. Instead, it operated at the behest of the studios and acquiesced to the paycuts and layoffs which hit Hollywood in the Depression. This culminated in the moguls demanding a 50 per cent cut in wages for all studio workers in March 1933. However, when the unionised carpenters and electricians refused to accept the proposal, the bosses targeted the better-paid creative workers and declared anyone who earned more than $50 a week would have their paycut on a sliding scale (Brownstein, 1990: 44).

For the writers' guild to be credible it had to protect its members' interests against the concentrated wealth of the studios. In March 1933, ten writers, including John Howard Lawson, gathered at the Roosevelt Hotel on Hollywood Boulevard to found the new SWG. By 5 April, over 200 writers had left the Academy to join the SWG. They established a constitution and series of by-laws to elect officers, the first of whom was Lawson, whose presidency was considered to be a triumph of collectivism. By October 1934, the membership of the SWG had swelled to 750.

This drive for collective bargaining included demands for higher wages, fewer hours, the standardisation of contracts, the regularisation of hiring practices and the arbitration of industrial disputes. In particular, the guild sought remuneration on a royalty basis for writers to make them part owners of the films made from their scripts. Through these goals, the writers believed they could offset the contention, '[the producers] owned you; you were their commodity; they were paying you so much a week, and you belonged to them' (Ogden Stewart, 1971: 94).

Cultural and ideological, as well as practical, imperatives shaped the writers' aspirations. No other group in America's writing community was as well paid, but had given itself over so completely to the production process as Hollywood's scriptwriters. Educated and articulate, the writers exhibited a militant political consciousness. This meant that the radical SWG would be threatened by the studio bosses who opposed its existence and by a small, but powerful, rightwing caucus which existed in the guild.

WRITERS VERSUS PRODUCERS

The New Deal established the National Industrial Recovery Act (NIRA) including the National Recovery Administration (NRA) to oversee the creation of trade and labour-management codes. The legislators anticipated that, through planning, fairness and cooperation, economic stability could be achieved. The SWG (along with the newly formed SAG) believed the NRA would force the studios to recognise it as the writers' sole representative in Hollywood, thereby enabling it to achieve collective bargaining status.

However, the NIRA codes gave the moguls greater flexibility to negotiate with what they perceived to be a volatile labour force. Several provisions reduced the writers' and actors' salaries, and the recognition the guilds had strived for was absent. The SWG and SAG criticised the codes in telegrams sent to Washington, and Roosevelt, fearing a public backlash against the agency, removed the controversial passages. Instead, writer–producer and actor–producer committees were formed to resolve pay and working conditions. However, the studio bosses opted out of these bodies and refused to recognise the guilds. Their cause was sustained by the 1935 Supreme Court's ruling of *Schecter Poultry Corp. versus United States* (295 US 495) which declared the NIRA to be unconstitutional.

Led by Louis B. Mayer and Irving Thalberg, the moguls opposed the SWG's demands. In September 1935, Mayer stated he would tear up the contract of any SWG member who was dissatisfied with his conditions at MGM. Thalberg attempted to sign MGM's key writers into personal service contracts, obliging them to be contracted to him rather than to the studio. The MGM production chief's contempt for the SWG was determined by his belief that every writer who joined the guild had engaged in an act of personal disloyalty. This fanaticism shocked many as Thalberg was seen as the most humane boss in Tinseltown. Yet '. . . the cries of personal betrayal and ingratitude clouded the issue which most producers, with their unerring feeling for the jugular, knew was decisive: control' (Ceplair and Englund, 2003: 31).

In November 1933, MGM became the first studio to enforce a unit system of control wherein writers were assigned to producers to work on assignments. This meant writers could be hired or fired on a weekly or picture-by-picture basis. By extending the pool of unemployed writers and threatening to end long-term contracts, the studios intimidated many scriptwriters. Militant bosses such as Thalberg, Zanuck and Warner then blacklisted SWG activists including Lawson, Lester Cole and Mary McCall (Buhle and Wagner, 2002: 46).

The passing of the National Labour Relations Act (NLRA), allowed the SWG to split from the Academy in 1935. Under the provisions of the law, it wrote to the studios informing them that it was the sole representative for screenwriters. However, the AMPP continued to deal with the Academy whose membership numbered thirty-eight writers in comparison to the SWG's 770. It gambled on the Supreme Court finding the NLRA unconstitutional and realised the SWG would have a limited influence as long as it remained isolated in Hollywood. The large pool of unemployed scriptwriters meant that the withdrawal of labour, its most potent weapon, was an untenable option for the SWG. The producers understood anyway that, in any potential strike, strike-breakers could be easily found and only the adaptation, rather than the acquisition, of material would be a concern.

The SWG's leaders decided that, if they were to challenge the studios' power, they needed to amalgamate with the national playwrights', authors' and journalists' guilds. The amalgamation could bring about unity, recognition from the studios and strengthen the union's negotiating position: ' "Just wait till we join the Authors' League, comrades!" Sammy shouted. "Then all us downtrodden writers can become producers and we'll punish the producers by making them get down on their hands and knees – and write!" ' (Schulberg, 1992: 135). However, it also made conspicuous the divisions between left and right which had percolated within the guild since 1933.

THE SCREEN PLAYWRIGHTS INC.

> Responding to a rising tide of resentment among the Guild members against their Executive Board for selling out their autonomy to the . . . Reds who controlled the Authors' League . . . the responsible element has formed a Committee of Five who had pledged themselves to rescue the writers' ship from the hands of crackpots and adventurers . . . The five distinguished gentlemen were Lawrence Paine, Harold Godfrey Wilson, John McCarter, Robert Griffin and – Sammy Glick (ibid.: 167).

It is instructive that the then Communist Budd Schulberg placed his all-American heel, Sammy Glick (who had previously made political capital by attacking the producers), on the side of the SP in *What Makes Sammy Run?* It also demonstrated how the divisions in the SWG reflected the 'Sammy-drive' values of money, prestige and power which he had made apparent in his novel.

The SP was composed of a well-paid cabal of rightwing writers who did not require union protection. They included Rupert Hughes, James K. McGuinness, John Lee Mahin, Howard Emmett Rogers, Frank Butler, Patterson McNutt and Herman J. Mankiewicz.

These writers left the SWG in May 1936 and eighty-one further resignations were announced in the trades shortly thereafter (*Variety*, 1936: 1–2). They opposed SWG's president Ernest Pascal's decision to amalgamate with the Authors' League, the Dramatists' Guild, the Newspaper Guild and the Radio Writers' Guild. For them, the merger reflected the perils of 'collectivism' and 'anti-American forms' of radicalism. They accused the SWG of engaging in 'a tyranny of writers over writers' (Hughes, 1936: 5).

This schism was long standing. Previously, the reactionary scriptwriters had engineered a form of 'polite unionism' which reflected their position as the better-paid and more privileged members of the workforce. They attempted to remove the guild's provisions concerning the assessment of their annual dues and its fining of writers who had acted in a prejudicial manner. Therefore, in the 1934 elections for union officials, they ran a 'liberal slate' that failed to win the day. Now these labour aristocrats believed they were being undermined by the SWG leadership's insistence that it should represent every scriptwriter, however lowly, working in Hollywood:

> They went on talking about the Guild. 'I'm all for the Guild,' Paine said. 'But I'll be damned if I like how it's being run. They're letting too many people in. What the hell, every lucky bastard who happens to sell one story isn't a screenwriter. The producers won't take us seriously until we limit the membership to writers who have been employed at least a year, or get a thousand dollars a week.' 'If this bunch of Reds have their way we'll be marching down Hollywood Boulevard in their May Day Parade,' Wilson said (Schulberg, 1992: 138).

These enmities heightened when the merger proposals came onto the agenda and the secessionists formed the SP to ally themselves with the studio moguls. Accordingly, they denounced the 'closed-shop' union practices which would emerge in the wake of the unification of the writers' guilds. Moreover, the SP received the support of MGM's front office and the studio promoted several of its members once they had joined the company union. In this way, the SP plunged Hollywood's screenwriting community into a civil war.

THE SCREENWRITERS' WARS

While declaring solidarity with the SWG in the spring of 1936, the SP members secretly allied themselves with Thalberg. Although the SWG withstood this treachery and its proposals for the amalgamation were supported by its membership in a vote of 193 to fifteen, the paucity of the electorate indicated a worrying collapse in the guild's militancy. The leadership's fears were exacerbated when the studio bosses provided SWG members with an ultimatum – either join the company union or be removed from the lot (Trumbo, 1970: 569).

Simultaneously, the mass resignation of rightwing screenwriters inflicted a crushing blow on the SWG and worried centrists found themselves caught between the union leadership and SP secessionists. Invariably, these moderates withdrew from the union or simply stopped going to meetings. Sensing victory, the SP held an inaugural meeting with the producers at the Beverly Hills Wilshire Hotel on 9 May 1936:

We do not believe in burning down the house to get rid of the rats. The better producers suffer from the rats as much as we do and are as eager for their suppression. The better producers believe that the happiness and security of the writers is an asset to their business. They have promised us complete cooperation in the solution of problems and the righting of wrongs (Screen Writers of Hollywood, 1936).

Although the scriptwriters left the SWG, they did not clamber to join the SP, whose membership only reached seventy-five. For the four years of its existence, this 'gentlemen's club' failed to achieve mass support as mid- or lower-ranking scriptwriters were told by their 'superiors' to remain grateful for the scraps given to them. Despite achieving several successes, the SP was perceived as a puppet of the studios. Its dissolution was inevitable, as average screenwriters were provided with little in terms of treatment, hiring, job security or control over the product (Ceplair and Englund, 2003: 44).

Yet, along with the moguls' intimidation, the SP's union-bashing tactics had undermined the workforce's solidarity and by June 1936, the SWG's active membership had fallen to fifty. Fearing they would be blacklisted, this rump met secretly to consider its options. As a direct confrontation with the studios was out of the question, there was only one hope – to regain credibility by petitioning the National Labour Relations Board (NLRB). However, while formulating its position, the SWG was given a boost when the Supreme Court upheld the constitutionality of the National Labour Relations Act (NLRA) in 1937. The decision enabled the SWG's leaders to run a ballot for unification and allowed screenwriters to return to the guild.

In June 1937, over 400 writers attended a meeting in which the decision to file the petition was passed and the NLRB's investigators came to Hollywood the following August. After a year's worth of hearings, it announced that the certification would be voted for on a studio-by-studio basis and through a secret ballot. This was a major achievement for the SWG, who, along with the SAG and SDG, won the election by a landslide. On 10 August 1938 the NLRB formally certified the reincorporated SWG as the sole body for the collective bargaining of writers in the motion picture industry. This decision was not disputed by the studios and represented a tremendous victory for the guild.

THE STUDIO CONTRACT AND THE LEGACY OF THE WRITERS' WARS
In 1939 negotiations between the SWG and AMPP began in order to create a fair and equitable studio contract. However, the producers remained reluctant to concede to the SWG and continued to recognise the SP despite the NLRB certification. This led to the SWG returning to the NLRB, which issued the producers with an unfair labour practice citation. This ended the AMPP's relationship with the SP as it voided the company union's contract with the studios. Still the producers dragged their feet and the negotiations lasted another two years until a deal, due to the oncoming war and the SWG's decision to call an all-out strike, was finalised in 1941.

In addition to the minimum wage, the end of speculative writing practices and the notice for termination rights won by the SP, the contract provided for an 85 per cent (rising to 100 per cent) union shop for the workforce, as well as 'exclusive control' over writing credits.

However, when the first contract was signed in 1942, it included a non-strike clause stating action could only occur when the SWG entered into its contractual negotiations with the studios. Furthermore, the rights to arbitrate over screen credits were divisive as the clause was written in such a way that writers could deal with the studios individually rather than through the guild.

Moreover, the negotiations were accompanied by the dismantlement of the SP. This led to several ironic episodes when the rightwing scriptwriters, who had fought to smash the guild, justified their return to the fold:

> . . . When we won the NLRB election . . . those writers who had left to join the company union had to come back . . . [and] it was a fascinating scene to sit there and watch as these people beat their breast in *mea culpa*. . . . [They harboured the ambition that someday the tables would be turned] . . . [and] that was openly said. . . . These . . . guys would never surrender. They were just grousing all the time about what had happened to them. [They] thought it was a mistake that we were so harsh with them; they should have been taken back without the *mea culpa* meeting (McGilligan and Buhle, 1997: 117–18).

The SP members never forgot their humiliation and, led by James McGuinness, sought their revenge by forming the Motion Picture Alliance with other Hollywood rightwingers in 1944. Despite the left's victory in achieving union recognition, these resentments would debilitate the SWG as a political force at the height of the HUAC investigations.

The 1946 Conference of Studio Unions (CSU) lockout

A volatile series of jurisdictional disputes occurred between the technicians' unions – the rightwing IATSE (IA), and the militant CSU. Once the battle lines were drawn only a catalyst was needed to expose these divisions. This occurred in 1946 when the studios enforced a violent 'lockout' of the CSU. As the strike escalated, the conservative leadership of the SAG, led by a board including Warner contract player Ronald Reagan, crucially withdrew its support for the CSU. In the wake of this collapse in union solidarity, left and rightwing divisions took hold.

THE INTERNATIONAL ALLIANCE OF THEATRICAL AND STAGE EMPLOYEES

The IA was formed in the 1890s to represent stage mechanics who were fighting wage cuts, intolerable hours and the abandonment of companies by defaulting tour managers. It was organised along industrial rather than craft lines to represent those electricians, carpenters, mechanics and painters who were part of a unique socio-economic formation: showbusiness. Its Los Angeles division, Local 33, became an affiliate of the American Federation of Labour (AFL) in 1908 and began organising in the film industry shortly afterwards. The studio employees faced similar problems to their theatrical counterparts: long hours, irregular working rights, no proper overtime rates, 'casualisation' and draconian hiring and firing practices. Films represented the stored work of theatrical workers because hundreds of prints could be struck and distributed from a master copy at a fraction of the cost of sending a performance out on the road (Nielsen and Mailes, 1995: 1).

From 1914 to 1926, the IA battled with the electrical and carpentry unions to gain control over Hollywood's technicians. This was achieved on 1 September 1926, when the IA negotiated a Studio Basic Agreement (SBA) with the moguls. The SBA was not a defined contract, but created the framework through which wages, hours, conditions and grievances could be negotiated. Consequently, pay and rights for studio craft workers improved in the 1930s and 1940s.

Simultaneously, the IA developed 'closed-shop' working practices in which its members would no longer be required to face the indignity of the 'shape-up' at the studio gates, but were employed through the union's offices. Despite this control over recruitment, further attempts at organisation and strikes were hampered because of New Deal labour legislation and the IA leadership's failings. Therefore, in 1934, the head of the Chicago IA local, George Browne, replaced president William Elliot as the leader of the union.

Browne's victory was uncontested, in no small part due to his role as the front man for mobster Willie Bioff. Both were heavily involved in the Chicago crime syndicate which was diversifying its interests from bootlegging to union racketeering after the abolition of Prohibition in 1933. And the gangsters realised they could use the IA to extort money from exhibitors, cinema owners and studio executives (Russo, 2001: 135–6).

BROWNE AND BIOFF: THE MOB TAKES OVER THE IA

Browne and Bioff, with the muscle of criminals like Johnny Rosselli, Nick Circella, Frank Nitti and Bugsy Siegel, pressurised the theatre owners by calling out cinema projectionists and threatening strikes by the stagehands to keep the studios in line. However, they realised it would be to their advantage to make a sweetheart deal with the producers to keep the legitimate technicians' unions at bay.[3] The IA leaders contacted studio executives Joe and Nicholas Schenck to formalise an arrangement in which the union would agree to a no-strike deal for seven years in return for $150,000 and 100 per cent recognition. As the moguls were concerned that the NLRA would establish collective bargaining rights for a variety of unions, thereby requiring a divestiture of their profits, they readily cooperated with the Outfit. However, the Schencks were worried that the authorities might become aware of the alliance if it was too hastily expedited.

In November 1935, Browne and Bioff called a phoney strike among projectionists after an International Brotherhood of Electrical Workers (IBEW) crew had been sent by Paramount to the IA's stronghold in New York to shoot aerial footage for the movie *Thirteen Hours in the Air* (1935). Only through the personal intervention of Paramount's head of production, Barney Balaban, could Browne be 'persuaded' to call the action off. The IBEW crew members were immediately dismissed and replaced by IA workers. In the meantime, the producers were 'forced' to accede to Browne's demands that the IA should be granted the sole rights to represent the industry's key workers.

This meant that the IA was given the first closed-shop agreement within the Hollywood studio system. On 2 January 1936, notices informed all grips, electricians, carpenters, property workers, camera crew and lab technicians that they would be required to rejoin their respective IA locals to keep their jobs. For the producers, this meant they could continue to hire workers on a casual basis. For the union's leadership, the agreement allowed them to embezzle the funds levied on the membership and to exchange bargaining favours with the producers.

However, the deal eroded the workforce's right to negotiate with the studios. Moreover, the mob could blacklist any uncooperative worker by refusing to grant, or revoking, a membership card. To stem dissent, Browne and his executive board declared the studio locals to be operating 'in a state of emergency', thereby banning meetings and employing 'lot checkers' (who were informers on a retainer) to oust troublemakers. The stitch-up was completed when Bioff and the AMPP's labour representative Pat Casey used a labyrinth of inter-union and producer-union rulings to thwart any legitimate collective bargaining agreements.

Browne and Bioff's racketeering eventually caught up with them when Jeff Kibre, an IA progressive, filed a formal complaint against the leadership with the NLRB. Kibre accused them of taking a bribe of $150,000 from Joe Schenck and the Fox president was forced to cut a deal with the federal investigators when it was discovered he had a huge, unpaid income tax bill. Consequently, he testified in the court case in which Browne and Bioff were found guilty of extortion, and they were sentenced to custodial terms of eight and ten years respectively. For the time being, the mob's influence in Hollywood was tempered and from then on was brokered by the shady lawyer Sidney Korshak. The government also believed the studios when they claimed that they had been the victims of organised crime rather than acting as co-conspirators in the disenfranchisement of the workforce.

For the IA, Browne and Bioff's legacy haunted the local shops as many of its officials owed their position to the regime. They ignored the charges of mob influence and, led by president Richard Walsh, pursued an extreme rightwing agenda. In response, many studio workers looked to the only democratic labour federation left in Hollywood – the Conference of Studio Unions (CSU): 'Willie Bioff made more Communists in Hollywood than any other Communist organiser could possible make. He . . . made them do things that they did not want to do, and they resented it' (Sorrell, 1948: 1874).

THE CONFERENCE OF STUDIO UNIONS

The CSU was formed in response to Browne and Bioff's corruption and the violence mounted by the mob's goons against workers on picket lines in 1937 and 1941. It was composed of five unions – the Screen Cartoonists Guild, the Screen Office Employees Guild, Film Technicians Local 683, Machinists Local 1185 and Motion Picture Painters Local 644. It also included IA progressives who hoped to unify all the non-IA locals in Hollywood and to collectively organise all non-unionised personnel.

The CSU was led by the militant Herb Sorrell, a business manager for the Painters Local 644, who had organised cartoonists in a strike at Disney in the early 1940s. Throughout the war, it supported many Popular Front and Communist organisations, who in turn backed the CSU in its disputes with the management. The CSU also won a key jurisdictional victory over the IA by securing an alliance with the SAG (May, 2000: 181). By 1945, the CSU had enrolled nearly 10,000 studio workers and the studios opposed Sorrell's radical convictions, criticisms of their employment practices and calls for collective representation. The CSU's growth undermined the IA, which still accounted for 16,000 members of the labour force.

Roy Brewer, the IA's rightwing Hollywood representative, realised the threat and denounced Sorrell as a Communist stooge. An accomplice to the moguls, he also sought to ensnare the CSU into a major, jurisdictional dispute and thereby break its strength (Horne, 2001: 156–7; Ceplair and Englund, 2003: 217).

THE 1945 CSU STRIKE

The 1945 CSU strike occurred over a seemingly insignificant dispute, over the union representation of seventy-five set decorators. The IA had refused to incorporate the Set Decorators' Guild in 1939 and this enabled the AMPP to refuse to recognise it in 1944. The set decorators decided to join the Painters, who were affiliated to the CSU and a petition was filed with the NLRB. In response the IA filed a counter petition stating that the decorators should be affiliated with its Local 44, allowing the AMPP to continue to refuse the decorators' application to join the CSU.

Sorrell promptly appealed to the War Labour Board (WLB), which upheld the CSU claim. However, the AMPP would not budge and the strike was launched in March 1945:

> The set decorators did not strike because the producers refused to change provision of a contract. They struck because the producers refused to act in conformity with a clear provision of the contract. . . . The set decorators . . . went out on strike only after the producers refused to abide by the award of the WLB arbitrator (CSU, 1945: 9).

Over the following eight months, this proved a divisive conflict. At Warner Bros., the Los Angeles Police Department's (LAPD) brutality against CSU pickets escalated and the affiliated Popular Front leaders sent off a torrent of letters and telegrams to an unresponsive Truman administration. The strike widened the gulf between the IA and CSU and created divisions between the Screen Publicists and Screen Office Employees Guilds. Finally, it demonstrated key dissensions between Sorrell and the Communist Party of the United States (CPUSA), which remained true to its wartime no-strike pledge. In response, Sorrell commented 'that war or no war we should not give up any basic American trade union belief' and the Party eventually supported the action (Nielsen and Mailes, 1995: 91).

These divisions were exploited by Brewer, who accused the CSU of being unpatriotic and, along with rightwing Californian Senator Jack Tenney, damned the Conference's leadership as being Communists dupes (ibid.: 132). He sent out threatening letters to those members of the Hollywood Independent Citizens Committee of the Arts, Science and Professions (HICCASP) who supported the strike. He accused them of being unAmerican and warned that IA projectionists would refuse to show their films. However, most shied away from the controversy and the SAG, now fronted by a rightwing board including Jack Dales, George Murphy, Robert Montgomery and Ronald Reagan, voted to cross the picket lines by a majority of 3,029 to eighty-eight.

Yet, in spite of the opposition of the bosses, rightwing trade unionists and politicians, Sorrell, with the limited support of the SWG, turned the tide. He did this by mobilising the Hollywood left after the NLRB had found in favour of the CSU, and by focusing the dispute onto one studio – Warner Brothers. This was met by hostility by the moguls who on 5 October decided to meet fire with fire: 'The riot at Warner Brothers hit Hollywood – and the nation – like a thunderclap. The cult of celebrity meant that . . . when news emerged from Hollywood about Reds and labour strife, it was bound to grab national attention' (Horne, 2001: 184–5).

The brutal force employed by the LAPD and sanctioned by the studio chiefs was a major miscalculation. It led to negative publicity for the studios and to stars such as Bette Davis refusing to cross picket lines. As public opinion favoured the CSU, the violence was seen as less of a consequence of Communist activity and more as a result of the producers' intransigence. Finally, as the pressure became unbearable, the AMPP agreed to recognise the decorators' right to affiliate with the CSU and that all strikers should be reinstated. Despite the favourable outcome, this was the Hollywood left's final victory and the right became more determined to rid itself of the CSU.

THE LOCKOUT AND COLLAPSE OF THE CSU

In September 1946, a further CSU strike occurred. This would last for three years and lead to its collapse, the eradication of the leftwing in Hollywood's unions and the end of democratic union representation in the motion picture industry. Again Brewer and the AMPP conspired to manufacture a dispute with the CSU. This had to do with the construction of sets and a convoluted distinction between who was responsible for 'erecting' or 'building' them. The IA claimed a scab carpenters' union should be recognised by the studios over an AFL-affiliated workshop. The CSU's painters refused to operate on the 'hot' sets and the majors barred all CSU workers from their lots, while simultaneously refusing to issue them dismissal slips.

In spite of warnings from CSU officials, who realised Brewer was spoiling for a fight, Sorrell could not be restrained in his response. He called for the producers to accede to the painters or there would be an all-out war, thereby playing into the hands of the right. As in the 1945 strike, the CSU's pickets were violently attacked and there was a strong degree of initial militancy. However, while the CSU's enemies may not have changed, their anti-Communist fervour proved effective in marginalising the Conference's leadership. The craft guilds including the SWG, whose board shied away from any political controversy, and the SAG, in which Brewer had the ear of leading member Reagan, refused to provide support:

> The actors . . . were the one single group which could automatically shut down the studios just by not appearing in front of the cameras. Roy Brewer was the one labour leader who talked as much about labour's responsibility as he did about its privilege. The class warfare boys would try to exploit this as a pro-boss attitude and, of course, they would . . . [exhume] . . . the ghost of all the Browne–Bioff evil (Reagan, 1965: 159).[4]

From his arrival in Hollywood in 1945, Brewer made it his mission to discredit all those 'subversives' he saw as his enemies. He conducted a witch-hunt against the IA's progressives and built bridges with the radical right. As his power base grew, Brewer smeared Sorrell and was aided by the SAG's rightwing leadership who argued that the lockout was caused 'not [by] a question of wages and hours . . . [but] because two international presidents of AFL unions [could not] agree which union should have jurisdiction over 350 jobs' (Montgomery, 1946: 7). Subsequently, the SAG voted to cross picket lines by 2,748 to 509.

Brewer colluded with the AMPP to keep the studios open by establishing scab locals to construct and paint their sets. As the CSU's pickets dwindled and its members reluctantly crossed the lines, the Conference was dismembered and Sorrell was run out of the industry when Brewer produced a Photostat copy of what he claimed to be Sorrell's signature on a Communist Party membership card. While the card was signed 'Herb Stewart', Brewer argued that for reasons of security the Party used pseudonyms and Stewart was Sorrell's mother's maiden name (Prindle, 1988: 45–6).

The collapse of the strike and the removal of the CSU leadership meant the radical right was in the ascendant and it turned its attention to liberals, fellow travellers and Communists with a renewed purpose. To this end, it achieved the support of Washington's political classes whose anti-Communist paranoia was reaching a crescendo in response to the Cold War.

The House Un-American Activities Committee and the Blacklist

As labour disputes divided Hollywood, the film industry was subjected to the House Un-American Activities Committee' (HUAC) investigations in the 1940s. The growth of the Hollywood Communist Party meant that the HUAC could subpoena Party members to its hearings. HUAC prosecuted ten Hollywood writers, producers and directors, the so-called 'Hollywood Ten', who refused to name other Communists and became 'unfriendly witnesses'. Its investigations in the 1950s led to friendly witnesses testifying against Communists who, along with unfriendly witnesses, were placed on the blacklist. The divisions between those who did or did not testify in front of the Committee would forever divide Hollywood and underpin its attitudes to politics to this day.

The Motion Picture Alliance for the Preservation of American Ideals

The Motion Picture Alliance was formed in February 1944 by Hollywood rightwingers, including Walt Disney, Sam Wood, Clarence Brown, Norman Taurog, Victor Fleming, King Vidor, James K. McGuinness, Rupert Hughes, Morrie Ryskind, Borden Chase, Gary Cooper and Robert Taylor. It argued that US films were being perverted by Communist intellectuals into becoming 'instrument(s) for the dissemination of un-American ideals and beliefs' (*Variety*, 1944a). Through highly publicised meetings its membership grew to include John Wayne, Ward Bond, John Ford, Leo McCarey, Clark Gable and Ginger Rogers. It received support from Leo Happ, the chair of the LA County's American Legion, and funds from William Randolph Hearst who employed the Alliance to sustain his attack on New Deal liberals.

However, the Alliance's association with the Legion and the Hearst press, along with its rightwing composition led to its being denounced by the Emergency Committee of the

Hollywood Guilds and Unions. This body questioned its political orientation and asked why it focused on Communist rather than fascist forms of unAmerican activity (Emergency Committee of Hollywood Guilds and Unions, 1944). The trade journals remained sceptical contending the Alliance was made up of rightwing 'crackpots' like Gary Cooper 'who [had] a knack for falling for such stuff' (McManus, 1944) and *Variety* concluded: 'Nuts! Name the Communists. Name the so-called intellectual supporters. What makes them "so-called intellectuals" and who are the Motion Picture Industrialists to whom they are superior?' (*Variety*, 1944b: 3).

The Motion Picture Alliance achieved legitimacy when Roy Brewer arrived in Hollywood. He employed it to organise an anti-left coalition in Hollywood's labour unions and would become its president in the 1950s. The Alliance's leaders realised they had to look beyond the film capital and, in their first major action, mailed a letter entitled 'From a Group of Your Friends in Hollywood' to the rightwing Senator Robert Reynolds of North Carolina, which he read into the Congressional Record. This treatise maintained that European and Asiatic aliens were placing anti-American propaganda into US films. The authors claimed that, as members of the Motion Picture Alliance, they had provided a bulwark against these malign forces and accused the moguls of 'coddling' the Communists (Reynolds, 1944: A1120).

The Alliance's allegations fell on fertile ground. Within Washington, a new generation of Republican politicians achieved electoral success in both houses of Congress in November 1946. Consequently, the HUAC was made a permanent and powerful House Committee under the pugnacious Parnell Thomas. It benefited from the international climate of the Cold War; the real or suspected subversion which had led to paranoia sweeping the nation; and the divisions which had come to the fore between Hollywood's right and left:

> By writing their letter to Senator Reynolds . . . the members of the Motion Picture Alliance had sent a loud and clear, if implicit, message to the Communist-hunters that the next time they came to Hollywood they would find a divided town, with a faction willing to cooperate (Prindle, 1988: 52).

THE HOUSE UN-AMERICAN ACTIVITIES COMMITTEE (HUAC) COMES TO HOLLYWOOD

HUAC paid particular attention to the film community owing to the role movies played in shaping attitudes and the publicity such an investigation attracted. Although the moguls had colluded with corrupt rightwing unions to undermine the workforces' rights, they had much to fear as the Committee's members were anti-Semitic and anti-liberal. As Hollywood was seen as a bastion of radicalism, the HUAC sustained an assault on New Deal liberalism and trade union reform.

In March 1947, Parnell Thomas and HUAC members John McDowell, John S. Wood and Richard M. Nixon arrived in Hollywood.[5] Publicly, the HUAC claimed it would investigate all types of unAmericanism including the Ku Klux Klan. In reality, the HUAC's rightwing Congressmen intended to smoke out Communists in Tinseltown. Moreover, HUAC committee member John S. Rankin of Mississippi was a rabid anti-Semite who conflated Judaism with Godless Communism:

Communism is older than Christianity. It is the curse of the ages. It hounded and persecuted the saviour during his earthly ministry, inspired his crucifixion, denied him in his dying agony, and gambled for his grace at the root of the cross, and has spent more than 1900 years trying to deny Christianity (Rankin, 1945).[6]

The HUAC's agents began by interviewing the 'friendly witnesses' drawn from the Motion Picture Alliance. Robert Taylor made clear his antipathy to all things Communist and when he was asked why he had appeared in the wartime propaganda feature *Song of Russia* (1944) which encouraged a sympathetic view of Russian comrades, he replied he had been pressurised into taking the role by Roosevelt official, Lowell Mellet. The Russian émigré and novelist of *The Fountainhead* (1943), Ayn Rand, testified that the film had misled American audiences by showing a distorted view of Soviet life. Similar anti-liberal biases emerged when Jack Warner was quizzed about his production of *Mission to Moscow* (1942), which had been based on the experiences of the former Ambassador to the Soviet Union, Joseph E. Davies, and had been made at the behest of the Roosevelt administration. Ginger Rogers also told the HUAC she had refused to learn a line of dialogue, 'Share and share alike, that democracy', written by Dalton Trumbo in *Tender Comrade* (1943) (Navasky, 1991: 79).

'Uncle Joe and Winston Churchill – Hollywood Style': Warner Brothers' *Mission to Moscow*

Acting on a tip from Brewer, the HUAC extended its scope by subpoenaing the 'subversive' film composer Hanns Eisler, a leftist Jewish refugee from Nazi Germany whose brother Gerhart was the Comintern delegate for the CPUSA. As far as the Committee was concerned, his guilt was beyond question and his passport was revoked. Eisler and his wife were deported to Czechoslavakia in 1948.

At first, there was a sizeable opposition to the HUAC because of the anti-liberal and anti-Semitic biases of its membership. For instance, Dore Schary, head of production at RKO, refused to ban Communists working at the studio and the Authors' League of America attacked the Committee for operating a form of political censorship. Louis B. Mayer informed the HUAC's agents he would run his studio as he saw fit, although he remained privately cautious. However, as the HUAC investigated stars such as Charlie Chaplin and John Garfield[7] and screenwriters like Lester Cole and Dalton Trumbo, this attitude changed. By June 1947, the anti-Communist Eric Johnston of the MPPDA commented: 'We ought to eradicate the so-called intellectuals who have made a good living denouncing those who believe the American system as having economic halitosis and political B.O. . . . Bluntly I think American Communists are treasonable and subversive' (Johnston, 1947).

When the HUAC returned to Washington to open its hearings in October 1947, Parnell Thomas informed the House that leftists had infiltrated the SWG and had been aided by New Deal organisations such as the NLRB. By this time Hollywood was turning on itself. Despite their initial hostility and the costs associated with losing some of their top screenwriters, the moguls realised the investigation would not go away. The HUAC agents provided dire warnings about their failure to cooperate and Parnell Thomas could not be sweet-talked into dropping his inquiries. Moreover, the studio executives were fearful of the negative publicity associated with being the employers of Communists. In addition, the Motion Picture Alliance's continual Red-baiting, the release of names and proscribed organisations by the Californian State House Un-American Activities Committee (chaired from 1941 by Jack Tenney) and the Hearst press kept the pressure on the studios.

To precipitate the storm which was about to hit the film community, the HUAC subpoenaed forty-three of Hollywood's writers, directors, producers and stars to appear at its hearings. This cohort comprised 'friendly witnesses' from the Alliance, but more importantly included nineteen Communists. By the time of the hearings, these 'unfriendly witnesses' were reduced to ten and dubbed the 'Hollywood Ten'. Their experience had a profound effect on the industry's internal politics and brought into question the extent to which individuals could maintain their rights in the US polity.

THE OCTOBER HEARINGS AND THE HOLLYWOOD TEN

The HUAC opened its hearings by cross-examining 'friendly witnesses' such as Warner, Mayer, Taylor, Cooper, Disney, Adolphe Menjou and the novelist Ayn Rand. The moguls provided the names of so-called Communists.[8] However, it was discovered that Warner had used the hearings to rid himself of non-Communists, such as Howard Koch, who had participated in the CSU strikes and had written the screenplay for *Mission to Moscow*. This would enable him to cut labour costs and protect his interests. The Motion Picture Alliance contingent spoke of a conspiracy of Communists who were out to subvert the film industry. For instance, Disney described the Cartoonists Guild's attempt to radicalise Mickey Mouse, and Taylor suggested the Party's members should be 'sent back to Russia or some other unpleasant place' (Navasky, 1991: 79), while Cooper commented he didn't like Communism 'because it's not on the level' (Olsen, 1947).

In the second week, eleven 'unfriendly witnesses' were called in front of the Committee. The first was the German playwright Bertolt Brecht who denied he had tried to join the Party and fled to East Germany only hours later. The remaining ten Communists included Dalton Trumbo, Albert Maltz, Alvah Bessie, John Howard Lawson, Ring Lardner Jr, Samuel Ornitz, Adrian Scott, Edward Dmytryk, Herbert Biberman and Lester Cole. They were among the most talented writers, producers and directors in the industry.[9] For instance, Trumbo had received an Academy Award nomination for his screenplay for *Thirty Seconds over Tokyo* (1944) and Lardner Jr was the co-author of the Oscar-winning screenplay for *Woman of the Year* (1942).

While they were members of the Party, their selection was arbitrary as other figures such as Donald Ogden Stewart, Michael Wilson and Abraham Polonsky could have been called. However, they were bonded by their hostility towards the HUAC, contending that they should defend their rights to be Communists, as the HUAC was composed of their political adversaries in the ongoing war between radicalism and reactionism. They refused to recognise its legitimacy and contested their interrogation under their rights to freedom of speech under the First Amendment (Ceplair and Englund, 2003: 266). In his statement, Maltz criticised the Committee as illegal and unjust for undermining his right to express his opinions (Maltz, 1947).

Furthermore, they were presented with the dilemma of being asked whether 'is it unAmerican to ask a man if he is Communist – or unAmerican to refuse to answer?' (Olsen, 1947). The prospects of becoming informers were unappealing, as Lardner Jr explained:

> Either you completely cooperated with the Committee which meant you said yes or no to whether you were a Communist . . . which in my case I had been . . . If the answer was yes, then you knew the next question [would be] . . . who else was? (Lardner Jr, 1978).

Although they did not explicitly claim the Fifth Amendment, they refused to answer any question by which they might perjure themselves.

This refusal to answer questions which they believed to be illegitimate and to name names, led the Hollywood Ten to become subject to Parnell Thomas's wrath. In an angry exchange with Lawson, he refused to allow the writer to read his criticisms into the record and interrupted Lawson's testimony when he broadened his answers from the narrow questions being asked by prosecutor Robert Stripling. Eventually, he cited Lawson to be in contempt of Congress and the sergeant at arms removed the screenwriter from the committee chamber. Parnell Thomas's scheduling practices and Lawson's explosive performance undermined the credibility of liberal groups such as the Committee for the First Amendment (CFA) who had sought a dignified response to the charges.

The CFA was led by directors William Wyler and John Huston, along with Philip Dunne,

Humphrey Bogart, Lauren Bacall, Danny Kaye, Gene Kelly, Fredric March and Paul Henreid. It was established to protest against the HUAC's violation of the Hollywood Ten's civil rights. However, its influence was limited by the HUAC's tactics, the reactionary testimony of MPPDA president Johnston and the collapse of solidarity in Hollywood. Subsequently, Bogart was forced to admit in a 1948 letter written to columnist Sidney Solosky 'I'm no Communist' that he had been a dope – albeit an 'American' dope who had not realised the CFA was composed of fellow travellers (Bogart, 1948). Similarly, the Hollywood Ten found the SWG's support had evaporated, while the SAG's new president, Reagan, appeared as a 'friendly witness' (Moldea, 1987: 32).

On 24 November 1947, the HUAC prosecuted the Hollywood Ten for being in contempt of Congress. In the light of this outcome, the accompanying press and the accusations of anti-Americanism, the MPAA convened the moguls to meet at the Waldorf-Astoria Hotel in New York. After two days, they issued a statement in which the Ten were suspended without pay and no Communists could be gainfully employed in Hollywood. The blacklist had begun. Subsequently, the Hollywood Ten were tried, found guilty, imprisoned and removed from the industry. However, in one of the ironies that accompanied the witch-hunts, Cole and Lardner Jr found themselves sharing Danbury Penitentiary with Parnell Thomas who, in the meantime, had been convicted for taking kickbacks.

The HUAC returns to Hollywood

In 1950 Senator Joseph McCarthy began the witch-hunts in the US government. The following year, the HUAC renewed its investigations into Communism in Hollywood. This time round, Congressman John S. Wood chaired the Committee and the scope of the investigations increased, as Communists, fellow travellers and members of proscribed organisations were required to testify. During the Wood Committee's period of investigation (1951–3), and the further inquiries led by Harold S. Veldt and Francis S. Walter, alongside the hearings revoking Paul Robeson's and Arthur Miller's passports, the divisions in Hollywood came to the fore (Vaughn, 1996).[10]

The first star to appear before the Committee was Larry Parks, who had made his name in the *The Jolson Story* (1947) and *Jolson Sings Again* (1949). Parks admitted that he had been a Communist and reluctantly named members of the Hollywood Communist Party (Navasky, 1991: ix). Despite his testimony, Parks was blacklisted and his career was over. Throughout the following years, with varying degrees of reluctance and conviction, informers were subpoenaed to appear. Some, like Sterling Hayden, informed to save their careers while others, such as Budd Schulberg, claimed they wanted to expose the evils of Stalinism.

Several film-makers and actors who refused to cooperate initially, including director Robert Rossen and actor Lee J. Cobb, returned to the Committee after their careers had been blighted. Such a recantation occurred in 1951 when the only member of the Hollywood Ten to break his silence, Edward Dmytryk, testified to try to revive his directorial career (Dmytryk, 1996: 160–9). According to Victor Navasky, several types of informer emerged: the espionage informer, the conspiracy informer, the liberal informer, the reluctant informer and the patriotic informer (Navasky, 1991).

'A canary or a stool pigeon?': the informer as hero in Elia Kazan's *On the Waterfront*

With regard to Navasky's last category, the most significant case of the era was that of Elia Kazan. Kazan was one of the talents of his generation both on the stage as a leading advocate of the Method school of acting and as an Academy Award-winning director of films such as *Gentlemen's Agreement* (1947), *Viva Zapata* (1952) and *A Streetcar Named Desire* (1951). In the 1930s, he had been active in the Communist Party and as an actor recited the final valediction calling for 'Strike' in Clifford Odets' agit-prop *Waiting for Lefty* (1935). As such a visible figure, he had it in his power to refuse to testify and to expose the HUAC as a corrupt edifice. Conversely, Kazan argued that he had left the Party in a disagreement over the Soviet Union's violation of human rights and believed it was his duty to inform.

However, while being lauded by the right as patriot and by centrists for doing the difficult, but right thing, it was revealed that Kazan had negotiated a major contract with Fox president Spyros Skouras contingent on his testimony (ibid.: 206).[11] For leftists, this was the ultimate act of betrayal as pecuniary rather than ideological convictions had determined his thinking. Moreover, Kazan had legitimised the HUAC's investigations as his testimony was a major coup and he betrayed many former colleagues whose careers were ruined.

Later, Kazan collaborated with fellow informer Schulberg on *On the Waterfront* (1954). While ostensibly presenting a picture of union racketeering in New York's docks, the film provided compelling motives for its protagonist Terry Malloy, played by Marlon Brando, to inform on his mobster bosses. However, for those who had refused to testify in front of the HUAC, the movie insulted their stance and equally talented film-makers, such as Abraham Polonsky, Jules Dassin, Martin Ritt and Joseph Losey were blacklisted. In some cases, they found work operating under pseudonyms or behind 'front' writers. Others were forced to leave the industry completely or flee to Europe to find work as the blacklist became the determinant factor for employability in Hollywood.

THE BLACKLIST

> And then came the blacklist. Suddenly [Hollywood was] reminded [that it] was the bastard of the family way. The anti-immigrant, anti-Semitic undercurrents that emerged had a devastating effect on Hollywood . . . however, the blacklist didn't work because of the attacks on Hollywood. Vichy France didn't work that way either. Vichy France worked because of what they did to each other. And that is the part about the blacklist which Hollywood never talks about (Chetwynd, 2000).

In institutionalising the blacklist, Hollywood's officialdom caved into the reactionary forces which enveloped the industry (Sharp, 2003: 301). This was exemplified by Cecil B. De Mille's thwarted attempt to oust Joseph Mankiewicz as SDG president by forcing a loyalty oath on directors at a volatile, extraordinary guild meeting in 1950 (Mitchell, 1998: 199–201). Such declarations of loyalty were also sought by the Motion Picture Industry Council (MPIC), which was initially chaired by MPAA president, Johnston, and whose membership included Reagan. The MPIC wanted to develop a public relations offensive in the light of smears concerning stars, actors, writers and producers circulating in scurrilous publications like *Red Channels*, and by reactionaries such as Myron C. Fagan, the failed playwright who set up the Cinema Educational Guild and accused Reagan and Gary Cooper of being Communists![12]

Throughout the 1950s, the entertainment lawyer Martin Gang, Roy Brewer (who by then controlled the MPIC) and the Motion Picture Alliance's secretary, Ward Bond, administered the blacklist. They were responsible for excluding from employment 200 or so Communists who had had refused to testify. They also held onto a 'graylist' of liberals and fellow travellers who belonged to proscribed organisations. They worked in tandem with Tenney's State Committee, the American Legion and a private company, American Business Consultants, to keep tabs on suspected subversives.

Gang, Brewer and Bond operated the clearance procedures through which individuals could provide names to the committee, so they might return to work. Once Gang was satisfied by a client's complicity, he would investigate why they had been blacklisted and William Wheeler, from the HUAC, was called to hear a formal recantation and to arrange an appearance in Washington. The procedure was supported by MCA's top agents Jules Stein and Lew Wasserman who used their relationship with Brewer to pressure clients such as Hayden into giving false testimonies or to clear the suspected Communist Jose Ferrer by requiring him to publicly criticise the singer and civil rights activist Paul Robeson (Sharp, 2003: 301–2). After this had been done, Gang informally told the studios the client could be re-employed through Brewer's MPIC or via Bond (Ceplair and Englund, 2003: 387–92).

Inevitably, in the administration of the blacklist, many individuals were found guilty purely on the basis of suspicion and mistakes were made. For instance, Edward G. Robinson, who was an active 1930s' liberal and member of the Popular Front, and had appeared in the left-leaning *Confessions of a Nazi Spy* (1939), could not find work in the first half of the 1950s. He was forced to admit to the HUAC that he had been duped by Communists into joining Front organisations before he was re-employed by De Mille in *The Ten Commandments* (1956). Similarly, the actor Paul Henreid, who had been a member of the Progressive Citizens of America (PCA) and CFA, discovered he was not cleared to write and direct several television episodes in the mid-1950s. Subsequently, he contacted Gang, signed a loyalty oath and complained:

> I am ashamed of nothing I have done although in the light of today's events . . . I would not today
> have joined everything I have done. All the speeches I made have clearly showed what I now state:
> that I am not a Fascist or Communist. I am a Lutheran, a liberal and registered Democrat (Henreid,
> 1955).

Yet, Henreid remained on the blacklist for five years and even Gang could not find the reason for his inclusion or indeed an admission by the HUAC that he had been placed on it in the first place. Then, as mysteriously as he had been put on the list, Henreid was removed from it and returned to work (Henreid, 1998). In an even more farcical display of bureaucratic intransigence, the screenwriter Louis Pollack was mistakenly blacklisted when his name was confused with that of clothing salesman and Communist Louis Pollock from San Diego (Pollock, 1961).

These contradictions extended to the employment of blacklisted writers who either operated behind 'front names' or without credit at all. Michael Wilson received an anonymous Oscar nomination for his work on *Friendly Persuasion* (1956), and with Carl Foreman wrote the Academy Award-winning script for *The Bridge on the River Kwai* (1957). This led to embarrassment when the film's producer Sam Spiegel awarded the credit to Pierre Boulle, the French author of the source novel who could not speak a word of English. Boulle had the good grace not pick up the Oscar, which was posthumously presented to Wilson's and Foreman's families in the 1980s. Similarly, Dalton Trumbo, one of the Hollywood Ten, operated as a screenwriter behind the name of 'Richard Rich'. Ironically, Rich was presented with an Oscar for Trumbo's screenplay *The Brave One* in 1957.

Indeed, the blacklist was only broken when Kirk Douglas and Otto Preminger gave Trumbo the credit for his work on *Spartacus* and *Exodus* respectively in 1960. Hollywood responded to the climate of 'New Frontierism' inaugurated by Kennedy's ascent to the presidency which had overtaken the national mood. A number of blacklistees such as Maltz, Polonsky, Will Geer and Lionel Stander returned to Hollywood to resurrect their careers. However, the deep divisions associated with the blacklist left a lasting wound in the industry that could not be easily healed.

Conclusion

The collective organisation of Hollywood's workforce occurred through the establishment of craft guilds and trade unions. However, the introduction of collective bargaining was controversial as the moguls refused to recognise the unions' rights to organise. With regard to the struggles to formulate the SWG, significant tensions arose between the left and right in the screenwriting community. The elitist attitudes associated with the scriptwriters who formed the SP, with the backing of studio executives, reflected their individualist instincts. The civil war among the screenwriters was venomous and while the SWG was eventually recognised in Hollywood, these difficulties were never fully resolved.

Similarly, the jurisdictional disputes that affected the technicians' unions reflected the deep-seated divisions between the right and left in the 1940s. The corrupt IA haemorrhaged members to the leftist CSU in the first half of the decade. Such a radicalisation of the labour force worried the moguls and the IA's reactionary leaders. When Roy Brewer came to Tinseltown in 1945 he mobilised the community's rightwing leadership through the formation of the Motion Picture Alliance and by gaining the support of Reagan at the SAG. This proved to be a vital link, as Reagan supported the interests of the business over those of the workers. Conversely, the CSU's leader Herb Sorrell was drawn into a series of disputes with the IA, which destroyed democratic trade union representation within the industry. This culminated with the lockout of the CSU between 1946 and 1949 and the collapse of the Hollywood left as a political force.

Meanwhile Hollywood's reactionary forces called for the HUAC to renew its investigations into Communist subversion. Led by Congressmen such as Parnell Thomas, Wood, Nixon and Rankin, the committee was aided by cooperative 'friendly witnesses' from the Motion Picture Alliance and the moguls. The HUAC further benefited from the paranoid winds of change which had swept the nation when it was institutionalised as a permanent House Committee. In conflating Judaism with Communism, it tapped into the vicious streak of anti-Semitism which had been used to attack the industry since its birth.

In its prosecution of the Hollywood Ten and its investigations into the film industry, the HUAC demonstrated a blatant disregard for the constitutional rights of suspects and press-ganged witnesses to take the stand. Because of the readiness of Hollywood's officials to comply with the inquiry and due to the high-profile nature of informants such as Kazan, the HUAC's anti-democratic stance was legitimised. A debate emerged between two members of the Hollywood Ten, Dalton Trumbo and Albert Maltz, about whether informers and blacklistees should both be seen as victims of the attack on the film industry. Hollywood's response to the HUAC raised concerns about the morality of those involved as careers and livelihoods were ruined.

The activities of the HUAC led to the collapse of political radicalism in Hollywood and the guilds remained permanently weakened as a consequence (Lewis, 2000: 13). A further legacy of the witch-hunt was to create a predominantly liberal political consensus in modern Hollywood. Yet the age-old divisions between left and right came to the fore in 1999 when the Academy awarded Kazan with a Lifetime Achievement Oscar. This was met with dismay on the left, but was supported by rightwing ideologues. On hearing the news, Polonsky declared the Oscar ceremony would provide the perfect opportunity to assassinate Kazan! Subsequently, at the awards, several actors including Nick Nolte and Ed Harris refused to stand and applaud Kazan, while Hollywood liberal and Kazan protégé Warren Beatty stood to clap his former mentor. Sitting on the fence, Steven Spielberg both applauded Kazan and remained in his seat. Despite the passage of time, the divisions associated with the blacklist remained potent and Hollywood's reaction to the honouring of Kazan demonstrated it had never fully recovered from the ravages wreaked upon it by the HUAC.

Notes

1. 'Red scares' had occurred in the United States ever since the 1917 Russian Revolution. In 1919, the Palmer Raids had sought out known activists and Communist conspirators. In 1941, Hollywood had been subject to Congress's Propaganda Hearings led by two conservative isolationists, Senator Burton Wheeler and Senator Gerald Nye, who argued the industry's anti-Nazism was a cover for its Semitic and Communist interests.

2. For the purpose of this chapter, I have concentrated on the struggles associated with the formation of the SWG. For details on the creation of the SAG and SDG, see Douglas Gomery (2005b), *The Hollywood Studio System: A History*, London: British Film Institute: 190–3.

3. Browne and Bioff tried to infiltrate the SAG. In response, the SAG threatened a national strike which stopped Browne and Bioff in their tracks. In 1955, Bioff died when he turned his key in the ignition of his car and was blown up by a bomb. As he said, 'Anyone who resigns goes out feet first.'

4. For further details see Lary May (2000), *The Big Tomorrow: Hollywood and the Politics of the American Way*, Chicago, IL and London: University of Chicago: 193–5.

5. Nixon pursued his own anti-Communist agenda in the case against the State Department official Alger Hiss. This forged his reputation in US politics.

6. Rankin delivered a series of anti-Semitic tirades during the hearings and considered citing Jewish stars who had changed their names such as Danny Kaye (David Daniel Kaminsky), Edward G. Robinson (Emmanuel Goldenberg) and Melvyn Douglas (Melvyn Hesselberg) as evidence of a political conspiracy.

7. Chaplin subsequently had his passport revoked and Garfield suffered an early death brought on by a massive coronary shortly after appearing in front of the HUAC in 1951.

8. The only mogul to criticise the HUAC was the independent producer Samuel Goldwyn. While the Committee subpoenaed him, the HUAC decided it would not call Goldwyn despite knowledge of his views.

9. The film director Billy Wilder quipped about the Hollywood Ten: 'Only two of them had talent, the rest were unfriendly.'

10. Californian Senator Tenney pursued his investigation of Communists and 'subversive' organisations like the Film for Democracy, the Hollywood Anti-Nazi League and the Progressive Citizens of America.

11. Skouras also pressured playwright Arthur Miller to name names when Miller was married to the studio's top star, Marilyn Monroe, in 1956. Miller refused and had his passport revoked.

12. *Red Channels* attempted to entrap Michael Blankfort, the Communist Party member who wrote the screenplay for *The Halls of Montezuma* (1950), when he received an anonymous call on 12 January 1951 praising his efforts for introducing subversive elements into the film.

6
Contemporary Hollywood Trade Unionism and the Rights of a Diverse Workforce

Introduction

Since the blacklist, the 'above-the-line' (writers, directors, actors) screen guilds and the 'below-the-line' (crews, technicians, painters, carpenters) craft unions have concentrated on industrial rather than ideological matters. They have focused on disputes over non-union productions, residual fees (payments for the reuse of films and television programmes) and possessive credits.

Modern Hollywood labour issues have reflected the changes in the studios' ownership because the global media corporations, who now own the studios, have used foreign production centres to reduce expenses, leading to a decline in the number of films being made in Hollywood. The guilds and unions have been concerned by runaway productions filmed in Canada, Australia and Eastern European states, where it is cheaper to film owing to devalued currencies, subsidies and tax incentives. These developments have undermined the Hollywood workforce, and the Film and Television Action Committee (FTAC), along with politicians including Californian Governor Arnold Schwarzenegger, have called for federal trade reforms.

Alternative collective bargaining structures have emerged in the wake of the studios' corporate ownership. Presently, the studios are represented by the Alliance of Motion Picture and Television Producers (AMPTP) and its negotiations with the guilds have been strained as the gulf has widened between the management and the workforce. The guilds have tried to reform themselves to respond to these changes. For instance, the SAG has undergone a civil war between modernisers and militants.

Another area of importance has been the guilds' attempts to effect changes in the film studios' employment practices regarding diversity. The SAG has advocated equality and fair representation since the inclusion of a non-discrimination clause in its 1963 Theatrical Agreement. The Writers Guild of America (WGA) Employment Access (EA) department has increased opportunities for writers who are drawn from an ethnic minority, women, the over-40s, and the gay and lesbian or disabled communities. However, for many minorities Hollywood remains impenetrable and the National Association for the Advancement of

Colored People (NAACP) has proposed greater access in front of and behind the camera.

This chapter will analyse Hollywood's contemporary industrial relations. It will consider how the multinational corporations who own the studios have altered the lines of demarcation through which labour issues are negotiated. Similarly, it discusses how the guilds have responded to royalties and residual question, the debates on possessive credits and the difficulties which have accompanied their responses. It examines the major dissensions over runaway productions. Finally, it addresses the extent to which a greater diversity within the film industry's workforce has been achieved.

The organisation of labour relations and modern trade union practice in Hollywood

The Hollywood film industry employs 582,900 people and owing to the labour-intensive nature of production is highly unionised. The studios are represented by the AMPTP which negotiates industry-wide collective bargaining agreements. Concurrently, the workforce has been organised on craft lines through 'above-the-line' guilds – the SAG, the American Federation of Television and Radio Artists (AFTRA), the WGA, the Directors' Guild of America (DGA) and the Producers' Guild of America (PGA) – and 'below-the-line' unions – IATSE (IA), the National Association of Broadcast Employees and Technicians (NABET) and the International Brotherhood of the Teamsters. Therefore, to make a film in Hollywood producers are required to be recognised by the unions and to employ union crews, actors, writers and directors. In effect, through its negotiation of the Studio Basic Agreement (SBA) the IA keeps the system going as it secures working conditions and pay for its members, who include grips, technicians, art directors and costumers. And every US film is required to have the IA's five-triangled 'bug' in its credits (Gomery, 2005b: 300). However, as Hollywood's monolithic status in film production has withered, the distance between the corporate-led studios and the guilds has grown.

LEW WASSERMAN AND THE ASSOCIATION OF MOTION PICTURE AND TELEVISION PRODUCERS

From 1966 to 1974, MCA chairman Lew Wasserman headed the Association of Motion Picture and Television Producers, whose predecessor, the AMPP, included television networks within its remit in 1964. During his reign Wasserman protected his studio Universal, which was the largest producer of television programming, from industrial action. Thus, to the advantage of the other majors as well, he kept labour disputes to a minimum.

In contrast to the previous moguls who opposed collective bargaining agreements, Wasserman understood that high levels of profitability could be maintained by working with the unions. He retained close links with IA President Richard Walsh and Teamsters' leaders Ralph Clare and Andy Anderson. In dealing with the Teamsters, he was aided by his long-standing friendship with mob lawyer Sidney Korshak (see Chapter 5) (Bruck, 2004: 361):

> . . . it was an *open* secret that Wasserman, through Korshak, could ensure labour peace with the Teamsters. And the Teamsters were the most powerful union by far, as well as the most feared.

Anderson emphasised that other unions' picket lines might be crossed without incurring mortal peril, but not the Teamsters' (ibid.: 361).

However, by the mid-1970s the other studio heads resented Wasserman who they believed had abused his position to Universal's advantage. To offset these accusations he resigned as chair of the AMPTP. Later the MCA chair placed Universal president Sid Sheinberg into the key position of labour power. The AMPTP continued to be run by a Wasserman appointee Billy Hunt. The changes were only cosmetic and in 1975 Steve Ross, head of Warner Communications, challenged Wasserman in a confrontation about the renegotiation of the IA's three-year contract.

As the previous deal had achieved little for the union membership, the IA demanded a more substantial contract. Moreover, the hard-line Walter Diehl who had replaced Walsh was determined to make up for the previous regime's concessions. To placate the IA, Hunt, with the approval of Wasserman and Sheinberg, proposed a staggering 15 per cent increase in wages in the first year, followed by consecutive 12 per cent pay rises in the second and third years of the deal. Normally the studio agreements had only specified 3 to 5 per cent increases in wages. At an extraordinary meeting of studio presidents, Ross led the other studio chief executives to challenge Hunt's offer, with only Paramount's Barry Diller backing the AMPTP. Infuriated, Wasserman resigned from the association on 3 September 1975. Subsequently, Wasserman, Sheinberg and Diller negotiated a unilateral deal with Diehl in which the IA received a 39 per cent pay increase over a forty-two-month period.

As the other studios' resolves became uncertain, they reluctantly supported the agreement leading to an escalation in production costs. The deal proved a mixed blessing for the 'below-the-line' employees as more independent producers, fronting studio-financed products, used non-unionised crews to cut expenses. However, to Wasserman's opponents it demonstrated his cunning when he absorbed the costs at Universal through its television production units.

Worse was to come when Wasserman formed a separate organisation, the Alliance, to deal with Universal and Paramount's labour relations. In 1977 MGM and Disney left the AMPTP to join the Alliance. Throughout the late 1970s and early 1980s, the guilds played the Alliance off against the AMPTP. And due to the collapse in cohesive bargaining there was an SAG strike in 1980 and a WGA strike in 1981. Finally, at the behest of Wasserman, who briefly revisited Hollywood's industrial relations to conclude the writers' strike and to avert the first ever DGA strike, labour lawyer J. Nicholas Counter III combined the AMPTP and the Alliance in 1982.

THE ALLIANCE OF MOTION PICTURE AND TELEVISION PRODUCERS

Counter remains president of the AMPTP and presides over a 'monolith of bargaining power' (Hiestand, 2005), representing 350 production companies, television networks and studios. The Alliance has effected eighty collective bargaining agreements on the basic studio contracts, specifying minimum salaries (or scale), working conditions and residuals with the guilds.

In 2004 to 2005, the AMPTP negotiated three-year deals with the WGA, the SAG, AFTRA and the DGA. For the WGA, the 2004 studio contract represented a 40 per cent increase on the 2001 negotiations and was worth $58 million including enhanced pension and health-care rights. The actors' unions, the SAG and AFTRA, agreed a new contract worth $200 million in January 2005 which was ratified by 76.5 per cent of the membership. The DGA accepted a deal that resolved the crisis on health benefits and provided creative protections for film and television directors when their work was released on DVD. The DGA president Michael Apted, however, decided not to pursue more complex issues concerning residuals over the different 'windows' of distribution (theatrical, DVD, home video, pay-per-view) arguing that 'The reality is that our members are earning unprecedented residuals. Residuals for our members have grown from $36 million in 1984 to $225 million in 2003' (Apted, 2004).

However, it has been the concerns over residuals and royalties that have strained the relations between the AMPTP and the workforce. As global media corporations have taken over the ownership of the studios, the guilds have sought recompense for their members' work across the range of different distribution technologies. Consequently, the AMPTP negotiators have reflected an anti-union antipathy in which

> rumours [have emerged] that not only can [the studios] withstand . . . strike[s], but they might be better off with one[s] that would give them the pretext to dump unprofitable projects – or divest themselves completely of the risky business of moviemaking (Mikulan, 2001: 28).

Conversely, Gerald Horne argued movie-making remains a key part of the media giants' activities and strike actions would be difficult to absorb (Horne, 2001: 29). Yet, beyond doubt, there has been a significant breakdown in communications between management and workforce:

> Ironically, the lament . . . is . . . over the absence of someone like Lew Wasserman . . . [who] . . . could knock heads during an impasse and . . . sign a contract. But the studio negotiating team, while containing titanic wealth and egos, has no such father figure to push the talks forward (ibid.: 29).

THE SCREEN ACTORS GUILD

The SAG was formed in 1933 and it represents 98,000 actors. In the first half of its history, it lobbied to remove the binding seven-year contracts over its membership.[1] In the 21st century, amid the digital revolution, its chief concern has been to protect its members' residuals. In 1987, SAG members received more than $1 billion from reruns of their films shown on broadcast television (Wasko, 2003: 43).

In 1992 the SAG combined with the Screen Extras Guild (SEG) to include the 3,600 registered extras who had lacked the strength to deal with the producers because they were non-unionised. In July 2003 the SAG membership was balloted on a merger between the SAG and AFTRA which organises the 80,000 performers working in radio and television.

However, despite a 76 per cent in favour vote from the television performers, only 58 per cent of the guild's membership supported the motion, which fell short of the 60 per cent short of the figure required to authorise the merger (Bates, 2003).

The failure of the SAG president Melissa Gilbert to deliver the vote reflected the difficulties facing the guild. One concern relates to A-list members such as Tom Cruise, Clint Eastwood or Mel Gibson who have formed production companies so that they can participate in the profits gained from their film's revenues. Because they operate as both workers and employers, their representation within the guild has become muddied. This has increased the gap between those who receive millions of dollars for their performances and the 85 per cent of guild members who are unemployed. From 2000 to 2001, the total number of acting jobs in film and television decreased from 53,134 to 48,167 representing a 9.3 per cent decline:

> All those superstars, character actors, bit-part players and wannabe waiters are in decline; they're an endangered species. Such is the state of affairs that it could be time for some emergency measures, like breeding a Gene Hackman in captivity, putting a hunting ban on Julia Roberts or creating special reserves for fast disappearing stocks of Steve Buscemis and Holly Hunters (Nathan, 2002).

The decline in roles affected the SAG's attempts to launch the Global One Rule on 1 May 2002. This states that no member may perform 'for any producer who has not executed a basic minimum agreement with the guild, which is in full force and effect' (Kiefer, 2002: 1–3). While a version of the rule has operated in Hollywood since the 1930s, the emphasis on international film production has brought into question how the SAG will police non-union productions filmed abroad. Therefore, through the introduction of the rule on a global basis, the SAG intended to effect stronger sanctions to ensure its members, producers and studios abided by the agreement. However, in practice, many difficulties have emerged as rank-and-file workers have circumvented the ruling, while A-list members have the monies to pay the fines incurred for appearing in films produced elsewhere. Furthermore, the AMPTP and the Canadian Film and Television Producers Association (CFTPA) threatened to sue the SAG if it pursued the ruling beyond US national borders.

This has led to tensions within the SAG's leadership about how to respond to this disparity at either end of its membership base. On the one hand, modernisers argue the guild should adapt to the changes in the studios' ownership and the extensive use of electronic technologies such as computer-generated imagery (CGI) in film production by transforming itself from 'a reactive to a service-orientated organisation' (Levey, 2000). In the mid-to late 1990s, SAG president Richard Masur advocated this position. On the other hand, Chuck Sloan formed a militant faction entitled the Performers Alliance (PA) which challenged the leadership's compliance with the studios. In November 1999, he backed the veteran character actor, William Daniels, who had appeared in *The Graduate* (1967) and the television series *St Elsewhere* but had no union experience, in a bitter election for the SAG presidency to remove Masur. Several PA members accompanied Daniels onto the SAG board and they took a more aggressive stance towards the studio management (Wienart, 2001).

Under Daniels the SAG engaged in the longest-running guild strike in Hollywood's history from 1 May to 31 October 2000. This concerned the royalties for performers working in commercials when the guild objected to the advertisers' attempts to replace the traditional 'pay-per-play' plan with payments proportionate to revenues drawn from products. Consequently, the SAG insisted on a fixed-rate payment formula and sought further incomes from adverts appearing across the range of media and multimedia outlets.

Throughout the dispute the SAG foundation relief fund received monies from stars such as Nicolas Cage, Harrison Ford, Helen Hunt, Kevin Spacey and Bruce Willis. The guild organised boycotts against companies like Procter & Gamble and SAG members lost over $100 million in abandoned contracts. The strength of feeling was such that when golfing superstar Tiger Woods (who was required to join the SAG to appear in commercials) and British actress Elizabeth Hurley broke rank to perform in non-union adverts they were heavily censured. Hurley was branded a 'scab' on the shock jock Howard Stern's radio show and both paid large fines to regain entrance into the guild.

Eventually, the AMPTP and the SAG reached an agreement over the payment formula from commercials. However, the process exacerbated tensions within the guild instead of bringing about unity. For instance, one of Daniels' opponents, SAG executive director Leonard Chassman, was subjected to a vote of no confidence by the militant board. And despite Daniels pleas to stop the infighting, his inexperience along with a damning report from consultants Tower Perrin, which labelled the union as being 'schizophrenic', fanned the flames of discord.

These dissensions became further conspicuous when Daniels' two-year tenure ended in February 2001 and his nominated successor Valerie Harper stood against the Restore Respect candidate Gilbert for the SAG presidency. After a fractious campaign Gilbert won the mandate by a margin of 1,500 votes. However, in the acrimonious fallout Harper declared Gilbert's victory to be fraudulent. This led to an even more divisive rerun ballot in March 2002 which was accompanied by such vicious character assassinations of both candidates that the prominent actor James Cromwell likened it to a 'cat fight'. Again, Gilbert was victorious winning 21,351 votes or 57 per cent of the electorate. Yet, as the SAG board was composed of modernisers and militants, her regime remained controversial.

A major difficulty was the Gilbert administration's relations with the Association of Talent Agencies (ATA). In particular, the ATA wanted the SAG to remove restrictions preventing agencies from owning stakes in production companies or in one another's businesses, which could lead to a possible conflict of interests. In return the guild's leadership argued the deal would enrich the Actors' Benefit Fund, thereby establishing improved conditions for the membership. However, despite the board's endorsement, SAG members, who were antipathetic to agents, rejected the deal. In spite of this setback and the failure to merge with AFTRA, Gilbert won another SAG presidential election in 2003. The PA faction reformed itself as MembershipFirst in 2004 to claim rank-and-file support over the leadership.[2] Therefore, while still Hollywood's largest talent guild, the SAG remains its most dysfunctional collective bargaining organisation:

Warren Beatty once toyed with . . . running for President of the United States. Now, some . . . have suggested [he should] consider . . . [the presidency] of the Screen Actors Guild. For Beatty, that's an effortless call: It would be easier to run for President of North Korea (Bates and Eller, 2001).

The Writers Guild of America

The WGA was formed in 1954 from the merger of the SWG and the Radio Writers' Guild. To cope with the growth in membership, the union was separated into a western branch (WGAw) with offices in Los Angeles and an eastern chapter (WGAe) based in New York. Presently, the Mississippi river acts as the dividing line for each branch's jurisdiction. Thus, a board of sixteen directors, including a president, vice-president and secretary–treasurer, oversees the WGAw. Simultaneously, a council of twenty-one members operating under a president, vice-president, and secretary–treasurer heads the WGAe.

The WGA represents writers working in motion pictures, television, cable, interactive media and the new media, and it affiliates with other writing bodies to protect its members' economic and creative rights. While it is a common misconception that screenwriters must belong to the guild to option or sell scripts or to be hired for assignments, it provides benefits including wage packages, proscribed minimum payments, a script registration service with a dated record of authorship and training workshops. To become a member, a scriptwriter must receive twenty-four credit units over a three-year period based on completed work or on the sale or licensing of original material produced for companies signed to the WGA Collective Bargaining Agreement (Morgan Wilson, 1998: 144)

Since the dissolution of the studios in the 1960s, Hollywood's screenwriters have operated in a fluid employment environment. There are a significant number of hyphenates – writer–directors or writer–producers – who have muddied relations between the guild and the AMPTP. While in most American labour situations, being a producer with the power to appoint and dismiss would make a person 'management' and ineligible for union membership, in Hollywood many creative people have invested in productions while simultaneously leading their unions. For example, former WGA president and 2001 negotiator John Wells was not only a writer, but also a millionaire executive producer of television shows including *ER* and *The West Wing*.

A limited number of writers make their living solely from selling screenplays and very few actually enjoy any real power. According to the WGAw, there was a 51.2 per cent employment rate in 2001 in which 4,525 guild members received an income from writing, of which 1,870 were designated as 'screen' writers. This fluidity has been reflected in the earnings received by scriptwriters ranging from $28,091 to more than $567,626. Along with the minimum amount of $29,500 that studios are required to pay for an original screenplay, WGA members receive fees for story treatments, first drafts, rewrites, and the doctoring of existing scripts.

The disparate nature of the guild's membership has impacted on its ability to effect collective bargaining arrangements with the AMPTP covering the Minimum Basic Agreement (MBA). On several occasions, these strains have led to a breakdown in labour relations.

In 1988, the WGA's 9,000 members engaged in a twenty-two-week strike when the guild could not agree to the studios' residuals formula designed to roll back the incomes writers received for each performance of their work (Dietz, 1991: 213). This led to divisions between the striking and non-striking factions. A group of high-profile writers including Lionel Chetwynd, John Hughes, Steven Bochco, Stephen J. Cannell and Bruce Paltrow called for the WGA to accept the AMPTP's offer, while a dissident faction filed a complaint against the guild at the National Labour Relations Board. At the end of the dispute, the union claimed victory as the producers' proposals became more palatable and this was reflected by the sales of scripts for $1 million each.

In 2001, the discrepancies over royalties in the MBA came to the fore once more. Throughout the negotiations the WGA faced opposition from Fox's Rupert Murdoch and Disney's Robert Iger when it pursued equal payments for writers when their films and television shows were transferred between the studios' subsidiary companies. The writers threatened to strike and the studios rushed several projects into immediate production including *Men in Black II* (2004) to offset the anticipated action.

However, in a last-minute compromise, the writers gained a new agreement in which increased payments amounting to $41 million were negotiated. The guild also achieved better residuals for its membership for programmes on pay and cable networks, for pay-per-view telecasts and for the foreign sales of films and television shows. The agreement covered work written directly for the online realm although the WGA and the AMPTP decided to put off negotiations for those residuals drawn from Internet downloads until the market had developed. The guild made only limited gains on the subject of royalties from DVDs and video releases.

Despite this flexing of labour muscle, writers continue to be aggrieved by their treatment from producers who view them as the most expendable members of the crew. This has led to bitterness in the WGA's rank-and-file membership about the guild's leadership, who they believe have allowed producers to freely employ screenwriters to write or redraft scripts on an *ad hoc* basis: ' "Writers are treated like dirt. . . . That's the whole attitude." [One executive says] "We use writers like Kleenex: Get another writer and another writer" – and they don't even tell the writer when they're doing it' (*Hollywood Reporter*, 2001: 1)

Scriptwriters have been concerned about protecting their creative rights and professional standards, and the WGA has sought to enhance their rights to visit a film set or attend cast readings. However, these remain only preferred options in the studio contracts. Moreover, in pursuing stronger creative rights, the WGA has entered into a collision course with the DGA, particularly over its opposition to the directors' possessive film credits (i.e. 'a film by . . .') (Cieply, 2001).

THE DIRECTORS GUILD OF AMERICA

The writers' conflict with the DGA first occurred in 1966 when the WGAw received the AMPTP's permission to bar directors from receiving the possessive credit if they had not written the script or authored the source material. In response, the DGA, led by 1st vice-president Delbert Mann, mobilised an action committee to protect its members' rights and threatened to strike. This pressure led to the DGA negotiating a contract with the studios in 1968 which guaranteed individuals and managers the right to negotiate for the special credit (Elrick, 1998).

The contract confirmed a practice which had been previously agreed on an individual or *ad hoc* basis. It heightened the status of film-makers as the industry embraced the French concept of directors being the 'auteur' or author of their films. In the 1960s and 1970s, this meant that film-makers such as Stanley Kubrick, Sam Peckinpah, Roman Polanski, Francis Ford Coppola, Martin Scorsese and Steven Spielberg became marquee names which sold their movies to the public. In 1981, in an attempt to reduce the number of credits cluttering billboards, the DGA and AMPTP decided to automatically give the possessive credit to the director when six or more people were credited on a film.

In recognition of its members' artistic and financial strengths, the DGA has jealously guarded the directors' possessive rights in its contracts with the AMPTP. Alternatively, the WGA has argued that as film is a collaborative art, directors should not be given possessive credits for a production. In 1994 it unsuccessfully tried to once more prohibit anyone but those film-makers who had written their own scripts from receiving possessive rights. Then, in the 2000 to 2001 contract negotiations, WGA officials sought to remove possessive credits altogether. These attempts were thwarted by the DGA whose attitude was parodied by Steve Martin:

> If I don't get 'a film . . .' I don't see how I can make the film. Oh yes, I could direct it. But I'm certainly not going to be able to supply the magic that makes a film. See, that's what the 'Directed by . . .' credit implies, that I'm standing around directing it. And what if, while I'm directing a film while not being given 'A film by . . .' credit, what if I passionately imbue it with my spirit and my personality and my élan? Won't this confuse the audience? Whose élan is this? they will wonder (Martin, 2001).

However, in February 2004, DGA President Michael Apted announced a series of proposals designed to appease the writers:

- The barring of first-time directors from receiving 'a film by' credit unless they were responsible for bringing the property to the production and provided substantial services in its development.
- The dropping of the 1981 provision automatically allowing directors to receive the 'film by' credit on billboard and poster advertising.
- The provision of non-binding guidelines to help studios granting possessive credits in which film-makers were required to have a marketable name, a signature style, the completion of at least three features and to have previously earned a 'film by' credit (Hiestand, 2004b: 64).

Through these compromises, the DGA intended to remove the barriers which had defined inter-guild relations. In response, the WGA president Charles Holland acknowledged the DGA's aims, but stated writers continued to oppose the possessive credit (ibid.: 64). The matter has also created consternation within the guild. In 1980, George Lucas and Irvin Kershner withdrew their membership and faced record fines when they refused to change the billing on *The Empire Strikes Back* (1980). More recently, Robert Rodriguez left the DGA as he chose to credit comic book writer Frank Miller as his co-director on *Sin City* (2005) in violation of the guild's codes.

In part, the possessive credit dispute reflects the conservative nature of the DGA. Although they were once considered to be 'hired hands' by the movie moguls, directors have always received a higher status in Hollywood than most writers or actors. These principles defined the formation of the SDG in the 1930s and its amalgamation in 1960 with the Radio and Television Directors' Guild to form the DGA. Like its predecessor, the DGA remains the only guild to have never called a strike.

The DGA's 12,000 members have often been more concerned about their artistic integrity than their pay, terms and conditions. In representing directors, unit production managers, assistant directors and technical co-ordinators in film and television, the DGA has been as concerned to ensure creative controls such as final cut as dealing with salary scales. For instance, with the colourisation of black and white films, the DGA lobbied for its members to prevent changes to their work. Similarly, the guild entered into a legal battle with the retailer Clean Films, which markets computer software to remove 'objectionable' language and scenes of a violent or sexual nature, alleging that copyright and trademark infringements had occurred (McNary, 2004).

In addition, the DGA has been concerned about the payment of residuals across different distribution technologies. To ensure members receive their dues, the guild requires production companies to become DGA signatories so residuals will be paid whether the producer has either released its interest in the film or has gone out of business. Such 'financial assurances' appear in assumption agreements and guarantees from parent companies, security agreements and residual reserves. While the process may be complex it has saved DGA members and pension-plan holders millions of dollars. And in 1998, the DGA successfully lobbied Congress to pass legislation to assure that, when a film's ownership is transferred, the new owners or distributors are obliged to pay residuals to directors, writers and actors as determined by their collectively bargained agreements.

Yet, unlike the WGA and the SAG; the DGA has launched contract negotiations well in advance of their expiration to secure its members' rights on DVD residuals and health-care benefits through bargaining rather than outright industrial action. Moreover, it was the only guild to support ex-MPAA president Valenti's decision to halt the practice of distributing DVDs and videotapes to Academy members during the Oscars so that no form of piracy or copyright infringement could occur.

Conversely, despite such moderation, the DGA has stood at the forefront of the guilds' battle with the studios over the proliferation of runaway productions. In the last decade, as a member of the Film US Alliance, it has explored a variety of tariff-based options with lobbyists, legislators, film commissioners, producers, small business owners and other guilds and unions (collectively organised as the California Coalition for Entertainment Jobs) to stem the tide of productions with American-based storylines being shot elsewhere for economic rather than creative reasons.

Runaway productions

The large budgets of blockbusters (see Chapter 2) have led to an escalation of runaway productions. Typically, these films employ Americans as producers, directors and stars, but the majority of the crew, supporting actors and extras are hired locally (Miller *et al.*, 2005: 126–70). In so doing, they have boosted the film labour and facilities markets abroad at the expense of Hollywood's workforce (Wasko, 2003: 41). In response, the guilds have led boycotts, demonstrations and protests to publicise the dangers to their membership and have lobbied Congress to pass bills creating favourable tax concessions.

IMPACT ON THE HOLLYWOOD FILM LABOUR FORCE AND THE GUILDS' RESPONSE

Although the outsourcing of US films overseas is not new, runaways have contributed to a sense of crisis in Hollywood's labour force (Klein, 2004).[3] In 1999, a DGA and SAG study reported that runaways had increased from 14 per cent of all US film and television productions in 1990 to 27 per cent in 1998. They had a negative economic impact totalling $10.3 billion per annum and meant over 125,000 jobs were lost in the 1990s. A more recent study by the Los Angeles Economic Development Corporation predicted another 4,000 jobs in the film industry would disappear by 2005 (ibid.).

The unions argue that runaways also undermine the businesses which service film productions. These include hotels, restaurants and caterers, post-production editing and music-scoring facilities, equipment rental and transport companies, and electrical contractors. The losses are not restricted to Southern California as other states such as Illinois, Texas and Florida have seen their once thriving film and television industries collapse, leading to bankruptcies, reduced tax receipts and a reservoir of highly skilled craftspeople whose incomes cannot be supplemented by work in other sectors.

Conversely, as Canada has hosted more than 80 per cent of all runaways, full-time employment in its film and television industries rose by 63 per cent from 1992 to 1998. The Canadian government has provided tax rebates and incentives which, combined with lower production costs, cheaper labour and a favourable exchange rate, mean a feature's budget could be reduced by 25 per cent. Cities such as Toronto and Vancouver can be dressed to appear as American locales and well-trained crews are readily available.[4]

With more runaways being filmed in Canada, the problems for the Hollywood labour force are exacerbated because Canadian technicians and performers have attained the requisite skills to match the greater number of productions. Canada itself has faced sustained competition from other countries offering lower wages and generous tax breaks. For instance, Australia and the Czech Republic have become popular, along with Hungary, Rumania and Brazil, in competing for US productions. These developments have undermined the tradition of craft practices in the Hollywood workforce:

> America has been the king of the movie business . . . and we have great craftspeople – set-builders, designers and painters – and we're losing those people who really know how to do that work, and we're training huge numbers of people in other countries (Coolidge, 2003: 4).

To offset these difficulties, the guilds have sought to outlaw runaways to protect Hollywood's labour force and its craft practices. In 1999, they led a mass demonstration of film workers in Griffith Park and a march on Hollywood Boulevard which congregated outside Mann's Chinese Theatre. There were further protests at the Hollywood Bowl and outside the Democratic National Convention in Los Angeles in 2000. In May 2001, the SAG lobbied the Bush White House and met with Republican Californian Congressman Bill Thomas, chair of the influential House Ways and Means Committee. Subsequently, in June 2003, forty leading DGA members met with Senate minority leader Tom Daschle to demand for federal legislation allowing for more favourable tax credits. Yet, as DGA president, Apted has demonstrated, several contradictions face industry workers with regard to runaway productions:

> We are a manufacturing industry, and people are going to go where they can get cheap labour. . . . I can't argue with a studio as a director if they say, 'We save 30 per cent of the budget if we go to Toronto.' What am I going to say to them? I can say that I'm not going to go, and they'll say, 'OK, thank you very much. Next!' So we want to keep working, we want to keep making films (Apted, 2003: 2).

THE FILM AND TELEVISION ACTION COMMITTEE: TRADE PETITIONS AND BOYCOTTS

In December 1998 the Hollywood unions backed the Film and Television Action Committee (FTAC).[5] This is a single-issue pressure group which seeks to recover US film jobs lost to other countries because of unfair trade practices. In Washington it is represented by a trade law company, Stewart and Stewart, which filed a section 301a petition to the US Trade Representative (USTR) to demand that nineteen foreign nations comply by the film trade agreements they have negotiated with the American government.

In pursuing the petition, the FTAC received opposition from the MPAA which argued that a 301a investigation would hurt American movie exports. However, the FTAC argues it is pursuing equity across the global film market by demanding that 46 per cent of the subsidies (used by the nineteen countries) should be abolished. It claims these subsidies violate international trade agreements and give an unfair competitive advantage to foreign motion picture industries (FTAC, 2002–5).

While the FTAC stands against 'economic' runaways (who relocate for reasons of cost), it does not oppose films shot elsewhere for creative purposes as it supports world labour solidarity between film workers across all nations and opposes corporate greed.[6] It reserves its wrath for films with American-based storylines which have been shot elsewhere to take advantage of subsidies. In 2004, it spearheaded an unheralded Internet and e-mail campaign against Anthony Minghella's *Cold Mountain* which was produced by Miramax. Although the movie was set in North Carolina during the Civil War, it was shot in Rumania. Despite Miramax's claims that it had scouted the Carpathian rather than the Blue Ridge Mountains owing to the contemporary industrial changes which blotted the American landscape, the FTAC smelt a rat:

> You can send a message that these economic losses and artistic choices compromised in the name of saving money are not acceptable to Americans. Do not contribute to *Cold Mountain* profiting literally at your expense by buying a ticket (Horn, 2004).

The Carpathians as the Blue Mountains: *Cold Mountain* – a runaway production

To harness the workforce's resentment, the FTAC included the postal addresses, e-mails and fax numbers of the producers on its website. It also forwarded a damning article entitled 'What You Need to Know about *Cold Mountain*' to 5,000 people on its mailing list. Other groups passed the report on in an e-mail chain. Concurrently, a similar survey was electronically circulated by the United States of America Coalition of Film and Television Workers to IA members.

Film workers were further incensed when the president of the International Cinematographers Guild (ICG) George Dibie informed them that *Cold Mountain*'s producers had ignored the US film unions' offers to reduce fees to keep the production within America. They therefore supported the ICG in its refusal to provide Miramax with a special screening of the film at its headquarters in December 2003. This stymied the momentum required for the picture to receive the positive buzz necessary for nominations at the 2004 Academy Awards.

Consequently, the *Cold Mountain* boycott diminished its chances at the Oscars and it only received a Best Supporting Actress Award for Renee Zellweger. For such a prestigious picture which relied on acclaim, this damaged its opportunities at the American box office. For the FTAC, the campaign demonstrated how the workforce could be galvanised to express its discontent. Subsequently, it focused attention on Ron Howard's *Cinderella Man* (2005), a biography of the American boxer Jim Braddock, which was filmed in Toronto. Yet, despite these strategies, the studios have continued to invest in runaways arguing that the tax credit system must be changed to make film production competitive within the US.

THE DEMAND FOR LEGISLATIVE REFORM: TAX INCENTIVES AND TARIFFS

The FTAC, along with the coalitions formed by the guilds, has pressed for reform at federal level, most especially regarding tax incentives. In this respect, there have been differences in opinion about what might prove to be the most effective form of tax legislation. For instance, the SAG proposed wage-based tax credits which were incorporated by Democratic Senator Blanche Lincoln in her reintroduction of the 2001 Film and Television Act during the 108th Congress. However, this initiative was lost when it was referred to the Senate's Finance Committee for further review.

Conversely, the DGA has favoured tax deprecations rather than income tax credits and its political action committee (PAC), led by Taylor Hackford, hosted meetings with Senators Edward Kennedy and Hilary Rodham Clinton to promote its policies in Capitol Hill. Clinton informed a DGA luncheon in September 2003 that runaway production is 'part of a larger global issue in keeping competitive with countries that have highly subsidised economies, such as Canada, as well as countries with low-cost production and labour' (Hiestand, 2004a: 27).

The DGA has lobbied several states including Louisiana, New Mexico (legislation in both passed in late 2002), Minnesota, New York, New Jersey, Florida, Illinois, Pennsylvania and Oregon for tax-incentive legislation. For instance, Hackford shot his feature *Ray* (2004) in Louisiana and saved $4 million through rebates. Subsequently, several producers who had scheduled their films to be made abroad relocated to Louisiana to take advantage of this windfall and the state reported its income from motion picture production rose from $20 million to $200 million per annum. Additionally, the guild worked with the Californian Governor and former film star Arnold Schwarzenegger to ensure his legislative portfolio included a significant focus on runaways.

The guilds have not only received support from Schwarzenegger, but also from George E. Pataki of New York, Rick Perry of Texas and Jeb Bush of Florida – who along with the 'Governator' wrote to Congress about the losses incurred as a result of runaways. The 'Big Four' lobbied for a runaway production incentive provision in Senate Bill 1637, which was part of the Jumpstart Our Business Strength (JOBS) Act. This would create an attractive tax reduction for US film and television producers in which qualifying movies (e.g. those productions which have 75 per cent of their resources based in the US) with budgets below $15 million could immediately write off all their costs. In turn, those films costing more than $15 million to produce would write off their expenses over a three-year period. Simultaneously, a sister export and manufacturing bill in the House of Representatives, HR2896, would require that 50 per cent of a film must be shot domestically to qualify for tax breaks on its foreign sales (ibid.: 27).

However, while receiving support from Washington, the guilds have had less success in the California State Legislature. In spring 2003, the California Assembly passed provision AB2747, which provided a 15 per cent production tax credit on the first $250,000 spent on wages for qualifying pictures and television programmes budgeted between $200,000–$10 million. But the bill was voted down in the State Senate. And even with Schwarzenegger in Sacramento, the state jettisoned its film-subsidy programme to trim its overall budget deficit (Longwell, 2003: 3–4).

Other problems faced the SAG when it petitioned for a federal inquiry into alleged unfair trade practices by the Canadian government. This argued that Canada's film subsidies and rebates were illegal as they had violated international competition rules. However, in supporting the FTAC's calls for countervailing tariffs against American producers shooting films in Canada, the SAG was attacked by MPAA ex-president Valenti over protectionism. The MPAA's position reflected the interests of its members who have sought profits abroad. And it opposed the FTAC proposals requiring producers to give up the subsidies they received from the Canadian government to the US Treasury as a condition for clearing a film for distribution in the US. The MPAA claimed the petition was unfairly protectionist and it was withdrawn in January 2002.[7]

There was also a lack of consensus within the trade unions when IA president Thomas Short contended such tariffs could lead to the loss of 50,000 jobs for his members. Similarly, the SAG faced the wrath of its Canadian counterpart, the Alliance of Canadian Cinema, Television and Radio Artists (ACTRA) which argued:

> It's isolationist protectionism at its worst . . . We're frankly shocked by it. This is going to have a negative effect not only on production in Canada but will hurt the US production industry . . . It will have a potentially hurtful effect on Canadian performers . . . [and] there was no consultation with AFTRA on this action (Kelly, 2001: 4).

Consequently, Canadian film officials argued that American outcries against runaways were overblown. They pointed out that Hollywood dwarfs every other indigenous film industry and Mark DesRoches, British Columbia's film commissioner, compared his state's income of $1.2 billion to the $28 billion per annum made in total film revenues in Southern California (Garvey, 2001). Because the guilds and FTAC have sought a legislative response to runaways, their strategies have led to accusations of 'Canada bashing'. And they face a complex balance in defending the rights of their labour force against accusations from competitors of protectionism.

Ethnic employment and diversity in modern Hollywood

The guilds have also become concerned about the diverse nature of the Hollywood workforce. For many ethnicities, the US film industry is perceived to be the bastion of white Anglo-Saxon or Jewish male interest. This has led to campaigns by the National Association for the Advancement of Colored People (NAACP) for a greater representation of ethnic workers in front of and the behind the camera, and in senior positions in the studios. The guilds have been proactive in providing surveys and initiatives to increase the rate of representation for minorities. However, due to the controversial nature of race relations between the black and Jewish communities in US society, these matters remain volatile in America's premier entertainment industry.

BLACK, LATINO AND MINORITY REPRESENTATION IN HOLLYWOOD: PERFORMERS AND WRITERS

The concerns about the under-representation of African-Americans, Latinos, Chinese, Asian/Pacific Islanders, Native Americans and other non-Caucasians in Hollywood emerged when the US embraced civil rights in the 1960s. In 1963 NAACP chair Herbert Hill threatened to coordinate a campaign of legal action, public protest and boycotts aimed at the studios. Instead of ignoring the NAACP, the studios launched negotiations when white stars including Marlon Brando threatened to withdraw unless more opportunities were given to black actors (Brownstein, 1990: 172–3).

Despite promises of reform, Hill was still complaining in 1967 that the six Hollywood IA locals were 'lily white' and the studios' hiring practices were discriminatory. In the same year, of the 3,508 roles on offer in film and television only 159 went to African-American actors. Hill accused the majors of engaging in 'tokenism' as they cast only a few black actors, often in stereotypical roles. Even the industry's most famous black star Sidney Poitier, who became the first African-American to receive an Academy Award for Best Actor in 1963, was presented with parts which were often determined more by his race than his talent.

It is sobering to reflect that the next black actors to win the Best Actor and Actress Oscars were Denzel Washington and Halle Berry in 2002.[8] Despite the visibility of stars such as Will Smith, Eddie Murphy, Samuel L. Jackson and Chris Tucker, and film-makers including Spike Lee, Reginald Hudlin and John Singleton, the NAACP and the film guilds remain critical of Hollywood's institutional racism.

In 1993 the SAG started to collate statistical information on the number of ethnic and minority actors appearing in American films and television programmes. Subsequently, the guild collected casting data on an annual basis from studios and producers on the race, gender and age of performers. These surveys found ethnic minorities were under-represented across the whole range of entertainment media. Additionally, in 1999 an SAG report 'Missing in Action: Latinos In and Out of Hollywood' focused on the under-representation of Latinos and the costs of losing the lucrative Latino market as a result. Advocacy groups pressed the industry to make films and television shows which reflected America's ethnic range and diverse communities.

In its 2000 annual survey the SAG announced that there had been 7 per cent increase in ethnic minority jobs and performances, with black actors accounting for 15 per cent of all characters appearing in film and television roles. Yet, in its 2002 to 2003 report, the SAG indicated the roles for performers of colour had decreased from 24.2 per cent to 23.5 per cent. More specifically:

- There was a 3 per cent reduction in African-American parts from 2002 to 2003. Although black actors made gains in starring roles, with an increase of sixty-four male and fourteen female leads in the 2003 data over 2002, there was a 35.12 per cent drop in African-American male roles. However, the black community's 15.3 per cent share of all appearances in film and television exceeded their 12.8 per cent representation in the US population.
- In 2003, Latino performers received 10.5 per cent fewer roles than the previous year and their overall 5.4 per cent share stood considerably below the Latino community's 13.7 per cent representation across the US population. The most notable drop occurred among Latino male leads, which declined by 31 per cent. There was, however, a 2.4 per cent increase in supporting roles for Latinas.
- Asian/Pacific Islanders represent 3.8 per cent of the American population, yet they only secured 2.5 per cent of the available film and television roles. Male Asian leads appearing in episodic television were hit hardest with a decrease from 104 lead roles in 2002 to sixty-one in 2003.

- Native Americans were the sole minority performers to increase their number of film appearances. In the 2003 data Native-American performers were cast in 128 roles – a 40.7 per cent increase from 2002 – with gains in male and female lead and supporting roles.
- Women remained under-represented as they secured 38 per cent of roles cast in film and television while accounting for over 50 per cent of the national population. There was an increase by 215 for supporting part roles over the previous year. However, the data indicated age acts as a barrier for women over forty who were cast in 11 per cent of the available roles compared to middle-aged men who gained 25 per cent of the roles cast (SAG, 2004).

Moreover, the NAACP's 2000 survey of scriptwriters discovered a mere 7 per cent of its 839 respondents were drawn from minority groups. It noted in this and subsequent reports the scarcity of multicultural writers, directors, producers, casting agents and crew members, and argued that this inequity behind the camera determined how minorities were represented on the screen. For instance, actor Garret Wang commented on how one casting director had informed him he did not have the correct Japanese accent until he used a Cantonese–Chinese tone of voice. Furthermore, the NAACP maintained that creative workers from the ethnic minorities had been ghettoised into making films primarily for black rather than crossover audiences.

INSTITUTIONAL RACISM: THE US BOX OFFICE, DISASSOCIATION AND CULTURAL ASSUMPTIONS

Such ghettoisation occurred as minorities remain, with the exception of Richard Parsons (the chairman and CEO of AOL/Time Warner), unrepresented in the decision-making positions which can 'green light' a film. In his PBS/BBC documentary *America Behind the Color Line: Black Hollywood*, Henry Louis Gates Jr demonstrated the financial implications for black power in Hollywood. He interviewed Samuel L. Jackson who contended that, while institutional racism existed, studios considered ethnicity in pecuniary rather than racist terms. Therefore, Gates posed the question – 'If the only colour that matters is green, what does that mean for black power in Hollywood?'

This led him to inquire of Arnon Milchan, head of New Regency Productions, how racism works at the Hollywood box office. Milchan explained that *Panic Room* (2002) which made $100 million at the US box office would have made half the amount if Halle Berry had starred rather than Jodie Foster. Gates asked what would be the financial implications for *Love Story* if it had starred Berry and Denzel Washington. Milchan again maintained the film might take half the revenues of an equivalent version with white leads. However, if Berry was paired with Russell Crowe he expected the picture could make $200–300 million. Milchan also considered why his company had so few black executives:

> It could be there is an assumption that Hollywood is closed to the black community. Maybe the club door is closed, but not by conspiracy. Maybe it's by disassociation socially – unless you get into that room, you don't have access. But if we hang out, we talk, and if we talk, we do business (Gates, 2004).

The disassociation between Hollywood's permanent government of executives, agents and producers with its ethnic minorities has led to studios backing films reliant on stereotypical representations of black rappers, hip-hop artists and sex which have limited appeal to wider audiences. Writer–director Reginald Hudlin argued that this creates a self-fulfilling prophecy in which the studio's power brokers constrain African-American film-makers by their belief that black movies can only attract black viewers. He contended that a black film's success becomes invisible as its financial power is attributed to its ability to fulfil the needs of the African-American constituency. If the movie has attracted a crossover audience, it is then conceived as a general success without any acknowledgement of black participation. Another problem raised by the studios is the limited international audience for black movies:

> The cultural gatekeepers are the problem. The distributors, the marketers on the international level, do not know how to take this product and sell it to these particular markets. . . . It's not racism at all. It's laziness, because when you have a new product and a new idea, someone's got to come up with a new marketing plan. . . . [Therefore with a black movie] they have to come up with a new plan [which they don't want to do]. Sometimes it's just people who are lazy, who don't want to do anything they're not accustomed to doing (ibid.: 275).

The film-maker Reggie Rock Bythewood explained how he had negotiated with the studios to make an action movie *Biker Boyz* (2003) with black leads. Eventually, he was offered $35 million to direct the film with a proviso: he would be required to replace the black actors with white leads. This gave him a dilemma – either he could direct a bigger movie or he could stick to his principles. He decided to make the film for half the proposed budget with African-American performers in the clear knowledge that this would affect the film's production and marketing opportunities. Because of the cultural assumptions of the Hollywood elite, chances for talent from the ethnic minorities have been limited and it remains difficult to break out of the cycle.

NAACP: CALLS FOR REFORM AND CONTROVERSIES

The NAACP has called for the removal of not only glass walls but also glass ceilings for black workers in Hollywood. It seeks to lever the studios into creating real opportunities and has proposed joint partnerships with the studios to enable ethnic minorities to compete on a level playing field. In 2000, this led to the development of a non-profit organisation Workplace Hollywood, which received $6 million from an offshoot of DreamWorks and other charitable societies to act as a clearing house for black, Asian and Hispanic talent.

However, in the NAACP 2003 report *Out of Focus, Out of Sync*, the president of the Hollywood/Beverly Hills chapter Ron Hasson commented that the film studios had refused to release statistics to track the progress of hiring minorities and their employment practices required reform (NAACP, 2003). More recently, the NAACP has engaged in dialogue with the MPAA to ensure the CARA board should be multicultural and that the studios be required to monitor how minority products are marketed both domestically and internationally. And a less strident tone has been established by national president Kweisi Mfume. Yet, despite this conciliation, Mfume remains adamant that the industry's attitude to race is retrogressive.

Therefore, the results of the NAACP's lobbying have been mixed. Its position in Hollywood was complicated by the turf wars that emerged between the local NAACP leaders and the national organisation in the 1990s. On several occasions, the NAACP's criticisms of the industry have blown up into controversies reflecting the strained relations between the US's black and Jewish communities. In July 1990, Legrand Clegg, president of the Coalition Against Black Exploitation, appearing on an NAACP panel, accused the studio executives of engaging in 'Jewish racism'. The black actress Marla Gibbs' comments about Jewish power in Hollywood were reported negatively in the *Los Angeles Times* and led to her being accused of racism. These difficulties led to a categorical denial of any such bias and a restating of their tenets from the NAACP leadership:

> We do not feel that any one group is responsible for the almost total exclusion of blacks from the decision-making ranks of the film . . . industry. [Yet] it is inconceivable that anyone could deny the existence of racism in an industry that after 80 years of business cannot point to one black who can give a green light to a film, hire or fire a producer or director – or sign a development deal (Gibson and Hooks, 1990).

Concurrently, the NAACP's lobbying has also created difficulties among black artists in Hollywood. Samuel L. Jackson has commented on how the NAACP criticised Steven Spielberg as a white director when he made a black story with an African-American cast, *The Color Purple* (1985), only to subsequently accuse the Academy of racism when it failed to win any Oscars despite eleven nominations. He noted that the NAACP has made unfair demands on awards bodies when a large amount of black film product has been aimed at the lowest common dominator (Gates, 2004: 249). The actor Don Cheadle felt that the black lobby has placed an extra burden on ethnic minority film-makers and performers as the calls for greater degrees of representation can backfire:

> Acting isn't bricklaying. If you have a skill for laying bricks, you can do it no matter what you look like – if they hire you. You can plumb a brick and put on the mortar, and then boom, do it. When it comes to casting, you can't just say. You have these five black people or these four Asian women, because not everybody can do it. Not everybody is right for every role. It's not as simple as saying we need more numbers . . . if the stories aren't intriguing, engaging, and entertaining, and if it doesn't hold together as a whole, then just sticking a bunch of people into a product that's ultimately not going to be that good doesn't help either. In fact, it does just the opposite (ibid.: 293–4).

THE GUILDS: AGREEMENTS, CONTRACTS AND ETHNIC MINORITIES

As the NAACP's impact on Hollywood has been qualified by industrial intransigence and controversy, the film guilds may effect a more lasting reform. The SAG has a long history in advocating equality, fair representation and inclusion. Along with the aforementioned collection and publication of casting data provided by signatory producers, the guild has tried to educate decision-makers through symposia, studies and face-to-face meetings. In addition, it has published directories for casting directors to increase their access to ethnic minority performers.

In 1963, a non-discrimination clause was negotiated into the SAG's Theatrical Agreement. Throughout the 1960s and 1970s, it extended its stance on affirmative action to include labour protections for African-Americans, the interests of women, Latino/Hispanics, Asian-Pacific Americans, Native Americans, seniors and the disabled. It also formed an Ethnic Minorities Committee in 1972, which has been followed by the establishment of several diversity committees.

In 1977, the SAG negotiated several provisions in its contracts to promote the diverse hiring of talent. The first required all signatories to regularly report their casting statistics, which would provide a measure of progress on minority hires. The second called for no discrimination on the grounds of race, creed, colour or national origin in the casting of any actor. However, despite being required to report on their casting statistics, the major studios and producers failed to provide this information. Consequently, in the 1980 negotiations, monetary penalties were written into production contracts between the SAG and the studios.

Simultaneously, the SAG became the first entertainment union to hire full-time employees to assure producer compliance with the affirmative action-provisions in its contracts. Presently, the guild's national director of affirmative action/diversity is Angel Rivera and he appointed Donald C. Richards as his associate national director in 2003. Both officials have developed and promoted educational programmes, conferences, workshops and symposiums to raise industrial awareness on diversity. They are also responsible for the enforcement of all SAG non-discrimination contractual provisions and the lobbying of studio executives to hire minority workers.

Similarly, the WGA's Employment Access (EA) department works with producers and studio heads to increase employment opportunities and the availability of assignments for writers who are black, Latino, Asian-Pacific Islander, Native American, women, over 40, gay, lesbian or disabled. The department administers seven committees to represent the minority writers as well as freelancers. The EA has developed access programmes, projects, events, panels and seminars to promote positive images of these historically under-employed writers. The WGA believes this will increase awareness and encourage changes in hiring practices.

Finally, the DGA has become conscious of ethnic minority rights for the Hollywood labour force. Its national executive director, Jay Roth, commented that diversity would be included in the negotiations between the DGA and AMPTP in its 2005 agreement. In particular, Roth argued the 'word of mouth' system of hiring directors needed to be overcome and the DGA president Apted confirmed the guild's support for its initiatives to extend minority opportunities. These have included the formation of the DGA's African-American steering committee which is co-chaired by LeVar Burton and Loretha Jones. This body has effected greater sensitisation through seminars and increased the black presence in the guild's ranks. It has also sought reforms for 'below-the-line' workers by co-sponsoring events with the WGA and the SAG.

Conclusion

The Hollywood film industry employs a highly skilled and specialised labour force. However, there have been difficulties in unifying industry workers because the labour organisations have been developed on craft rather than vertically integrated lines. This has created juris-dictional divisions between the guilds which have been exacerbated by a high degree of unemployment (e.g. 85 per cent of actors are out of work for most of the time). With the globalisation of the film market, these internal difficulties have been heightened by concerns over residuals and reforms in guild practices.

The workforce therefore, has been subject to a volatile history in its industrial relations. In part, this has been reflected in the conflict between the WGA and DGA over possessive credits. More crucially, several contentious disputes have emerged with the militant studio managements who have risen in the wake of the multinational corporate ownership of the majors. Consequently, the AMPTP's negotiating stance has hardened, most especially with regard to residual payments. For all the film guilds, the assurance of revenues drawn from alternative mediums of a film's output (theatrical, television performances, video, DVD, pay-per-view, Internet downloads) have been deemed vital for their members' finances. Thus, contractual negotiations have become complex and breakdowns have occurred leading to strikes and associated action.

Another concern has been the growth of runaway film productions. Again the multi-national nature of studio ownership has meant executives have cut production costs by making films abroad to take advantage of subsidies, tax rebates, exchange rates and cheap labour. This has led to campaigns, boycotts and intense lobbying by the guilds for tax incen-tives to keep film production in the US. However, countries such as Canada have accused the US labour force of engaging in protectionism to reinforce the financial dominance of the Hollywood film.

Finally, Hollywood has failed to respond to the needs of ethnic minorities. Despite attempts by the guilds to include contractual provisions on minority hiring, black film workers remain critical of the studios' institutional racism. Similarly, while black, Hispanic and Asian performers and film-makers have achieved visibility, opportunities remain limited because ethnic minorities have been excluded from the senior decision-making positions (i.e. those who can 'green light' a production). Therefore, they have been forced to produce stereotypical films which tap into black rather than crossover markets. Consequently, it remains to be seen whether the guilds' employment and sensitisation initiatives will reform attitudes to race in the industry.

Notes

1. For further details on the history of the SAG, see David F. Prindle (1988), *The Politics of Glamour: Ideology and Democracy in the Screen Actors Guild*, Madison: University of Wisconsin Press. In particular, Prindle covers the internal wars in the 1980s between SAG president Ed Asner and rightwingers, including Charlton Heston, over the politicisation of the guild in its opposition to Reagan.

2. On 3 August 2005, Gilbert confirmed she would not be standing for a third term. The relations between the Restore Respect and MembershipFirst factions remain strained as there have been disputes over bargaining positions on residuals, increases in dues, the AFTRA merger and the ATA alliance. For further details, see Kimberly Speight (2005) 'SAG Candidates Heat up Election', *Hollywood Reporter*, 3 August.

3. As far back as 2 December 1961, Heston as the third vice-president of the SAG presented evidence in front of the Sub-Committee on the Impact of Imports and Exports on American Employment House Committee on Education and Labor stating:

    > I go where the work is, whether it's somewhere south of Suez, or the San Fernando Valley. But I can't act in Hollywood, if nobody makes movies there. This seems to be the one point on which there is no disagreement: not enough films are made in Hollywood to maintain there the craftsmen and artists that once made it great. We all know some action must be taken.

4. Vancouver is now North America's third largest production centre and is the home to such studios as Lion's Gate and the Vancouver Film Studios.

5. The FTAC is endorsed by these unions: IA Locals 695, 871, 44, 728, 720, the Screen Actors Guild (SAG), Labourers' International Union of North America (LIUNA), Studio Utility Employees Local 724 (LIUNA), International Brotherhood of Teamsters and Locals 399, 355, 391, 509, 592, IBEW Local 40, Plasterers Local 755, UA Plumbers Local 78. In addition, it receives support from the Florida Motion Picture and Television Association, the cities of Burbank and Santa Monica, CA, Pittsburgh, PA, Jersey City and Clifton, NJ, Hollywood Centre Studios, Michaelsons Catering, Fantasy II Film Effects, International Studio Services, History for Hire and Jackson Shrub Supply.

6. Consequently, they have not complained about productions such as *The Lord of the Rings: The Return of the King* (2003) which was made in New Zealand, or *Lost in Translation* (2003), filmed in Japan.

7. See Janet Wasko (2003) *How Hollywood Works*, London, Thousand Oaks, CA and New Delhi: Sage: 219.

8. Several black actors including Louis Gossett Jr, Cuba Gooding Jr, Whoopi Goldberg and Morgan Freeman have won Oscars for Best Supporting roles and Sidney Poitier received a Lifetime Achievement Academy Award in 2002.

7
Campaign Politics, Activism and Hollywood Showbiz

Introduction

The relationship between US politicians and the film community reflects close affiliations between Washington and Hollywood. These links are vital to the international film trade, the success of which is beneficial for the American government and the motion picture industry. They have been shaped by the interests that have structured relations between Hollywood and the political elite.

Therefore, modern Hollywood has fostered contacts with the political classes. For instance, Lew Wasserman raised campaign funds through celebrity dinners. Industry players such as Wasserman, Sid Sheinberg, David Geffen, Steven Spielberg and Jeffrey Katzenberg contributed to Bill Clinton's presidential campaigns in 1992 and 1996. Consequently, they established influential relations with politicians enabling them to promote their interests and reflecting the Jewish complexion of modern Hollywood's leadership (Hoberman and Shandler, 2003: 206).

Hollywood's political relations have primarily been with the Democratic Party owing to the liberal consensus in place after the blacklist and the anti-Semitism exhibited by the HUAC (see Chapter 5). Shrewd executives cultivated conservatives, most especially President Ronald Reagan for whom Wasserman and registered Republican Taft Schreiber operated as MCA agents when he was a Hollywood star. Despite William F. Buckley Jr's claim that 'there are fewer closet conservatives than closet homosexuals in Hollywood' (Buckley Jr, 1995), a sizeable number of Republicans have emerged. Most recently Arnold Schwarzenegger became the Republican Governor of California.

The relations between Hollywood and politicians have been a two-way street as the political classes have realised that stars can help them to appeal to a wider constituency. This occurred in the presidencies of John F. Kennedy (JFK), Reagan and Bill Clinton and led to celebrity endorsements, the organisation of inaugural events and participation in the campaign process. Celebrity activism has provided political capital by offering an ideological shorthand to the American public. Stars have been involved in causes, on the left (Jane Fonda, Donald Sutherland, Robert Vaughn and the anti-Vietnam movement), in civil rights (Harry

Belafonte, Sidney Poitier, Sammy Davis Jr), for Native Americans (Marlon Brando) or for the libertarian right (Charlton Heston and the National Riflemen's Association (NRA)). Robert Redford and Warren Beatty produced films attacking the plutocratic nature of American politics. However, since 9/11, Hollywood liberals' have been vilified rather than deemed credible.

This chapter outlines the relations between modern Hollywood and the political elite. It considers how the industry's leaders established inroads into the centres of power. Furthermore, it analyses how celebrities provide practical and symbolic support in campaigns. It has been posited that entertainment values have been detrimentally incorporated into the political process. Finally, it discusses how celebrity, in the cases of Reagan and Schwarzenegger, brokered their entrance into mainstream politics.

The cultivation of politicians

The Hollywood establishment has cultivated politicians to ease the industry's interests in Washington. In the 1960s moguls Lew Wasserman and Arthur Krim gained access to President Lyndon Johnson's inner circle. Wasserman, in particular, organised campaign contributions for Democratic politicians and was regularly invited to the White House. In the wake of Wasserman's demise, executives such as Mike Medavoy and David Geffen became crucial figures in the Hollywood–Washington nexus while gatherings organised by liberal stars and executives contributed to fundraising.

CORPORATE–POLITICAL CONNECTIONS: WASSERMAN AND KRIM ENTER THE POLITICAL FRAY

Wasserman and Krim gained access to the citadels of power when they were drawn into politics by the Kennedys. Throughout the 1960s, Wasserman became Hollywood's acknowledged power in the West, while Krim was based in New York and became its Eastern representative.

Wasserman's involvement was provoked by the Justice Department's anti-trust suits against MCA's purchase of Universal and Decca Records (see Chapter 2). Although the case collapsed, he was traumatised by government intervention and 'shed his political passivity [to acquire] powerful allies to prevent a recurrence' (Brownstein, 1990: 187). Wasserman's motives were also shaped by his diversification of MCA's assets which left the corporation subject to larger forces. Therefore, he contributed to the Californian Democratic Party through Chairman Eugene Wyman and established a political machine from his contacts. This enabled him to access the key centres of political, business and labour power in Southern California (Bruck, 2004: 214).

Krim entered politics with his partner at United Artists (UA), Robert Benjamin, because he had liberal ideas on education and civil rights. Both supported Adlai Stevenson's third bid for the Democratic nomination in 1960. However, when JFK won the nomination they became fundraisers for the Kennedy campaign in New York. In the wake of JFK's victory, Benjamin withdrew from partisan politics to become a member of the United Nations (UN) Association. Krim became an active fundraiser for Kennedy as the President's advisors realised the value of support from the business community.

In 1962, Krim orchestrated the all-star birthday gala for JFK at Madison Square Gardens where the President was (in)famously serenaded by Marilyn Monroe. In the same year, he established the President's Club in New York in which a $1,000 membership fee went to JFK's coffers, thereby circumventing the local party which had held back funds in 1960. As the club was successful, Krim set up a Californian branch in 1963 and approached Wasserman:

> Yes [there is an inter-studio fraternity] that [is] comparable to a university or social club. . . . I've known Arthur twenty-five or thirty years since he first started in the industry. And as a result, his career progressed and mine progressed – we hold similar titles in different corporations – why, you tend to have a fraternity spirit (Wasserman, 1973).

Wasserman and Krim: Fundraising, innovations and access to power

In June 1963, Wasserman emerged as a national political force when he organised a $1,000-a-plate dinner for Kennedy at the Beverly Hills Hotel. In this fundraiser, Wasserman, Wyman and real estate entrepreneur Mark Boyar established a practice in which ten out of eleven chairs were filled at each table, allowing the President to move from one table to another at five-minute intervals. As head of the Californian President's Club, Wasserman escorted JFK between tables reminding him of the names of each guest. Impressed, Kennedy invited Wasserman to join the board of the National Cultural Centre. He developed another innovation wherein each section of the entertainment industry – film, theatre, music, nightclubs and high arts – donated the proceeds from an assigned night to the Cultural Centre (Bruck, 2004: 210–11).

After JFK's assassination in 1963, Krim and Wasserman's link to the Democratic Party were enhanced during Lyndon Johnson's (LBJ) presidency. In LBJ's 1964 election both moguls worked hard to secure contributions. In May 1964, Krim organised another presidential extravaganza at Madison Square Gardens which was preceded by a campaign dinner with Johnson and his supporters. Because Wasserman recruited over 500 members to the Hollywood branch of the President's Club, the film community became the Party's second most lucrative stopover after New York.

Thus, Wasserman and Krim enjoyed a unique entrée to the President after he had won a landslide against rightwing Senator Barry Goldwater. In their equation that money bought access they shared similarities with the Texan oil tycoons who bankrolled LBJ's rise to the Senate and presidency. Owing to their personal affiliations with LBJ, they became advisors in his inner circle:

> [LBJ] thought Arthur Krim and Lew Wasserman were two of the smartest people he knew. He thought they had great judgement about people, about things and about events. Just because you were running a movie company doesn't mean you are not knowledgeable about the great international events of the time (Valenti, 2000).

LBJ AND HOLLYWOOD: WASSERMAN AND KRIM AT THE TOP TABLE

LBJ offered both moguls positions in his Cabinet – Wasserman as Secretary of Commerce and Krim the UN ambassadorship. While honoured to be considered, they declined. However, in the final stages of the presidency, Krim became Johnson's 'special consultant'.

Although Wasserman held sway in Hollywood, it was Krim who enjoyed greater favour in Washington. LBJ understood that Wasserman wanted to secure favourable conditions for MCA. So, he kept him at arm's length and Wasserman was deployed for strategic meetings with business leaders. To keep the mogul sweet, Johnson gave him special attention and Wasserman admired the President's Texan horse-trading qualities. Moreover, being based in Los Angeles, Wasserman's visits to Washington were an event rather than commonplace.

Conversely, Krim became LBJ's most trusted advisor counselling the President on a range of issues from his personal problems to international affairs. He was such a fixture by the President's side that he often lived in the White House, attended church with LBJ despite his Jewish heritage, and built his home next to Johnson's ranch in Austin, Texas:

> In the last year of Johnson's presidency, Krim saw or spoke with the President on at least 151 different days; he vacationed with him at his ranch in Texas twelve times; [and] he had dinner with him eleven times in . . . [a] month. Few Cabinet officers had as much contact with their Chief Executive; for a private citizen to spend so much time with a sitting President is almost unimaginable (Brownstein, 1990: 199).

Johnson respected the UA chief's discretion and lack of ego. In turn, Krim shielded himself from any publicity so that no inkling of his influence emerged. However, the Johnson administration was unpopular owing to the escalation of the Vietnam War and Krim was unable to persuade LBJ to contest the 1968 Presidential election.

HOLLYWOOD'S ZEUS: WASSERMAN AND THE HOLLYWOOD CAMPAIGN MACHINE

Johnson's withdrawal marked Krim's retreat from national affairs and Wasserman's ascendancy as Hollywood's most powerful political broker from the 1960s to the 1980s. After LBJ's retirement, Wasserman and Wyman organised the party's grandees to stand behind Vice-President Hubert H. Humphrey. Despite opposition from Eugene McCarthy and Robert F. Kennedy (RFK, who was assassinated during his presidential bid), their support ensured Humphrey the nomination and Wasserman loaned him $250,000 in the election against Richard Nixon. This proved to be ineffective as Nixon won the vote.

While Wasserman remained committed to the Democrats, he maintained links with the Republican Party through MCA chair Jules Stein and vice-president Taft Schreiber.[1] Stein and Schreiber provided six-figure contributions to Nixon's 1968 and 1972 campaigns, and were the Grand Old Party's (GOP) principal Hollywood supporters along with Jack Warner and Bob Hope. Schreiber became a fundraiser for Nixon and made friends with campaign managers Maurice Stans and Leonard Garment. With Stein, he mobilised Hollywood's support for former MCA client and Republican candidate Ronald Reagan in his 1966 campaign to be Governor of California. In this manner, MCA covered both sides of the political divide.

Later on, these relations with the Republicans enabled Schreiber and Wasserman to negotiate investment tax credits with the Nixon administration (see Chapter 2). Wasserman kept his distance from Nixon as Schreiber was the key link and because his long-standing friendship with mob lawyer Sidney Korshak did not sit well with the GOP. For Nixon, Schreiber motivated older members of the Hollywood establishment to side with the Republicans including James Stewart, John Wayne and Clint Eastwood. However, the film community's relations with Nixon remained ambiguous and Schreiber's death in 1976 limited further inroads into Republican politics.

Concurrently, a liberal formation called the 'Malibu Mafia' briefly threatened Wasserman's pre-eminence. This affluent, loosely coordinated group lived in the Malibu colony and comprised television producer Norman Lear, philanthropist Stanley K. Sheinbaum, industrialist Max Palevsky and the chairman of Warners, Ted Ashley. At its edges stood stars such as Beatty and Paul Newman and its shared goals included opposition to Vietnam and support for McCarthy, RFK and George McGovern.

Wasserman, however, retained his dominance by supporting Democratic leaders including Senators Ted Kennedy and Lloyd Bentsen and Governor of California Jerry Brown. This meant that, whenever any legislation threatened the industry, he was immediately contacted. In 1976, he decisively supported Jimmy Carter, the little-known Governor of Georgia, during his bid for the Democratic nomination. Wasserman's instincts proved correct as Carter's momentum built up during the primaries so he won the election. Throughout Carter's disastrous presidency he remained loyal and was offered a Cabinet position.

In 1988, Wasserman provided Governor Michael Dukakis with his first major campaign contribution of $100,000 enabling his candidacy to take-off. However, his most deft manoeuvre occurred when he used his relationship with Reagan, once he became President in 1980, to lobby for the rescinding of syndication rules governing television networks (Gomery, 2005b: 216).

During the 1970s and 1980s, Wasserman turned his funding skills into a fine art. Ironically, the rules designed to constrain presidential candidates from earning excessive campaign contributions increased the parties' interests in raising revenues through alternative sources. Within this growth of 'soft' money, Wasserman organised campaign dinners of over 1,000 guests with a military-like precision. He also hosted fundraisers for presidents, members of the Democratic National Committee, and senators and congressmen who sat on the important Finance, Commerce and Judiciary Committees. In this way, Wasserman launched the careers of legislators and built up goodwill in order to advance MCA's interests (Bruck, 2004: 364–7). His friendship with Reagan remained secure and he was the ex-president's first official appointment after he left office in 1989. In turn, he found the site for and contributed to Reagan's Presidential Library which opened in 1991 in Simi Valley.

Wasserman's power waned when he lost control of MCA in 1992 allowing younger Hollywood executives to take command. However, his lasting position in Democratic politics was reflected in the attendance at his funeral in 2002 of Clinton, Californian Governor Gray Davis and LA Mayor James Hahn. At the event, MPAA president Jack Valenti commented, 'If Hollywood was Mount Olympus, Lew Wasserman was Zeus' (ibid.: 473).

A NEW GENERATION: HOLLYWOOD'S RELATIONS WITH GARY HART AND
ITS LOVE AFFAIR WITH BILL CLINTON

In autumn 1983, Senator Gary Hart asked Orion executive Mike Medavoy to become the
financial co-chairman of his Democratic presidential nomination bid. Hart had received
Hollywood's support during his 1980 senatorial campaign when he met Medavoy through
Robert Redford. However, while Medavoy was flattered, he was reluctant to become
involved believing only Wasserman could provide the monies:

> Gary cut me off. 'Mike, those people aren't going to help me,' he said. 'I need to form a brand-
> new group of people across the board. This is about the next generation. The only way I'm going
> to win is by tapping into a younger group of Americans of all ethnic backgrounds both at the polls
> and in my core group of supporters' (Medavoy, 2002: 144).

Throughout 1984, Medavoy arranged fundraisers with Redford, Goldie Hawn, Barbra
Streisand, Sherry Lansing and Thom Mount. For Medavoy, access provided him with status,
relationships with legislators and the rules about selling a politician: keep messages simple
and do not talk down to the audience. In contrast to Wasserman, the new generation of
Hollywood activists wanted to articulate their interests in their Jewish heritage, environmental matters, multiculturalism, health care, abortion and gay rights.

Ultimately, Hart lost to former Vice-President Walter Mondale who stopped his rival
with the sound bite 'Where's the beef?' Medavoy demurred from being Hart's finance director in his 1988 bid for the presidential nomination. In this ill-fated campaign, in which Hart
became involved in a sexual scandal, Warren Beatty acted as an advisor. Subsequently,
Clinton became the main beneficiary of Hart's efforts to secure a power base in Hollywood
and enjoyed the support of Medavoy, Columbia Chief Dawn Steel, television producers Lear
and Harry Thomason, and stars such as Streisand and Richard Dreyfuss. This group were
titled the Friends of Bill (FOBs) and became aware of his ambitions to run for the presidency
in the late 1980s.

During the 1992 campaign, the impresario David Geffen bankrolled Clinton's war-chest
which was plagued by a deficit of $1 million. For the homosexual Geffen, Clinton promised
to represent gay rights, and became one of his closest friends. In tandem, Streisand hosted a
$1.5 million Beverly Hills fundraiser which was broadcast by satellite in New York,
Washington, Atlantic City and San Francisco. Clinton was also shrewd enough to contact
Wasserman who, in his last major act of campaign funding, organised a $10,000-a-couple
dinner raising $1.7 million. He appealed to Wasserman because of his charisma and savvy.
And Clinton's charm extended to other executives and film-makers including Mike Ovitz,
Peter Guber and Spielberg as they were as much in awe of him as he was of them (Dickenson,
2002).

Throughout his presidency, Clinton invited actors such as Christopher Reeve, Michael
Douglas and Harrison Ford to the Oval Office, while Streisand spent the night at the White
House after performing at his inauguration. Spielberg, Geffen and Katzenberg, who formed
the new studio DreamWorks, were also extended overnight invitations. By the 1996

election, celebrities such as Robin Williams, Paul Newman, Dustin Hoffman, Whoopi Goldberg, Sharon Stone and Sarah Jessica Parker endorsed the President. In the campaign, Clinton received soft money contributions from Seagrams, Disney and DreamWorks. Additionally, the Democratic National Committee received $7 million in 1996 from three fundraisers organised by Geffen, Spielberg and Katzenberg. These were emceed by Tom Hanks and featured Don Henley, Maya Angelou, Geffen and Streisand (West and Orman, 2003: 55). No other president was as closely associated with the film communities' liberal values or moved with such ease in its leading circles as Clinton, creating reports that he would run a studio once his term had ended (Medavoy, 2002: 273; Hoberman and Shandler, 2003: 271).

However, as Hollywood donations to the Democrats were twice the amount the Republicans received, Clinton's proximity to the film community became the source of rightwing vilification. His 1996 opponent Senator Robert Dole criticised the depraved nature of films claiming they undermined the nation's character (Sayre, 1995–6: 51). Hollywood executives responded that Dole ignored the films produced by stars with Republican links such as Schwarzenegger, Bruce Willis and Sylvester Stallone. They argued his comments were hypocritical in the light of Dole's support for the NRA and his purposes were akin to those of the HUAC witch-hunts. In particular, his criticisms fed fundamentalist groups whose anti-Semitism insulted Hollywood's Jewish heritage and painfully reminded it of its problematic status in the US polity (Hoberman and Shandler, 2003: 269–72).

AFTER CLINTON: HOLLYWOOD'S RELATIONS WITH AL GORE AND JOHN KERRY

With varying degrees of enthusiasm, Hollywood liberals backed President George W. Bush's losing Democratic opponents Vice-President Al Gore in 2000 and Senator John Kerry in 2004. Gore's relations with the film community were strained by his running mate Joe Lieberman's calls for a voluntary ratings system. He appeared to only be interested in raising campaign contributions from the industry (Pollack, 2000).

However, Gore could rely on Streisand performing at a $1,000-per-ticket Democratic National Committee fundraiser. He raised over $1 million in hard money contributions from Hollywood corporations such as Seagrams, Time Warner, Disney and Saban, along with celebrity endorsements from Spielberg, Katzenberg, Geffen, Hanks, Beatty, Jack Nicholson and Kevin Costner (West and Orman, 2003: 40–1). In supporting Gore, Hollywood's interest was determined as much by status as it was by ideological fervour: 'If the big guns – the Geffens and Eisners – have any agenda, it has more to do with business than ideology. . . . The relationship between Hollywood and Washington is that of two mutually admiring elites. Celebrities collecting other celebrities' (Cooper, 1999).

In a determined effort to rid America of Bush, the Hollywood liberal community raised funds for the Democrats during his presidency and galvanised itself to support Kerry (Broder, 2002). This led to the vilification of the Bush administration, of its relations with the religious right and of its involvement in Iraq. Many celebrities criticised Bush for his stupidity and at a Kerry rally in New York an inebriated Whoopi Goldberg made an extended sexual pun on the President's surname! While Kerry distanced himself from such attacks, he aligned himself with Hollywood liberals including Ben Affleck who made an appearance at the Democratic National Convention.

Moreover, the advocacy group MoveOn.org enlisted directors Rob Reiner and Richard Linklater, writer Aaron Sorkin and musician Moby to produce anti-Bush adverts. It also promoted Michael Moore's *Fahrenheit 9/11* (2004), through which the polemicist hoped to oust Bush from office. This led to politically driven films being released in the summer and autumn of 2004 including Jonathan Demme's remake of *The Manchurian Candidate* (2004) which attacked corporate America. Finally, musicians such as Bruce Springsteen and Steve Earle performed concerts to motivate the electorate to vote for Kerry.

However, despite Hollywood's support of Kerry, he lost the 2004 presidential election by a substantial margin. This led to rightwing demagogues such as Fox News's Bill O'Reilly claiming Hollywood was 'out of touch' and filled with 'political dilettantes'. In some respects, the film community became the conservatives' whipping boy as 'most of the money handed out by the entertainment industry is ideological money and buys its giver nothing' (Alterman, 2004b).

It should be remembered though that Bush had supporters in Hollywood, including former Time Warner CEO Terry Semel, who organised a reception for the then Governor of Texas in 1999. And the producer Jerry Weintraub's links with the Bush family extended to overnight stays in the White House with George Bush Sr, funding for the presidential library and the raising of campaign funds for 'Dubya' in 2000 and 2004.

Celebrity activism

Film stars have drawn attention to anti-war causes, environmental activism, civil rights and personal liberties. In the age of media and celebrity, Hollywood and politics have combined so that stars have stood on platforms, attended inaugural events and participated in campaigns. In 1972, Beatty and his sister Shirley MacLaine worked for McGovern's presidential campaign. Robert Redford, however, distrusted politicians, preferring to operate as a citizen activist. As a liberal bastion with an underlying Jewish complexion, Hollywood has been vilified by conservative politicians, the fundamentalist right and the media. Yet, a sizeable, if smaller and more loosely organised, rightwing film constituency has emerged.

CELEBRITY POLITICIANS AND POLITICAL CELEBRITIES: THE MERGING OF IMAGES AND INTERESTS

John Street has divided celebrity politicians (CPs) into two categories. CP1s for politicians who use popular culture to enhance their pre-established functions, goals and ideologies. This began in 1952 when Robert Montgomery coached Dwight Eisenhower for spot ads and reached its apotheosis in Reagan's presidency and Schwarzenegger's election as governor. CP2s describe entertainers who represent causes without seeking an elected mandate (Street, 2004: 437–9).

Throughout the relationship between Hollywood and Washington, CP1s have benefited. As the first televisual Commander-in-Chief, JFK realised how Frank Sinatra and his 'Rat Pack' allowed him access to a glamorous world which enhanced his matinée idol status. Since Kennedy, the predominance of imagery, sound bites and style in political communication

'What is this campaign all about?': Robert Redford as *The Candidate*

have blurred the lines between celebrity and politics. Clinton played the saxophone on the *Arsenio Hall Show* and the political classes have glad-handed celebrities.

CP2s have articulated their support for politicians, publicised causes and pressurised the public policy process. Since the 1960s stars have attracted media attention for their views. In 1968, Newman, Tony Randall, Leonard Nimoy, Robert Vaughn and Robert Ryan worked for McCarthy. The director of the original *The Manchurian Candidate* (1962), John Frankenheimer, made campaign films for RFK.

In 1972, Beatty and MacLaine put their careers on hold to work for McGovern, whose anti-Vietnam stance drew a line between the older generation of Hollywood conservatives and a younger group of liberal superstars. For MacLaine, her front-of-house activism led to her appearing at rallies, canvassing the electorate, criticising a derisive media and extending her interests in the Women's Movement. For Beatty, who operated as McGovern's campaign manager, the experience led him to pioneer fundraising concerts with Streisand, James Taylor and Quincy Jones netting $1 million for the Democratic nominee (Schroeder, 2004: 130–1). He also coordinated friends such as Nicholson, Gene Hackman, Julie Christie and Goldie Hawn to canvass voters and usher at rallies.

With this star power, Beatty enabled McGovern to attract attention and provided a formula for lesser-known candidates. In 1976 Carter, in the early part of his campaign, relied on southern country musicians such as the Allman Brothers, the Marshall Tucker Band and

The Two Bobs: Woodward and Redford on the set of *All the President's Men*

Charlie Daniels before receiving monies from traditional donors. Concurrently, Linda Ronstadt, Jackson Browne and the Eagles jump-started Jerry Brown's Californian gubernatorial campaign.

However, by the second half of the 1970s, stars withdrew from such intense activism. During this period, the aloof Redford's political involvement became the CP2 model of choice. He preferred to narrate documentaries, support petitions, make speeches and raise funds for environmental causes. Redford's scepticism was reflected in his decision to make *The Candidate* (1972) which portrayed an idealistic lawyer sacrificing his beliefs to win a senatorial election. A potent critique of modern political campaigning, the film was shown at the 1972 Democratic Convention. After this, he produced and starred in *All the President's Men* (1976) which dramatised Bob Woodward and Carl Bernstein's reporting of Watergate. Although these films placed Redford into the national consciousness, he did not seek office and preferred environmental politics. Eventually, he appeared on platforms for Hart and Senator Bill Bradley whose ecological stance he agreed with. This was his closest friendship with a mainstream politician. He continued to lobby as a citizen activist rather than associate with a party or particular group.

Conversely, Beatty remained Hollywood's most regular fixture in liberal Democratic politics. In 1999, there was speculation he might run for the White House when he made several inscrutable comments in an article for the *New York Times* entitled 'Liberties: Will You Warren?' (Dowd, 1999: 15). However, while doing little to dispel these rumours, he preferred to use the publicity to promote *Bulworth* (1998) his satire on a corrupt Senator who tells the truth about race relations and political greed through rap music. In a case of biting the hand that fed him, Beatty provided parting shots at a venal Hollywood:

> Q: Senator, do you think us in the entertainment business needs government help in determining limits on the amount of sex and violence in today's films and television programmes?
>
> Bulworth: You know the funny thing is how lousy most of your stuff is. You know you make violent films, you make dirty films, you make family films but most of them aren't very good are they? Funny, that so many smart people could work so hard and spend so much money on them. What do you think it is? It must be the money, it turns everything to crap. I mean, Jesus, how much money do you people need?
>
> Q: Just between us Senator do you think it is advisable to schedule campaign stops with industry leaders when you have such a low opinion of their product?
>
> Bulworth: My guys are not stupid. They always put the big Jews on my schedule. I mean you're mostly Jews here. Look, I'm sure Murphy put something bad about Farrakhan in here (Beatty and Pikser, 1998).

Beatty's reticence reflected his colourful background and his womanising. He had seen how the media had brought down Hart's 1988 campaign with revelations about the Senator's affair with Donna Rice. For many, Hart's demise occurred because he crossed the boundary between what the public might deem acceptable from a film star but not from a politician. Even JFK hid his sexual conquests from a more compliant press and realised his friendship with Sinatra had to be curtailed when the entertainer's links to organised crime became an embarrassment rather than an asset.

With the exceptions of Reagan, Schwarzenegger, Senator George Murphy and to a lesser degree Eastwood (who was the Mayor of Carmel for a short period in the 1980s), showbiz and electoral politics has functioned most effectively when each side has honoured the other's uniqueness:

> Politicians . . . want the most popular guy, girl or singer . . . on a platform at a campus. They want them to write a cheque for a lot of money. However, when they ask them to write a cheque they feel they have to listen to them. And there are a lot of people who feel because they write a cheque for $25,000 they have a valuable opinion. Sometimes they do and sometimes – boy oh boy – do they not! (Pollack, 2000).

This realisation led to most of Hollywood's activists using their clout for causal rather than partisan effect.

CIVIL RIGHTS

In 1956 Harry Belafonte met Dr Martin Luther King and participated in civil rights marches. In the early 1960s, he worked with black artists including Sidney Poitier and Sammy Davis Jr to support the movement by raising funds, performing at concerts, crafting strategy and liaising with the Kennedy White House. He bailed out King when he was imprisoned by

Birmingham's racist police chief Bull Connor. As the cause spread Belafonte enlisted white stars such as Paul Newman, Charlton Heston, Burt Lancaster, James Garner and Marlon Brando. This celebrity delegation attended the Million Man March on 28 August 1963. This was no small feat as J. Edgar Hoover had ordered Federal Bureau of Investigation (FBI) agents to dissuade them from attending. Their activism marked Hollywood's political reawakening after the HUAC.

For Brando, civil rights proved a clarion call. Throughout the 1960s, he marched in Maryland to protest against the brutal treatment of blacks by the National Guard and took part in an LA demonstration against discriminatory housing. Subsequently, he promoted brotherhood with New York Mayor John Lindsay in Harlem and worked strenuously to provide aid to India to alleviate the famine. In 1968 he was distraught when King was assassinated and attended a Black Panther funeral to demonstrate against racial intolerance.

This led to Brando sending Sasheen Littlefeather to the 1973 Academy Awards to explain his refusal of a Best Actor Oscar for *The Godfather* as a protest about the treatment of Native Americans in film and history. In violating the ceremony he was castigated by old-line Hollywood, but had shown his disgust in front of a television audience of millions. But, as Brando became more reclusive, his activism waned and was nothing compared to those who opposed the war in Vietnam (Brownstein, 1990: 229).

HOLLYWOOD AND VIETNAM

In the late 1960s, America reached a boiling point in the wake of assassinations, race riots, bloody demonstrations, campus radicalism, home-grown terrorism and the Vietnam War. At first, the film industry sent conservatives such as Wayne and Hope to Vietnam to rally troops and backed Wayne's flag-waving *The Green Berets* (1968). However, when Nixon recanted on his 'Peace with Honour' promises and the fighting escalated, such patriotism became redundant. A growing contingent of film activists articulated their opposition to Vietnam.

Easy Rider (1969) producer Bert Schneider supported the Black Panthers and housed Jerry Rubin when he was on the run. On receiving an Academy Award for the 1975 documentary *Hearts and Minds*, Schneider shocked the audience by conveying 'greetings of friendship to all American People from Ambassador Dinh Ba Thi', chief of the Provisional Revolutionary Government delegation to the Paris Peace Talks (Biskind, 1998: 275).

The first star to criticise the US commitment in South-East Asia was Robert Vaughn, best known as *The Man from U.N.C.L.E.* In January 1966, he made an anti-war speech at a Democratic rally in Indianapolis and became the chair of the Dissenting Democrats who worked to remove LBJ. His scepticism indicated a sea change in Hollywood's previous deference to politicians, leading to entertainers openly questioning the government:

> By the late 1960s, the stars feel involved enough and the politicians have been diminished enough, that they look across the stage and say, 'Hey, maybe I belong up there. If people will listen to me, the act of giving me the microphone validates me.' . . . Ultimately, Jane Fonda [provided] a cautionary note demonstrating what happens when you take off all the restraints and see how far you can go (Brownstein, 2000).

Fonda's activism represented a spectacular change in her image from sex star into spokesperson for causes including women's rights, multiculturalism and opposition to militarism. In 1969, she supported the occupancy of Alcatraz Island by Native Americans. Shortly afterwards, she allied with Huey Newton and the Black Panthers littering her speeches with references to the police as 'pigs' and closing with 'Power to the people'.

However, it was as the darling of the anti-war movement that she achieved notoriety. Throughout the early 1970s, she attended marches and raised monies for the Vietnam Veterans Against the War. In addition, she performed Fuck or Free the Army (FTA) shows with Donald Sutherland, Dick Gregory and Peter Boyle. In 1972, she visited North Vietnam to speak out against US imperialism, attacking American POWs who had bombed Hanoi and accusing Nixon of 'war crimes'. On the trip, she was photographed laughing while seated on an anti-aircraft tank and became known as 'Hanoi Jane'. Fonda's unapologetic support of the Viet Cong led to her being placed under domestic surveillance by Nixon and to the studios' refusal to hire her, despite her 1971 Best Actress Oscar for *Klute*.

Although she resurrected her career and became better known for her fitness videos while apologising for her activism, she remained a pariah to many Vietnam veterans. In April 2005, on a book-signing tour, Michael Smith spat tobacco juice into her face, claiming Fonda was a 'traitor who has been spitting in the faces of war veterans for years [and] there are a lot of veterans who would love to do what I did' (Vendel, 2005).

THE 1980S: HOLLYWOOD ACTIVISTS AGAINST REAGAN

The vilification of Fonda tied in with a backlash against the Democrats as Carter's administration plunged the US into 'stagflation' and engaged in a disastrous attempt to free hostages in Iran. For Hollywood's liberals, the 1980 election of the rightwing Reagan as President was an affront. They believed the former actor was a fraud who gave his greatest performance by pretending to be a politician. However, his victory also perpetuated the belief that stars had a legitimate role in political affairs.

Therefore, liberal celebrities queued up to oppose the administration's rightwing ideologies and hawkish position in the Second Cold War: 'Everyone in Hollywood is basically a Democrat. Reagan's a conservative Republican and a Barry Goldwater conservative Republican to boot, talk about a traitor to your own class. That's why everyone hated him so much' (Cadell, 2000). Lear headed a group entitled 'People for the American Way' composed of religious and communal leaders who sought to reinvigorate civic virtues and criticised the religious right for its intolerance. He recruited Demme to edit commercials showing discussions on tolerance and freedom of thought. There was also a major battle in the Screen Actors Guild (SAG) when its president Ed Asner politicised the guild to oppose Reagan against the wishes of rightwingers led by Heston.

Others criticised Reagan for supporting dictators in Central America. For instance, Mike Farrell, the star of the television sitcom *M*A*S*H*, worked to support refugees and Richard Gere campaigned for the Sandinistas in El Salvador. The Hollywood left founded the Committee for Concern for Central America, which deployed lobbyists to Capitol Hill, invited Daniel Ortega to speak in LA and hosted star-studded galas to mobilise opposition to US foreign policies. Simultaneously, Newman and Sally Field campaigned to freeze nuclear weaponry, while Christopher Reeve and Alec Baldwin established the Creative Coalition.

In addition, Hollywood's 'brat-packers' including Rob Lowe, Tom Cruise, Rosanna Arquette and Sarah Jessica Parker were approached by Fonda and her second husband Californian State Senator Tom Hayden to support environmental legislation such as the clean water ballot, Proposition 65. Eventually, Hayden directed the network of young stars to work for Dukakis (Brownstein, 1990: 285–300).

The most powerful group to oppose Reagan was the Hollywood Women's Political Committee (HWPC) formed by Fonda, Streisand, Lily Tomlin and Paula Weinstein during Geraldine Ferrara's Democratic vice-presidential candidacy in 1984. By 1986, the HWPC had seventy-two members who each paid an annual fee of $2,500. It maintained a militant agenda which was both courageous and foolhardy. On one infamous occasion, HWPC's members attacked Ted Kennedy so much that he exploded in indignation. However, the HWPC proved its mettle to Democrats when Streisand raised $1.5 million at a dinner to protest against nuclear power. Yet, even with its access to finance, the HWPC could not compete with the special interest groups in the 1990s. Moreover, as Bill Carrick, the Democratic campaign consultant in LA, argued: '. . . the Clinton presidency . . . had a great moderating effect. Hollywood hadn't had a close relationship with the White House. . . .The ideological heat of the eighties evaporated overnight' (Cooper, 1999: 2)

CONTEMPORARY POLITICAL ACTIVISM: TIM ROBBINS, SUSAN SARANDON AND MICHAEL MOORE

Since the 1990s, Hollywood liberals including Tim Robbins, Sean Penn, Susan Sarandon, Oliver Stone, Michael Moore, Alec Baldwin, Ed Begley Jr, George Clooney and Martin Sheen have come to the fore. They have criticised the American justice system, supported pro-choice rights on abortion, led projects to shelter the homeless, explored anti-globalisation causes and targeted the Bush administration's 'realist' foreign policy since 9/11.

Hollywood's most visible attachment has been to environmentalism. In 1999, Woody Harrelson joined protesters who mounted the Golden Gate Bridge to the chagrin of passing motorists. In May 2004, the National Resources Defence Council (NRDC) received contributions totalling $3 million at a Brentwood fundraiser which included Tom Hanks, Leonardo DiCaprio, Rob Reiner, Martin Short, Michelle Pfeiffer, Tobey Maguire, Steve Bing and Ray Romano. It was overseen by Laurie David, a former television producer turned full-time activist, and wife of *Seinfeld* co-creator Larry David.

In feature films, Oliver Stone remained Hollywood's leading polemicist making *JFK* (1991) and *Nixon* (1999), while Robbins directed movies including *Bob Roberts* (1992), *Dead Man Walking* (1995) and *The Cradle Will Rock* (1999) which explored fascism, capital punishment and anti-Communism. And Robbins and his partner Sarandon supported the repeal of the death penalty and protested against the internment of HIV-carrying Haitians at Guantanamo Bay. In 1999, they organised anti-globalisation activists demonstrating against the World Trade Organisation (WTO) in Seattle. They protested over Amadou Diallo's death in police custody in New York and campaigned for Ralph Nader at the 2000 presidential election. Sarandon also headed the international women's organisation MADRE, while Robbins was a board member of the Nation Institute (Dickenson, 2002).

However, their activism became more controversial during the 2003 War in Iraq when Robbins castigated US forces for indiscriminate bombing, war-mongering and destabilising democracies. In 2004 he wrote a play entitled *Embedded* satirising the compliant coverage of 'Operation Iraqi Freedom' and caricaturing Donald Rumsfeld, Richard Perle and Paul Wolfowitz as neo-con plotters taking over the world. As a result, Robbins and Sarandon were disinvited to the Baseball Hall of Fame's celebration to commemorate the fifteenth anniversary of *Bull Durham* (1988) in which they had played leading roles (Anthony, 2004: 14).

At the 2003 Oscars, Robbins and Sarandon made peace signals to the crowds outside the Kodak Theatre. Inside, Chris Cooper finished his acceptance speech for Best Supporting Actor by calling for 'peace to us all' and Adrien Brody, in accepting his Best Actor award for the *The Pianist* (2002), received a standing ovation when he commented on 'the sadness and dehumanisation of people in times of war' (Dickenson, 2003a). However, their actions were nothing compared to Moore's criticisms of Bush when he received an Oscar for his anti-gun documentary, *Bowling for Columbine* (2002). He ended his speech with, 'We are against the war, Mr Bush . . . shame on you, shame on you, shame on you' (ibid.: 2003).

Subsequently, Moore became Hollywood's most outspoken polemicist when he produced *Fahrenheit 9/11*. This was a blistering attack on Bush's foreign policy, his links with the Bin Laden family and his use of America's underclass as cannon-fodder. In publicising the documentary, Moore attacked the Republican administration and declared it to be an agitprop for Kerry's cause. He accused Disney of refusing to distribute the film and gained international respect by winning the Palme D'Or at the 2004 Cannes Film Festival. In this way, Moore, who had achieved a cult audience through books, documentaries and television programmes, became a national figure who was equally patronised and demonised. In particular, Senator John McCain admonished him when he attended the 2004 Republican convention (Bachrach, 2005: 108–15).

CRITICISMS OF CELEBRITY ACTIVISM AND RIGHTWING HOLLYWOOD

In attacking Bush's foreign policies, Hollywood activists claimed they were being effectively blacklisted either by losing roles or by being informed that they should keep their views private. To some degree, the film community brought these criticisms upon itself:

> Social problems present themselves to many of these people in terms of scenario, in which, once certain key scenes are linked . . . the plot will proceed inexorably to an upbeat fade. . . . If poor people march on Washington and camp out there to receive some bundles of clothes gathered on the Fox lot by Barbra Streisand, then some good must come of it . . . and doubts have no place in the story (Dideon, 1998: 519)

As the gap between expectation and resolution has widened, celebrities have been criticised for their simplistic responses to complex issues. And the liberal consensus in Hollywood was parodied in Trey Parker and Matt Stone's puppet satire *Team America: World Police* wherein

Robbins, Penn, Sarandon and Baldwin represented the Film Actors Guild (FAG) which provided unconditional support to the North Korean dictator Kim Ill Song.

Since 9/11, the centre-left sensibility in Hollywood has been vilified as national divisions became conspicuous. Reactionary radio talkshow hosts and websites have damned celebrities for their lax morals and anti-Americanism. For instance, Penn was castigated when he visited Iraq before the war to publicise the plight of ordinary Iraqis. In the 2004 presidential election campaign, rightwingers tarnished Kerry by cloning his photo into a photo of the platform of an early 1970s' anti-Vietnam rally attended by Fonda. Robbins' controversial reputation even determined how an interviewing reporter was dealt with at his point of entry in LAX:

> When I finally convinced the customs officer that I was not seeking . . . the destruction of the free world, she asked me who it was I had come to interview. Tim Robbins, I replied. 'But . . . he hasn't got a movie coming out.' I told her that I was there to talk to him about a play he had written. 'Right . . . Just don't be taken in by his politics' (Anthony, 2004: 14).

Along with these attacks, Hollywood's rightwing constituency has become more vocal. For many years, its leading advocate was Heston who shed his former liberalism in the civil rights movement to become an arch conservative during the 1970s. As an articulate commentator, he debated with Newman about nuclear weapons, affiliated with Reagan, formed a political action committee and extended his criticisms of multiculturalism and political correctness. In 1995, he became the president of the NRA and defended his constitutional right to bear arms by coining the phrase 'Take my gun from my cold, dead hands.'

Following Heston's lead, other celebrities revealed rightwing sensibilities for either personal or ideological reasons. For instance, having fallen out with the Kennedys, Sinatra converted to the Republicans and organised inaugural events for Nixon and Reagan. His influence led to Sammy Davis Jr renouncing his interests in civil rights and appearing on platforms with Nixon. John Wayne's fervent anti-Communism and conservative values were evident in films such as *Big Jim McClain* (1952) and *The Alamo* (1960). He became an icon for rightwingers and was asked by Republicans to stand for office. Additionally, Eastwood made his views on law and order clear when playing vigilante cop Harry Callaghan in *Dirty Harry* (1971).

In 1992, rightwing activist David Horowitz and writer Lionel Chetwynd formed the Wednesday Morning Club to host informal gatherings where Hollywood's conservatives could meet Republican leaders. According to Horowitz the club offset the leftwing bias in the film community. However, when Chetwynd, Tom Selleck and Kurt Russell maintained they had not suffered for their views, Horowitz moderated his position arguing the group occupied a vacuum in Hollywood's politics (Corn, 5 April 1999).

Although celebrities, such as Willis, Chuck Norris and Kelsey Grammer, associated with Republican politicians, Hollywood conservatives have not been well organised. Rightwing personalities have kept their views to themselves, provided small contributions and occasionally appeared on platforms. Generally Republicans have used stars like Sylvester Stallone, whose *Rambo* movies became a byword for Reagan's hawkish foreign policies, for jingoistic purposes. Consequently, it is an irony that while Hollywood remains a bastion of liberalism, its two most famous actors-turned-politicians have been Republicans – Reagan and Schwarzenegger.

Celebrities as politicians

Throughout the 1940s and 1950s, Reagan was a virulent anti-Communist who employed the skills he attained as president of the SAG between 1947 and 1952 and 1959 to 1960 to jump-start his political career. In 1966, he was persuaded to run as Governor of California by a combination of business interests, his success as a public speaker and the surprise election of fellow Republican and star George Murphy as Senator of California in 1964. He used his period in office to prepare himself for the White House. While Reagan followed a more traditional route into politics, Schwarzenegger became the 'Governator' during the 2003 Californian recall election by using celebrity as his main form of political capital. In both cases, the mixture of star power and televisual communications techniques led to the questioning of the validity of the modern US political process.

RONALD REAGAN'S CAREER AS A COLD WARRIOR AND TRADE UNIONIST IN HOLLYWOOD
Reagan's conversion from liberal Democrat to rightwing Republican occurred during the labour troubles that rocked Hollywood after World War II (see Chapter 5). In becoming an arch conservative, he received his political education from Roy Brewer, the reactionary IATSE representative in Hollywood.[2] When Reagan joined the SAG board he opposed Katharine Hepburn and Edward G. Robinson who argued that guild members should not cross Conference of Studio Unions' (CSU) picket lines.

In 1947, Reagan became a friendly witness for the HUAC and an informer for the FBI (Moldea, 1987; Prindle, 1988: 50). In the same year, he was elected SAG president and removed radicals from the guild. Additionally, he sat on the anti-Communist Motion Picture Industry Council (MPIC) for which he served as president for two terms. In 1950, his stock rose when he joined a ten-man committee formed from an alliance of the MPIC and Motion Picture Alliance for the Preservation of American Ideals. This body demanded that Hollywood workers should take a mandatory loyalty oath. He also persuaded Edward Dmytryk, a member of the Hollywood Ten, to inform on Communist sympathisers. Similarly, he was the 'one-man' gang who urged Sterling Hayden to name names, a decision Hayden later admitted caused him shame (Bourne, 1981: 4).

Throughout his period in office, Reagan aligned himself with the industry by signing the SAG waiver which enabled MCA to transform itself from a talent agency into a producer of television programmes. In exchange, he received a lucrative deal to present *The General Electric Theater*. Although his film career declined after he stepped down as SAG president, he advanced his political ambitions by appearing as a GE spokesman to civic groups condemning Communist infiltration in the film industry.

In his second term as SAG president, Reagan stemmed an actors' strike by securing better residuals in the Studio Basic Agreement (SBA) for his membership. However, there was dissent in the guild's ranks over the leadership's acquiescence to the studios over pension and health plans. Most especially, Reagan characterised a form of sweetheart unionism which suited the needs of the executives rather than the workforce (Prindle, 1988: 87). Moreover, he could not remember negotiating the MCA waiver when he was subpoenaed to testify at the 1962 anti-trust case (see Chapter 2). During his period as a trade unionist, he learned how to negotiate the power structures in Southern California and these abilities, along with his strength as a communicator, held him in good stead when he sought electoral office.

REAGAN SEEKS OFFICE

Although Reagan's ideologies shifted dramatically, he did not become a registered Republican until the early 1960s. Indeed, when seeking the Governorship of California in 1966, he maintained his convictions remained the same and it was the Democratic Party's leftward drift which forced him to cross the political divide. In 1964, he legitimised his position as a leader in the Republican Party by co-chairing the Californian citizens for Goldwater-Miller and by delivering a well-received speech supporting Goldwater's presidential nomination. He denied the existence of the blacklist by arguing 'Hollywood does have a list handed to it by millions of moviegoers who have said "we don't want and will not pay to see pictures made by or with . . . people we consider traitors"' (Reagan, 1960).

To effect his entrance into the 1966 campaign, Reagan published his autobiography *Where's the Rest of Me?* (the title referred to his most famous role as an amputee in *Kings Row*) and informed Hollywood's rightwing gossip columnist Hedda Hopper of his intentions to run. In this interview, he declared he was against discriminatory business taxes and excessive public spending, that he supported US involvement in Vietnam and admitted his performing skills helped him to communicate to the electorate (Hopper, 1965). He stressed how his values of individualism, family, community, Judeo-Christianity and the American way were shaped by the films he had appeared in as a Warners contract player (Vaughn, 1994: 235–6).

During the campaign, Reagan received support from three LA millionaires: car dealer Holmes Tuttle, financier Henry Salvatori and oil tycoon A. C. Rubel. Together they formed the Friends of Reagan committee which included MCA vice-president Schreiber as chief fundraiser and chairman Stein, who mobilised other businessmen to finance the campaign. MCA covered both sides of the political divide as Wasserman organised support for Governor Edmund 'Pat' Brown.

Throughout the election, Reagan used television to present himself as an honest man uncorrupted by vices, thereby turning Democratic criticisms over his inexperience on their head. He appealed to Californians despite Brown's criticisms of his Hollywood background, an ad from Gene Kelly which called for a clear line between politics and celebrity and a campaign documentary called 'Man versus Actor':

> A certain local actor is now between pictures, but next November he will be out of work. I have always said that one unemployed person in California, is one too many. I hope you will call and help him in the profession in which he is qualified (Brown, 1966).

As Wasserman backed Brown, his relationship with Reagan soured and would only be resurrected in his former client's presidency. However, when Reagan won the vote, Wasserman,

Stein and Schreiber secured the Governor-Elect's fortunes in a complicated land deal with 20th Century-Fox so the standing joke became 'MCA even had its own governor' (Moldea, 1987: 239).

Reagan used his celebrity to provide an ideological shorthand to the Californian electorate. His fame, looks and skills as a communicator proved vital in winning the 1966 gubernatorial election. He took advantage of television's growing importance in US politics by developing a likeable image and by keeping his message simple. His stardom attracted donors whose funds allowed him to buy airtime for spot-ads and press coverage. Throughout his governorship (1966–1974) Reagan refined these skills and reinforced his links with the business elite. After leaving office, he remained in the media spotlight by making speeches, writing columns and seeking the Republican nomination in 1976. In the 1980 presidential election Reagan defeated Carter having had 'the benefit of some forty years of being in the public eye' (West and Orman, 2003: 46).

PRESIDENT REAGAN: THE GREAT COMMUNICATOR

Throughout his 1980 campaign, Reagan's communication skills served him well. He could repeat a line many times over and make it sound fresh and he was the master of the sound bite, putting down Carter in the televised debates with 'There you go again!' He hit his marks with practised ease. Again the Democrats criticised his background as an actor. However, with a skilful public relations team, Reagan carefully cultivated his relations with the film industry by only occasionally surrounding himself with Republican stars such as Heston, Hope, Sinatra and Stewart, and preferring to emphasise his effective leadership. Yet he was not frightened to acknowledge his Hollywood career when he invoked Wayne as the symbolic representation of the American Dream, thereby challenging Carter's arguments that a malaise had sapped the nation of its will (Brownstein, 1990: 276–7).

During his two-term presidency, Reagan's hawkish agenda was mediated by his image as the 'Great Communicator'. He demonstrated a masterful use of television, photo opportunities and phrases drawn from films such as Eastwood's line, 'Go ahead and make my day' or his own line as George Gip in *Knute Rockne All American* (1940) 'win one for the Gipper'. His administration was praised for bringing glamour back to the White House, the celebrity status of the First Lady Nancy Reagan who led the 'Just Say No' anti-drug campaign and for the coverage Reagan generated as the Commander-in-Chief.

Because of his folksy popularity, Reagan became the 'Teflon President' to whom the mud did not stick even after the Iran-Contragate in which he claimed, with shades of the 1962 anti-trust case, to have lost his memory. Moreover, Reagan's minders worked hard to ensure he did not answer reporters in off-the-cuff exchanges as fears abounded about his senility. In 1985, when Reagan suggested 'One man's terrorist is another man's freedom fighter', press secretary Larry Speakes issued an extraordinary release, 'Ladies and gentlemen, the President's statements do not reflect the policy of the Reagan administration' (West and Orman, 2003: 47). For many commentators: '[Reagan] became the quintessential media president who elevated style and image over substance with the help of an uncritical, protective American establishment media' (ibid.: 48).

ARNOLD SCHWARZENEGGER: CELEBRITY POLITICS AND THE 2003 RECALL VOTE

Since Reagan, the phenomenon of celebrities becoming politicians has increased as the American political system exhibited partisan de-alignment and voter disengagement. This meant it became open to media representations, sophisticated political marketing and a huge increase in campaign costs. Therefore, former wrestler Jesse Ventura was elected the Governor of Minnesota and the late Sonny Bono (of Sonny and Cher fame) became a Republican Congressman.

The most famous star-turned-politician was Schwarzenegger who successfully campaigned for the Californian governorship during the 2003 recall vote. He had been associated with Bush Sr who called him 'Conan the Republican' (West and Orman, 2003: 69). In contrast to Reagan though, who used his celebrity in tandem with a long career as a trade unionist, party politician and policy-maker, the 'Governator' was a political neophyte.

He partly achieved office through his connections. For instance, his marriage to Maria Shriver, a television journalist and the daughter of McGovern's running mate Sargent Shriver and Eugene Kennedy, drew him into the Kennedy clan and the political realm. In 1991, he became the chairman of the Presidential Council for Physical Fitness and Sport, and in 2002, he sponsored Proposition 49, a Californian state bill to provide after-school child care. More importantly, he used his fame to generate voluminous media coverage and money for his campaign (West, 2003). Schwarzenegger proved a shrewd communicator but unlike Reagan whose film career had been eclipsed, he remained an 'A' list star appearing in *Terminator 3: The Rise of the Machines* (2003) shortly before announcing his candidacy on Jay Leno's *The Tonight Show*.

Schwarzenegger's opportunity to run for office occurred in one of the most bizarre campaigns in American politics. In 2002, the incumbent Democratic Governor Gray Davis, a colourless technocrat, was re-elected in a dirty election in which he concealed the economic crisis affecting the state. As California plunged into deficit, Davis slashed health, education, transport and policing budgets.[3] San Diego Republican Congressman Darrell Issa devoted several million dollars to raise the signatures required for a recall petition against Davis, which referred to an obscure state law passed in 1849. This led to voters being asked two questions: first, should Davis be recalled and second, who should replace him?

Along with Schwarzenegger, 135 candidates stood in the election. They included former child performer Gary Combs, *Hustler* publisher Larry Flynt, porn star Mary Carey and Arianna Stassinopoulos Huffington, the 'highest-flying Greek since Icarus' and ex-wife of the Texan oil billionaire Michael Huffington. In the ensuing media circus, allegations about Schwarzenegger's promiscuity, harassment of women and father's membership of the Nazi Party surfaced. He offset these accusations by employing campaign strategists, such as Sean Walsh, who had worked for Reagan and Bush:

Schwarzenegger is the political equivalent to the Beatles. [He] has brought Beatle power to the American and California political system, and you know the music was getting a little stale before the Beatles came on the scene, well I'd say politics was getting a little stale before Schwarzenegger came on the scene (Walsh, 2003).

Schwarzenegger used his fame to gain unprecedented national and international media exposure. Along with his wife, who neutralised charges of sexist behaviour, he appeared on *The Oprah Winfrey Show* and had airtime on *The Tonight Show*, Larry King and Howard Stern. He also appeared on talk radio shows, used the Internet and was helped by his business associate Joe Weider who suppressed negative tabloid coverage. Instead the American media produced a glossy supplement entitled *Arnold, the American Dream*.

To sustain his message, Schwarzenegger's consultants orchestrated press conferences, public platforms, photo opportunities and sound bites, enabling him to attack the high levels of taxation in California. He cited his background as an Austrian immigrant who became a champion body builder and movie superstar as the personal representation of the American Dream. Yet, along with fiscal conservatism and US mythology, he embraced a liberal agenda which promoted pro-choice and gay rights demonstrating his independence from mainstream Republican thinking. By marketing himself to the Californian electorate, he used his celebrity status to receive widespread support.

In the event, the Californian electorate voted to recall Davis and Schwarzenegger won the second election with 48 per cent of the popular vote. He benefited as disenchanted voters created an unusual opportunity through which he exploited his fame. His inexperience, however, brought into question his suitability for governing the sixth largest economy in the world.

SCHWARZENEGGER AS THE GOVERNATOR

To effect his political agenda, Schwarzenegger mobilised a formidable Republican brains trust including former Governor Pete Wilson, monetarist Milton Friedman and billionaire Warren Buffet. And for the first year of his term, his star power maintained his effectiveness. He developed a credible economic plan and criss-crossed the state to cajole sceptical voters into supporting two referendums. The first secured a $15 billion bond deal to refinance the Californian state debt and the second enabled him to balance the budget.

However, the limits of using his star persona became apparent in the summer of 2004 when his $103 billion budget plan unravelled. In his frustration, he accused his opponents in the state legislature of being 'girlie men'. After this, Schwarzenegger offended protesting nurses in December 2004 by claiming they were against him because he 'kicked butts'. These *faux pas* led to public sector unions complaining about Schwarzenegger's bullying tactics against the Californian Teacher Association, the police, fire-fighters and state workers. As his popularity waned, he shored up his core vote by favouring fiscal conservatism over a liberal social agenda (Wright, 2005).

A frustrated Schwarzenegger called for a referendum on 8 November 2005 to give Californians the chance to vote on policy measures allowing him to control the state budget and to curtail union power. He hoped the referendum would prove an opportunity to use his communication skills to appeal to the electorate. For his opponents, it demonstrated his inadequacies as a legislator and enabled them to mobilise their support against him. In the event, Schwarzenegger lost the four budgetary amendments he had publicly backed and his governorship entered a new phase of crisis. Schwarzenegger's period in office demonstrated the limitations of employing celebrity to deal with the complexities of modern governance.

Conclusion

The relationship between American show business and politicians remains vital in modern US political affairs. Moguls such as Wasserman nurtured this link to secure favourable conditions to protect their business interests. Hollywood's glamour has promoted a symbolic form of communication reflecting American values and concerns. Thus, a considerable degree of the film community's political involvement has been driven by ideological fervour. In particular, its relations with Kennedy and Clinton reflected a mutual understanding of imagery and interest-based politics.

This adherence to causes has led to stars using their celebrity to promote civil rights, personal liberties, opposition to wars and freedom of speech. Invariably, the liberal complexion of the Hollywood film industry created closer affiliations with the Democratic rather than the Republican Party. Stars supported reforms to what they perceived was an unrepresentative and corrupt system. These positions have been controversial leading to reactionary opponents questioning the validity of actors' opinions. In particular, star support for the 2004 Kerry campaign and opposition to the war in Iraq often resulted in outright vilification. Once more, Hollywood's contradictory position in the American polity became conspicuous. On one hand, it is celebrated as the quintessential US mythologiser. On the other, it is damned as a Semitic outsider to the mainstream WASP majority.

The film community's paradoxical role in US politics has increased as celebrity and image have become greater forms of capital. Often, in modern American political communications, style has triumphed over substance and performing skills are mandatory for seeking office at a local or national level. In this context; it is not surprising that stars have become politicians themselves. Yet, despite its liberal credentials, Hollywood's most successful actors-turned-politicians have been conservatives – Reagan and Schwarzenegger. Both demonstrated a mastery of imagery, symbolism and drama by using television to communicate their messages to the electorate. Reagan's career followed a standard trajectory, while Schwarzenegger's fame was his principal asset and this created difficulties for him in office.

The use of celebrity in politics leads to questions about whether the American electorate has been unduly influenced by the merging of imagery, glamour and ideology. A key allegation has emerged that style has impoverished the rights of US citizens as the democratic polity has been undermined Consequently, critics such as Neil Postman 'accuse those in the political realm of internalising a media-inspired desire to be palatable and entertaining' (Higgins, 2005). They claim there has been a decline in rationality as televisual style dominates substantive debate. Conversely, Street argues, by rendering themselves as celebrities, politicians legitimise the breach between their public and private personas. This enables them to make their motives more transparent, thereby providing the public with a greater insight into their conduct (Street, 2004). While a significant debate exists in the academy, Hollywood has played a profound role in shaping the modern US political communications process. Most especially, it has blurred the lines between celebrity and political discourse in contemporary American affairs.

Notes

1. In 1969, Stein and Schreiber would team up against Wasserman in an aborted bid to take over MCA.

2. In 1984, Reagan appointed Brewer as the Chairman of the Federal Service Impasse Panel which brokered disputes between federal employers and the workforce.

3. Schwarzennegger's links with the late Kenneth Lay, the convicted, fraudulent ex-Chairman of Enron, was revealed in the 2005 documentary film *Enron: The Smartest Guys in the Room*. In this film, it was shown that a significant degree of California's budgetary crisis had resulted from manipulation of the state's energy business by Enron, which had led to power outages and inflated energy prices. Guy Davis indicated a major financial deficit had resulted from Enron traders' illegal profiteering – and in electoral terms, Schwarzenegger had been the beneficiary of this collapse in the state economy.

Conclusion

The 20th century was deemed the 'American century' as the US emerged as a superpower in economic and global affairs. In this context, the Hollywood film industry reflected and informed the trends in American capitalist development. The motion picture system emerged from the waves of immigration, industrialisation and urbanisation which shaped the nation's development in the first decades of the century. It was run by Jewish immigrant entrepreneurs who relocated from New York to Hollywood owing to the space and light in the Los Angeles basin and because of the lax Californian labour rules. This westward movement was a symbolic extension of the American experience in which new or alternative visions of the country emerged.

In a short period the embryonic industry was defined by a system of vertical integration between distribution and exhibition, and a Fordist form of production in the major studios. The 'studio system' was created by Adolph Zukor of Paramount who incorporated 'block-booking' and 'blind-bidding' requirements from cinema chains to secure profitability. The moguls developed the studios from a firm financial base and ensured monies were returned to their holding companies in New York. This structure remained in place until the 1960s, although its decline was a result of a number of factors; the 1948 Paramount Decrees which dismantled the anti-competitive forms of vertical integration founded by Zukor, the growth of television as a rival medium and the HUAC's ravages of the system.

In the next stage of corporate development, two figures dominated. First, Lew Wasserman, who realised agencies could become studios and transformed MCA into a producer of television programmes. He purchased Universal in 1958 and the studio became the largest producer of films and television series from the 1960s to the 1980s. The second power player was United Artists' executive Arthur Krim, who, with his business partner Robert Benjamin, revolutionised the production process by distributing independent films. These films found new audiences who embraced the visions of the counterculture or movie-brat generation of film-makers. Eventually, these directors would make 'blockbuster' or 'high-concept' movies which could be released across thousands of screens and marketed through exploitation techniques to ensure extraordinary returns. This phase of profitability tied in with a change in the studios' ownership as transnational corporations including Gulf and Western (Paramount), the Kinney Corporation (Warner Bros.) and Transamerica (United Artists) bought the studios in the 1970s.

The modern Hollywood majors are owned by global media conglomerates. They have consolidated their interests throughout a range of services so films appear across a variety of 'windows' of distribution including free-to-air, pay-television and video-on-demand. They have diversified their concerns so that blockbusters often make greater revenues from associated forms of merchandise than at the box office. This diversification has meant the studios maintain a close control over the value chain of their films from their inception to their exhibition. Moreover, the US film industry dominates the international film market and Hollywood pictures generate significant revenues in foreign territories.

The international dimension of US motion picture trade remains its greatest strength, but may foment its most dangerous weakness. The expansion of global communication systems such as the Internet means information may be instantly disseminated and downloaded. In the digital era, Hollywood's greatest fears are the illegal copying of its films as piracy has proliferated. Despite the growth of more effective mechanisms through which to police intellectual property rights, the losses have been astronomical and demonstrate the reliance the studios place on retaining controls over the distribution of content.

The globalisation of the film industry has had significant implications for the Southern Californian economy. As Hollywood is a major source of employment in Los Angeles, the ability of the conglomerates to shift film productions elsewhere has troubled the guilds and unions. Runaway productions have proliferated and proved cheaper because of favourable labour rates, facilities and tax returns in rival production centres in Canada, Australia and Eastern Europe. These strategies have undermined the Hollywood workforce and the Film and Television Action Committee (FTAC), along with Californian Governor Arnold Schwarzenegger, has called for federal trade regulations to effect reform.

The impact of the corporate diversification on the film workforce has been further felt with regard to the residual incomes which are generated once a film has played out its theatrical run. The guilds have engaged in strikes to secure the relevant monies for their members in studio basic agreements so that the corporations cannot avoid or circumvent appropriate payments to the workforce.

Throughout the phases of Hollywood's industrial development, it has received support from the US government as its dominance in the international marketplace has these benefits for the American economy:

- As an exporter of US product, Hollywood helps to stem the nation's balance of payments deficit.
- Hollywood films advertise US goods abroad through their focus on American products.
- Hollywood films present American values and cultural artefacts to an international audience.

Thus, from the 1920s to 1940s, the Department of Commerce supported Hollywood's advance into the post-World War I European territories. In World War II and during the

Cold War, the State Department realised film's ideological worth when it sought to export American values to European states to stem the growth of Communism. From the 1960s, the affiliations between the motion picture industry and Washington were extended further as industry leaders such as Wasserman and Krim raised campaign funds and cultivated presidents, senators and congressmen to broker their interests.

This relationship has been coordinated by the studio's trade representative – the Motion Picture Association of America (MPAA) and its international arm the Motion Picture Association (MPA). This powerful body has only had four presidents; Will Hays, Eric Johnston, Jack Valenti and Dan Glickman. Each one was experienced in political affairs and could negotiate for Hollywood in Washington. In particular, Hays and Valenti proved to be the industry's most able lobbyists as they presided over the expansion of the international motion picture trade. Because they enjoyed contacts with presidential regimes and key figures in Capitol Hill, they received government support for their attempts to liberalise the global film trade to the advantage of the majors and at the expense of foreign rivals.

Under the stewardship of Valenti, the MPAA/MPA provided a unified front for the studios and advocated the liberalisation of US film trade through bilateral and multilateral agreements. This led to trade disputes, most notably the standoff between US and EU negotiators during the 1994 Uruguay Round of the GATT. The MPA's position in the GATS 2000 negotiations is one in which a clear vision of the free market, due to the interests of global market pressure, undermines the viability of local cultural identities.

The global power of the US film industry has meant American products, values and ideologies have dominated in the world marketplace leading to accusations of cultural imperialism. And it is the social, cultural and democratic dimensions of the motion picture trade which have differentiated Hollywood from other American industries. The film community has a strong symbolic worth in US political affairs as Hollywood's films have had a profound effect in socialising the national audience, thereby attracting both celebration and criticism. For instance, the movie moguls shared a common Jewish immigrant working–class heritage. They embodied the American Dream, rising from immigrant ghettos to make their fortunes in the new medium of the cinema. Having sampled the extremes of poverty and wealth, they preserved their fortunes, downplayed their Jewish heritage, and assimilated themselves into mainstream American society.

The MPAA has been better known for its role in film classification than in fostering Hollywood's industrial interests at home and abroad. The calls for censorship came from WASP and Catholic organisations whose anti-Semitic beliefs led them to accuse Jewish moguls, stars and directors of corrupting the nation. Thus, the Production Code Administration (PCA) was headed by the Presbyterian Hays and Catholic Joseph Breen to ensure moral and political conformity to conservative interests. The moguls went along with this as it protected their financial assets and qualified any federal intervention over content.

More profoundly, the debates surrounding the introduction of the Production Code reflected Hollywood's outsider status among American elites in the first half of the 20th century. They demonstrated how the film industry was subject to forms of anti-Semitism as Hollywood occupied a central position with regard to the Jewish question in US life. And these developments would impact on the political ideologies and divisions which emerged in the 1930s and 1940s.

The accusations of subversion were intensified as there was a politicisation of the film workforce through an ideological fervour for liberal and radical causes, and for labour struggles. These conservatives' fears exacerbated the anti-Communist witch-hunts. Through its prosecution of the Hollywood Ten and its investigations into the film industry, the HUAC demonstrated a blatant disregard for the constitutional rights of suspects and press-ganged witnesses to take the stand. Because of the readiness of Hollywood's officials to comply with the inquiry and the high-profile nature of informants such as Elia Kazan, the HUAC's anti-democratic stance was legitimised.

In conflating Judaism with Communism, although a considerable number of radicals came from Jewish backgrounds, the HUAC tapped into the vicious streak of anti-Semitism which had been used to attack the industry since its birth. Hollywood has never fully recovered from the blacklist which ended many careers and reflected the industry's deep-seated fears of being perceived as a pariah. The blacklist also exposed brutal industrial divisions as moguls and rightwingers engaged in a form of super patriotism at the expense of the liberties and rights of their colleagues. The ravages of the HUAC led to the depoliticisation of Hollywood trade unions and the predominantly liberal sensibility within the industry.

In the 21st century similar fears have been articulated by Hollywood activists concerning their rights to criticise the Bush administration. As national divisions have escalated since 9/11 and the war in Iraq, Hollywood has become the arena for some of the country's most vigorous debates. Most especially, celebrities such as Tim Robbins, Susan Sarandon and Michael Moore have articulated their criticisms over the state of American political life. Moore's unprecedented success with his blockbuster documentary *Fahrenheit 9/11* which won the Palme D'Or at Cannes and made over $100 million at the domestic box office demonstrated that a sizeable constituency of Americans were critical of the Bush administration's foreign policies. However, America's rightwing political, social and religious constituencies have damned Hollywood for its lax morals, liberalism and its critical stance. And the conservative composition of the US news media, led by Rupert Murdoch's Fox News, has undermined dissent and questioned the legitimacy of celebrities' rights to influence debate.

The film industry occupies a peculiar position in the American body politic. On one hand, politicians have courted film stars to provide lustre to their campaigns because of the prominence of celebrity in US culture. Stars have appeared on platforms or have been involved in the campaign process. Celebrity activists have used their fame as an asset when being identified with causes such as environmentalism, civil liberties and opposition to the wars in Vietnam and Iraq. Conversely, many conservatives have accused the film community's 'pampered' multimillionaires of being hypocritical in their identification with oppressed minorities. For instance, in September 2005 when Sean Penn promoted aid to the predominantly black disaster victims of Hurricane Katrina in New Orleans he was vilified by some for using the situation for his own self-aggrandisement. In this way, stars have been simultaneously lauded and condemned for their opposition to wars, engagement in civil rights' struggles and demands for political rights. And the polarities in attitudes to Hollywood appear to be growing, rather than diminishing.

Finally, as celebrity politics has become more pronounced in a climate of mediated political communication, Hollywood's glamour has been used to promote different ideologies, political allegiances and to determine a symbolic form of political communication which has reflected and informed the concerns of US society. This trend demonstrates a wider phenomenon of celebrities becoming politicians in their own rights (Ronald Reagan, Arnold Schwarzenegger, Sonny Bono, Jesse Ventura and Clint Eastwood) as the de-alignment in the US political system has grown owing to the power of media representations, sophisticated political marketing and the increased costs involved in campaigning.

Ironically, despite Hollywood's liberal stance, its most successful actors-turned-politicians have been Republicans. Reagan launched his political career as a Cold Warrior and trade unionist during the HUAC witch-hunts. He built up sufficient stock with rightwing politicians and Californian business interests to run for the governorship. Ultimately, he developed his likeable style through television appearances and employed ideologies drawn from his films to create the template he required to run for the White House. While Reagan followed a more traditional career path, Schwarzenegger's capital with the Californian electorate was drawn solely from his celebrity and he traded his stardom for office.

Hollywood's role in modern political affairs brings into question celebrity, popular culture and interests in civic and social affairs. For some commentators, the film industry has been criticised for contributing to the erosion of US public life as the differences between high politics and campaigning have evaporated. Neil Postman suggests that political discourse has been permanently undermined by the media and that an uncritical form of populism has replaced the democratic value systems of the past (Postman, 1987). John Street argues that any discussion of citizenship needs to consider its relationship with culture:

> This is not just a matter of seeing representation as a cultural performance, of noting the use of icons and images of popular culture in politics, but of seeing both as symptomatic of the link between politics and popular aesthetics (Street, 2004: 449).

Consequently, the film industry has been a vital fulcrum in American communications, re-coordinating the links between the political elite and electorate. In this respect, while blame has been attached to the film industry for simplifying political discourse, it is more appropriate to consider Hollywood as only one causal factor of many (mass media coverage, partisan realignment and general voter decline despite the upsurge in the 2004 presidential election) in the evolution of modern political communications.

This study has sought to reconcile the different approaches accorded the US film industry on its role in America's political, cultural and social life. At the level of political economy and the international flow of product, the Hollywood film industry has evolved from national champion into global phenomenon. It has received support from the US government which has realised its economic and ideological worth nationally and internationally.

Simultaneously, Hollywood's relationship with the US political elite has been characterised by a paradoxical gulf in social and cultural interests. The predominantly Semitic complexion of the industry has been praised and condemned in equal measure. As purveyors of the American Dream, film celebrities have taken on a heightened role in US affairs, but their views have been eviscerated over the years. Hollywood's position in the US democracy exhibits a range of contradictions about economic power, social worth and conceptions of liberty. Consequently, it has been the purpose of this book to contribute to the debate about the American film industry's social worth by making conspicuous its importance to the nation's cultural existence, its position within the world order and its value to US citizens.

Bibliography

Allen, Jeanne Thomas (1976), 'The Decay of the Motion Picture Patents Company', in Tino Balio (ed.), *The American Film Industry*, Madison and London: University of Wisconsin Press.

Alterman, Eric (2004a), 'The Hollywood Campaign: Want Big Money to Get Elected to National Office? If You're a Democrat, You Need to Head for the Hills – Beverly Hills. A Miner's Map for the Liberal Gold Rush', *Atlantic Online*, September (downloaded from http://www.theatlantic.com/doc/prem/200409/alterman on 12 September 2005).

Alterman, Eric (2004b), 'Money for Nothing', *The Nation*, 13 December (downloaded from http://www.thenation.com/doc/20041213/alterman on 12 September 2005).

Anthony, Andrew (2004), 'Acting up: Why Tim Robbins Won't Be Silenced', *Observer Magazine*, 29 August: 14–17.

Apted, Michael (2003), 'Dialogue with Michael Apted', *Hollywood Reporter*, 18 August: 2 and 12.

Apted, Michael (2004), 'DGA Signs Contract with TV, Film Producer', *Studio Briefing*, 24 September, Internet Movie Database (downloaded from http://www.imdb.com/news/sb/2004-09-24 on 12 September 2005).

Arnold, Thomas K. (2004), 'DVDs Hit the Campaign Trail Hard: *Fahrenheit 9/11* Isn't Fanning Flames Alone', *USA Today*, 10 August: 3.

Atkin, Hillary (2004a), 'Growing Up: The Hollywood Bureau of the NAACP Celebrates Its First Anniversary', *Hollywood Reporter*, 5–7 March: S-14.

Atkin, Hillary (2004b), 'Dialogue: Notes from the Field – Interview with NAACP Chairman Julian Bond and President and CEO Kweisi Mfume', *Hollywood Reporter*, 5–7 March: S-18.

Bach, Steven (1986), *Final Cut: Dreams and Disaster in the Making of* Heaven's Gate, London: Faber and Faber.

Bachrach, Judy (2005), 'Moore's War: After Skewing a Sitting President, a Detroit Mogul and a Cultural Icon, Michael Moore is Taking on the Health Care Industry', *Vanity Fair*, March: 108–115.

Balio, Tino (ed.) (1976), *The American Film Industry*, Madison and London: University of Wisconsin Press.

Balio, Tino (ed.) (1990), *Hollywood in the Age of Television*, London: Unwin Hyman.

Bates, James and Claudia Eller (2001), 'Casting the Leads in SAG a Challenge', *Los Angeles Times*, 16 July: C1–C3.

Bates, James (2003), 'SAG-AFTRA Consolidation Falls Just Short of Approval: Majorities of Both Vote "Yes", but Screen Actors' Guild Backing Doesn't Reach 60 Per Cent Needed', *Los Angeles Times*, 2 July.

Beatty, Warren and Jeremy Pikser (1998), *Bulworth*, Los Angeles: 20th Century-Fox.

Biskind, Peter (1998), *Easy Riders, Raging Bulls: How the Sex-Drugs-and-Rock 'N' Roll Generation Saved Hollywood*, New York: Simon and Schuster.

Biskind, Peter (1999), 'When Worlds Collide', *The Nation*, 5 April (downloaded from http://www. thenation.com/doc/19990405/biskind on 12 September 2005).

Biskind, Peter (2004), *Down and Dirty Pictures: Miramax, Sundance and the Rise of Independent Film*, New York: Simon and Schuster.

Bjork, Ulf Jonas (2000), 'The U.S. Commerce Department Aids Hollywood Exports, 1921–33', *The Historian*, vol. 62 (downloaded from http://www.findarticles.com/cf_dls/m2082/3_62/62828735/p1/article.jhtml on 12 September 2005).

Black, Gregory D. (1994), *Hollywood Censored: Morality Codes, Catholics and the Movies*, Cambridge: Cambridge University Press.

Blankfort, Michael (1951), 'Red Channels Entrapment Attempt Recorded Telephone Conversation', House of UnAmerican Activities Committee Special Collection, 12 January, Academy of Motion Picture Library, Beverly Hills, CA.

Bogart, Humphrey (1948), 'I'm No Communist', *Photoplay*, March.

Boliek, Brooks (2003), 'NAACP Looks Behind the Scenes: Study Cites Lack of Minority Writers, Helmers, Producers', *Hollywood Reporter*, 29 October: 3 and 10.

Boliek, Brooks (2005), 'MPAA Head Rode Out Rocky First Year', *Hollywood Reporter*, 1 September (downloaded from http://www.hollywoodreporter.com/thr/imdb/article_display.jsp?vnu_special_account_code=thrsiteimdbpro&vnu_content_id=1001052846 on 12 September 2005).

Borneman, Ernest (1976), 'United States versus Hollywood: The Case Study of an Anti-trust Suit', in Tino Balio (ed.), *The American Film Industry*, Madison and London: University of Wisconsin Press.

Bourne, Tom (1981), 'The Hollywood Blacklist Starring Ronald Reagan: He Says the Blacklist Never Existed . . . the Facts Say Otherwise', *Los Angeles Free Weekly* vol. 3 no. 16, 13 February: 1–14.

Bowser, Kenneth (2000), *Hollywood DC: A Tale of Two Cities*, Fremantle Corporation (Broadcast on Bravo cable network, November).

Bowser, Kenneth (2003), *Easy Riders, Raging Bulls*, Fremantle Corporation/BBC (DVD).

Breen, Joseph I. (1934), 'Report: Hays Papers', 13 March, quoted from Leonard J. Leff and Jerold L. Simmons (1990), *The Dame in the Kimino*, New York: Grove Weidenfeld.

Broder, John M. (2002), 'Streisand Helps Raise Money for Democrats and Tells Them to Play Offense', *New York Times*, 30 September (downloaded from http://www.nytimes.com/2002/09/30 on 12 September 2005).

Bromley, Carl (2003), 'The House That Jack Built', *The Nation* vol. 270, no. 13, 3 April: 39.

Brown, Edmund 'Pat' (1966), 'Campaign Commercial: Man versus Actor', National Museum of Television and Radio, Beverly Hills, CA.

Brownstein, Ronald (1990), *The Power and the Glitter: The Hollywood–Washington Connection*, New York: Pantheon Books.

Brownstein, Ronald (2000), 'Interview', quoted from Kenneth Bowser, *Hollywood DC: A Tale of Two Cities*, Fremantle Corporation (Broadcast on Bravo cable network, November).

Bruck, Connie (2004), *When Hollywood had a King: The Reign of Lew Wasserman, Who Leveraged Talent into Power and Influence*, New York: Random House.

Buckley Jr, William F. (1995), 'Interview with Charlton Heston', *Firing Line*, National Review Productions, National Television and Radio Museum, Beverly Hills, CA.

Buhle, Paul and Dave Wagner (2001), *A Very Dangerous Citizen: Abraham Lincoln Polonsky and the Hollywood Left*, Berkeley, Los Angeles and London: University of California Press.

Buhle, Paul and Dave Wagner (2002), *Radical Hollywood: The Untold Story Behind America's Favourite Movies*, New York: New Press.

Buhle, Paul and Dave Wagner (2003), *Hide in Plain Sight: The Hollywood Blacklistees in Film and Television, 1950–2002*, Basingstoke: Palgrave Macmillan.

Cadell, Pat (2000), 'Interview', quoted from Kenneth Bowser, *Hollywood DC: A Tale of Two Cities*, Fremantle Corporation (Broadcast on Bravo cable network, November).

Cagney, James (1940), 'Cagney's Two-Shirt Theory on Communism', *Hollywood City News*, 20 August.

Carr, Steven Alan (2001), *Hollywood and Anti-Semitism: A Cultural History up to World War II*, Cambridge: Cambridge University Press.

Castleman, Amanda (2005), 'Hollywood North by Northwest: Drawn in the Drizzle. Vancouver B.C. Has Nurtured Boris Karloff, *Star Trek*'s Scotty, Pam Anderson and the Continent's Third Largest Production Center', *Movie Maker: The Art and Business of Making Movies* vol. 12, no. 59, Summer: 42–4.

Ceplair, Larry and Steven Englund (2003), *The Inquisition in Hollywood: Politics in the Film Community, 1930–60*, Urbana and Chicago: University of Illinois Press.

Champlin, Charles (1967), 'Movie Chief Jack Valenti – Seal of Approval, So Far', *LA Times*, 5 February: 5.

Chapman, Peter (2000), 'Monti Grabs Lead Role in the EU Media Show', *European Voice*, 6–12 July: 21.

Chetwynd, Lionel (2000), 'Interview', quoted from Kenneth Bowser, *Hollywood DC: A Tale of Two Cities*, Fremantle Corporation (Broadcast on Bravo cable network, November).

Chomsky, Noam (2002), *Media Control: The Spectacular Achievements of Propaganda* (2nd edn), Open Media.

Chung, Winnie (2003), 'DVD Pirates Storm through Asia – Report: Illegal Film Copies Nearly Doubled in Past Year', *Hollywood Reporter*, 19–25 August: 2.

Cieply, Michael (2001), 'Creative Tensions: The WGA–DGA Divide', *Los Angeles Times*, 22 July.

Clark, Danae (1995), *Negotiating Hollywood: The Cultural Politics of the Actors' Labor*, Minneapolis and London: University of Minnesota Press.

Clegg II, Legrand H. (1990a), ' "Jewish Racism" in H'wood Alleged', *Hollywood Reporter*, 12 July: 2.

Clegg II, Legrand H. (1990b), 'Letter to Editor: Black Charges of Jewish Racism in Entertainment Industry', *Los Angeles Times*, 20 July: 15.

Conant, Michael (1976), 'The Impact of the Paramount Decrees', in Tino Balio (ed.), *The American Film Industry*, Madison and London: University of Wisconsin Press.

Conference of Studio Unions (1945), 'Pamphlet: The Government of the United States Give You the Facts! Read This and Find Out Why the Hollywood Strike Is Legal', Roger MacDonald Special Collection, 12 June, Academy of Motion Picture Library, Beverly Hills, CA.

Coolidge, Martha (2003), 'Interview', *Daily Variety*, 27 February: 4.

Cooper, Marc (1999), 'Postcards from the Left', *The Nation*, 5 April (downloaded from http://www.thenation.com/doc/19990405/cooper on 12 September 2005).

Corn, David (1999), 'Looking for Mr Right', *The Nation*, 5 April (downloaded from http://www.thenation.com/doc/19990405/corn on 12 September 2005).

Crowdus, Gary (1994), *A Political Companion to Film*, Chicago, IL: Lakeview Press.

Davies, Philip John (2002), 'Hollywood in Elections and Elections in Hollywood', in Philip John Davies and Paul Wells (eds), *American Film and Politics from Reagan to Bush Jr*, Manchester: Manchester University Press.

Davis, Mike (1998), *City of Quartz: Excavating the Future in Los Angeles*, London: Pimlico.

Dickenson, Ben (2002), 'Goodbye Warren, Hello Tim: How Clinton Demobilized Liberalism and Anti-Capitalism Came into Hollywood', *Bright Lights Film Journal* no. 38, November (downloaded from http://www.brightlightsfilm.com/38/endlib.htm on 12 September 2005).

Dickenson, Ben (2003a), 'Tongues Untied: Art, Politics and Business Collide', *Bright Lights Film Journal* no. 40, May (downloaded from http://www.brightlightsfilm.com/40/ oscars.htm on 12 September 2005).

Dickenson, Ben (2003b), 'The Trouble with the Governator: The Ascension of Arnold – Salvation, Apocalypse, or Trigger for a Resurgent Left', *Bright Lights Film Journal* no. 42, November (downloaded from http://www.brightlightsfilm.com/42/arnold.htm on 12 September 2005).

Dideon, Joan (1998), 'Vacant Fervor', in Christopher Sylvester (ed.), *The Grove Book of Hollywood*, New York: Grove Press.

Dietz, David (1991), 'Comparison between the 1985 and 1988 Writers' Guild of America Theatrical and Television Basic Agreements – What Did the Guild Obtain from the 1988 Strike?', *Federal Communications Law Journal* vol. 43: 185–214.

Dmytryk, Edward (1996), *Odd Man Out: A Memoir of the Hollywood Ten*, Carbondale and Edwardsville: Southern Illinois University Press.

Doherty, Thomas (1999), *Pre-Code Hollywood: Sex, Immorality, and Insurrection in American Cinema 1930–1934*, New York: Columbia University Press.

Dowd, Maureen (1999), 'Liberties: Will You Warren?', *New York Times*, 15 August: 15.

Duncan, Paul (2004), 'Review of *Cinema Today* by Edward Buscombe', *Times Educational Supplement*, 2 July: 28.

Edwards, Anne (1987), *Early Reagan*, New York: William Morris and Company Inc.

Elrick, Ted (1998), 'A film by', *DGA Magazine*, June–July (downloaded from http://www.dga.org/thedga/ cr_gi_wga.php3 on 12 September 2005).

Emergency Committee of Hollywood Guilds and Unions (1944), 'Letter: Announcement by Emergency Committee of Hollywood Guilds and Unions to General Industry', *Hollywood Reporter*, 23 June.

Entertainment Industry Coalition for Free Trade (2003), 'Press Release: Entertainment Industry Coalition for Free Trade Hails Signing of US–Chile Free Trade Agreement', 6 June (downloaded from http://www.mpaa.org/jack/2003/2003_06_06.pdf on 12 September 2005).

Erickson, Hal (2005), 'Review of *The Miracle of Morgan's Creek*', *New York Times* (downloaded from http://movies2.nytimes.com/gst/movies/movie.html?v_id=32822 on 12 September 2005).

European Commission, Directorate-General X. (1999), *GATS/WTO New Round Consultation on Audiovisual Services: Report of the Hearing of 23 February, 1999*.

Film and Television Action Committee (2002–5), *Film and Television Action Committee Website* (downloaded from http://www.ftac.net on 12 September 2005).

Ford, Henry (1921), 'The Jewish Aspect of the "Movie" Problem', *The Dearborn Independent*, 12 February.

Gabler, Neal (1988), *An Empire of Their Own: How the Jews Invented Hollywood*, New York: Crown Publishers.

Garvey, Megan (2001), 'SAG Says Canada Film
    Policies Illegal, Seeks Federal Inquiry', *Los Angeles
    Times*, 22 August.

Gates Jr, Henry Louis (2004), *America Behind the
    Color Line: Dialogues with African Americans*, New
    York and Boston, MA: Warner Books.

Gems, Jonathan (2005), 'Is British Film Dead? A
    Once Prolific Industry is Being Strangled by
    Hollywood and Apathetic UK Governments',
    Independent, 15 April: 8.

Gerston, Larry N. and Terry Christensen (2004),
    Recall! California's Political Earthquake, Armonk
    and London: M. E. Sharpe Inc.

Gibbs, Marla (1990), 'Letter to Editor: Black
    Charges of Jewish Racism in Entertainment
    Industry', *Los Angeles Times*, 20 July: 15.

Gibson, William F. and Benjamin L. Hooks (1990),
    'Letter to Editor: Black Charges of Jewish
    Racism in Entertainment Industry', *Los Angeles
    Times*, 20 July: 15.

Gomery, Douglas (1986), *The Hollywood Studio
    System*, London: British Film Institute.

Gomery, Douglas (1992), *Shared Pleasures: A History
    of Movie Presentation in the United States*, London:
    British Film Institute.

Gomery, Douglas (2005a), 'Economic and
    Institutional Analysis: Hollywood as Monopoly
    Capitalism', in Mike Wayne (ed.), *Understanding
    Film: Marxist Perspectives*, London and Ann Arbor,
    MI: Pluto Press.

Gomery, Douglas (2005b), *The Hollywood Studio
    System: A History*, London: British Film
    Institute.

de Grazia, Victoria (1998), 'European Cinema and
    the Idea of Europe, 1925–1995', in Geoffrey
    Nowell-Smith and Steven Ricci (eds), *Hollywood
    and Europe: Economics, Culture, National Identity:
    1945–1995*, London: British Film Institute.

Guback, Thomas H. (1976), 'Hollywood's
    International Market', in Tino Balio (ed.), *The
    American Film Industry*, Madison and London:
    University of Wisconsin Press.

Guttman, Robert J. (1998), 'Going to the Movies
    with Jack Valenti', *Europe* no. 379, September: 25.

Henreid, Paul (1955), 'Letter to H. William Fitcher
    Law Offices', House Committee of UnAmerican
    Activities Special Collection, 2 May, Academy of
    Motion Picture Library, Beverly Hills, CA.

Henreid, Paul (1998), 'That Washington Trip', in
    Christopher Sylvester (ed.), *The Grove Book of
    Hollywood*, New York: Grove Press.

Hiestand, Jesse (2004), 'Direct Orders: As the DGA
    Prepares for its Annual Awards Ceremony its
    Leadership Takes a Larger Industry View',
    Hollywood Reporter, 6–8 February: 27.

Hiestand, Jesse (2004a), 'Dialogue – The
    Professionals DGA: Interview with Jay Roth',
    Hollywood Reporter, 6–8 February: 37.

Hiestand, Jesse (2004b), 'DGA Alters Auteur
    Theory: Guild Offers New Guidelines for
    Possessive Credits', *Hollywood Reporter*, 10
    February: 64.

Hiestand, Jesse (2005), 'Diplomatic Community:
    The Studios Set Aside Their Differences to Gain
    Bargaining Clout', *Hollywood Reporter*, 31 March
    (downloaded from http://www.
    hollywoodreporter.com/thr/film/feature_display.j
    sp?vnu_content_id=1000863178 on 12
    September 2005).

Higgins, Michael (2005), 'The "Public Inquisitor" as
    Media Celebrity', Unpublished paper presented
    at the Media and Politics Specialist Group (MPG)
    Panel at the Political Studies Association (PSA),
    Conference, 5–7 April, University of Leeds.

Higson, Andrew and Richard Maltby (eds) (1999),
    *Film Europe and Film America: Cinema, Commerce
    and Cultural Exchange 1920–1939*, Exeter:
    University of Exeter Press.

Hill, John and Pamela Church Gibson (eds) (2000),
    *American Cinema and Hollywood: Critical
    Approaches*, Oxford: Oxford University Press.

Hoberman, J. and Jeffrey Shandler (2003),
    Entertaining America: Jews, Movies and Broadcasting,
    Princeton, NJ: Princeton University Press.

Hollywood Reporter (2001), 'Rewriting the Rules: Contract Negotiations Continue Between the WGA and the Studios as Guild Members Seek Creative and Financial Compensation', *Hollywood Reporter*, March: 1–4.

Holt, Jennifer (2001), 'In Deregulation We Trust: The Synergy of Politics and Industry in Reagan-era Hollywood – The Business of Hollywood, Ronald Reagan and the Motion Picture Industry', *Film Quarterly*, Winter (downloaded from http://www.findarticles.com/p/articles/mi_m1070/is_2_55/ai_83477537 on 12 September 2005).

Hopper, Hedda (1965), 'Interview with Ronald Reagan', Hedda Hopper Special Collection, 6 May, Academy of Motion Picture Library, Beverly Hills, CA.

Horn, John (2004), 'A "Cold" War over Foreign Filming. Frustrated by Job Losses, Industry Workers Launch an Internet Campaign against *Cold Mountain* for Choosing Romania as its American Stand-in', *Los Angeles Times*, 4 February (downloaded from http://www. ftac.net/html/2-lat-2-4-04.html on 12 September 2005).

Horne, Gerald (2001), *Class Struggles in Hollywood 1930–1950: Moguls, Mobsters, Stars, Reds and Trade Unionists*, Austin: University of Texas Press.

Hoskins, Colin, Stuart McFayden and Adam Finn (1997), *Global Television and Film: An Introduction to the Economics of the Business*, Oxford: Oxford University Press.

Hughes, Rupert (1936), 'Sez Roy Howard to Rupert Hughes: Sez Rupert Hughes to Roy Howard', *Variety*, 12 May: 5.

Jarvie, Ian (1992), *Hollywood's Overseas Campaign, the North Atlantic Movie Trade 1920–1950*, Cambridge: Cambridge University Press.

Jarvie, Ian (1998), 'Free Trade as Cultural Threat: American Films and Exports in the Post-War Period', in Geoffrey Nowell-Smith and Steven Ricci (eds), *Hollywood and Europe: Economics, Culture, National Identity: 1945–1995*, London: British Film Institute.

Jeancolas, Jean-Pierre (1998), 'From the Blum-Byrnes Agreement to the GATT Affair' in Geoffrey Nowell-Smith and Steven Ricci (eds), *Hollywood and Europe: Economics, Culture and National Identity, 1945-1995*, London: British Film Institute.

Johnston, Eric (1947), 'President of MPAA Statement', *Variety*, 5 June: 2.

Jones, Kent (2004), 'Fahrenheit 9/11', *Film Comment*, July–August: 18–26.

Jowett, Garth (1976), *Film: The Democratic Art*, Boston, MA: Little Brown.

Kelly, Brendan (2001), 'Canuck Tariff Tiff: ACTRA Attacks SAG over Anti-runaway Measures', *Daily Variety*, 24 August: 4.

Kerr, Paul (ed.) (1986), *The Hollywood Film Industry: A Reader*, London: Routledge and Kegan Paul in association with the British Film Institute.

Kerrigan, Finola and Nigel Culking (1999), *A Reflection on the American Domination of the Film Industry: An Historical and Industrial Perspective*, Paper 15, Hertfordshire: University of Hertfordshire.

Kiefer, Peter (2001), 'Acting Gains for Minorities: SAG Report Finds There's Still Plenty of Room Left for Diversity', *Hollywood Reporter*, 14 August: 1–2.

Kiefer, Peter (2002), 'Rule One, Take One: Globalization Hits the Screen Actors' Guild, and the Organization Stands Firm in Implementing a Rule that Protects Its Members', *Hollywood Reporter*, 27 February: S-1–S-3.

Kiefer, Peter (2003), 'Dialogue with Michael Apted, President of DGA', *Hollywood Reporter*, 18 August: 12.

King, Tom (2000), *David Geffen: A Biography of New Hollywood*, London: Hutchinson.

Klady, Leonard (2005), 'Switching Food Chains. New MPAA Chief Dan Glickman Made his ShoWest Debut This Week. Bill Clinton's Former Agriculture Secretary Talks about the Challenge of his New Role', *Screen International*, 18 March: 6.

Klein, Christina (2004), 'The Hollowing out of Hollywood: "Runaway Productions" Boost Profits but Also Take Jobs Abroad', *Yale Global Online*, 30 April (downloaded from http://www.yaleglobal.yale.edu/display.article?id =3794 on 12 September 2005).

Klein, Julius (1926), to H. C. Maclean, 17 August, BFDC motion picture records, 'General'.

Koppes, Clayton R. and Gregory D. Black (1977), 'What to Show the World: The Office of War Information and Hollywood, 1942–1945', *Journal of American History* vol. 64 no. 5, June: 87–105.

Lardner Jr, Ring (1978), 'Thirty Years after the Hollywood 10', *New York Times*, 18 March.

Lasky, Jesse L. with Don Weldon (1957), *I Blow My Own Horn*, Garden City, NY: Doubleday.

Leff, Leonard J. (1998), 'A Test of American Film Censorship: *Who's Afraid of Virginia Woolf?*', in Peter C. Rollins (ed.), *Hollywood as Historian: American Film in a Cultural Context* (rev. edn), Lexington: University of Kentucky Press.

Leffall, Jabulani (2003), 'Diversity Gains are in the Eye of the Beholder', *Variety*, 28 April: A4.

Levey, Collin (2000), 'An Actors Union's SAGging Fortunes', *Wall Street Journal*, 2 May.

Lewis, Jon (ed.) (1998), *The New American Cinema*, Durham, NC: Duke University Press.

Lewis, Jon (2000), *Hollywood versus Hardcore: How the Struggle over Censorship Saved the Modern Film Industry*, New York and London: New York University Press.

Litwack, Mark (1987), *Reel Power: The Struggle for Influence and Success in the New Hollywood*, London: Sidgwick and Jackson.

Longwell, Todd (2003), 'Runaway Productions', *Hollywood Reporter*, 27 February: 3–4.

Maltby, Richard (1995), *Hollywood Cinema: An Introduction*, Oxford: Blackwell.

Maltz, Albert (1947), *Statement of Albert Maltz to the House Committee of UnAmerican Activities*, William Wyler Special Collection, Academy of Motion Picture Library, Beverly Hills, CA.

Martin, Steve (2001), 'A Film by Steve Martin: A Pot Shot at the DGA's Firm Stand', *Daily Variety*, 23 January.

May, Lary (2000), *The Big Tomorrow: Hollywood and the Politics of the American Way*, Chicago, IL and London: University of Chicago Press.

McCrum, Robert (2003), 'The Total Recall: Fear and Loathing on the California Campaign Trail', *Observer Magazine*, 28 September: 22–32.

McDonald, Paul (1999), *World Film Distribution Report (Volume 1–5)*, London: EMAP Media.

McDougal, Dennis (1998), *The Last Mogul: Lew Wasserman, MCA, and the Hidden History of Hollywood*, New York: Crown Publishers.

McGilligan, Patrick and Paul Buhle (1997), *Tender Comrades: A Backstory of the Hollywood Blacklist*, New York: St Martin's Griffin.

McManus, John T. (1944), 'Motion Picture Aliiance', *Variety*, 15 February.

McNary, Dave (2000), 'A Lack of Latinos: SAG Study Reports Role Dearth, Stereotypes', *Variety*, 25 May: 4 and 23.

McNary, Dave (2001), 'SAG Sees Cast Gains: Report Finds Increase in Minority, Overall Roles', *Variety*, 14 August: 2 and 22.

McNary, Dave (2003), 'Daschle, DGA to Talk Runaway Prod'n', *Variety*, 30 May: 3.

McNary, Dave (2004), 'Guild Targets Global Goals: Foreign Partners Sought to Support DGA Members Working Abroad', *Variety*, 6 February.

Medavoy, Mike with Josh Young (2002), *You're Only as Good as Your Next One*, New York, London, Toronto, Sydney and Singapore: Atria Books.

Medved, Michael (1993), *Hollywood versus America*, London: HarperCollins.

Medved, Michael (1996), 'Hollywood's Four Big Lies', in Karl French (ed.), *Screen Violence*, London: Bloomsbury.

Mikulan, Steven (2001), 'Tinsel-Town Rebellion: Writers, Moguls and Hollywood's Day of Reckoning', *LA Weekly* 27 April–3 May (downloaded from http://www.laweekly.com on 12 September 2005).

Milius, John (2003), 'Interview', quoted from Kenneth Bowser, *Easy Riders, Raging Bulls*, Fremantle Corporation/BBC (DVD).

Miller, Toby (1996), 'The Crime of Monsieur Lang: GATT, Screen and the International Division of Labour', in Albert Moran (ed.), *Film Policy: International, National and Regional Perspectives*, London and New York: Routledge.

Miller, Toby, Nitin Govil, John McMurria and Richard Maxwell (2001), *Global Hollywood*, London: British Film Institute.

Miller, Toby, Nitin Govil, John McMurria and Richard Maxwell and Tina Wang (2005), *Global Hollywood 2*, London: British Film Institute.

Mitchell, Greg (1992), *The Campaign of the Century: Upton Sinclair's Race for Governor of California and the Birth of Media Politics*, New York: Random House.

Mitchell, Greg (1998), *Tricky Dick and the Pink Lady: Richard Nixon vs. Helen Gahagan Douglas – Sexual Politics and the Red Scare, 1950*, New York: Random House.

Moldea, Dan E. (1987), *Dark Victory: Ronald Reagan, MCA and the Mob*, New York: Viking Penguin.

Monaco, James (1979), *American Film Now: The People, the Power, the Money, the Movies*, New York, London and Scarborough, Ontario: New American Library.

Montgomery, Robert (1946), 'SAG President Speaks', *Variety*, 9 October: 7.

Moran, Albert (ed.) (1996), *Film Policy: International, National and Regional Perspectives*, London: Routledge.

Morgan Wilson, John (1998), *Inside Hollywood: A Writer's Guide to Researching the World of Movies and TV*, Cincinnati, OH: Writer's Digest Books.

Morris, Betsy (2004), 'Arnold Power: He Accumulates It. He Wields It. He Wins over Voters with It. But Is the Governor's Star Power Enough to Win the War of Wills with His California Opponents?', *Fortune: The Power Issue*, September, Fortune Group: 77–88.

Muscio, Guiliana (1997), *Hollywood's New Deal*, Philadelphia, PA: Temple University Press.

Nathan, Ian (2002), 'Look Who's (not) Working', *The Times*, 4 July.

National Association for the Advancement of Colored People (2003), *Out of Focus, Out of Sync, Take 3: A Report on the Film and Television Industry*, November, Baltimore: NAACP.

Navasky, Victor S. (1991), *Naming Names* (rev. edn), New York: Viking Penguin.

Neale, Steven and Murray Smith (1998), *Contemporary Hollywood Cinema*, London and New York: Routledge.

Neve, Brian (1992), *Film and Politics in America: A Social Tradition*, London and New York: Routledge.

Nielsen, Mike and Gene Mailes (1995), *Hollywood's Other Blacklist: Union Struggles in the Studio System*, London: British Film Institute.

Nowell-Smith, Geoffrey (1998), *Hollywood and Europe: Economics, Culture, National Identity, 1945–95*, London: British Film Institute.

Olsen, Sidney (1947), 'Congressional Committee Poses a Question: Is it Un-American to Ask a Man if he is Communist or Un-American to Refuse to Answer', *Life Magazine*, 24 November.

Parry, Chris (2003), 'The "On Crack" Files: Isn't it Time Someone Explained the World to Jack Valenti', *Hollywood Bitchslap*, 2 October (downloaded from http://www.hollywoodbitchslap.com/feature.php?feature=807&highlight=Jack+Valenti on 12 September 2005).

Pirie, David (ed.) (1981), *Anatomy of the Movies*, London: Windward.

Pollack, Sydney (2000), 'Interview' quoted from Kenneth Bowser, *Hollywood DC: A Tale of Two Cities*, Fremantle Corporation (Broadcast on Bravo cable network, November).

Pollock, Louis (1961), 'Letter to Writers' Guild of America, West Council', 20 March, Howard Estabrook Special Collection, Academy of Motion Picture Library, Beverly Hills, CA.

Postman, Neil (1987), *Amusing Ourselves to Death: Public Discourse in the Age of Show Business*, London: Methuen.

Powers, Stephen, David J. Rothman and Stanley Rothman (1996), *Hollywood's America: Social and Political Themes in Motion Pictures*, Boulder, CO: Westview Press.

Prindle, David F. (1988), *The Politics of Glamour: Ideology and Democracy in the Screen Actors Guild*, Madison: University of Wisconsin Press.

Puttnam, David (1997), *The Undeclared War: The Struggle for Control of the World's Film Industry*, London: HarperCollins.

Pye, Michael and Lynda Myles (1979), *The Movie Brats: How the Film Generation Took Over Hollywood*, London: Temple Smith.

Pye, Michael (1980), *Moguls: Inside the Business of Show Business*, London: Temple Smith.

Randall, Richard S. (1970), *Censorship of the Movies: The Social and Political Control of a Mass Medium*, Madison, Milwaukee and London: University of Wisconsin Press.

Rankin, John S. (1945), *Congressional Record*, 18 July, Washington: US Congress.

Raymond, Emilie Elizabeth (2003), 'From My Cold, Dead Hands': A Political and Cultural Biography of Charlton Heston, Unpublished PhD thesis, University of Missouri – Columbia.

Reagan, Ronald (1960), 'Letter from Ronald Reagan to Hugh Hefner' (downloaded from http://www.labournet.net/docks2/0107/reagan1.htm on 12 September 2005).

Reagan, Ronald with Richard G. Hubler (1965), *Where's the Rest of Me?*, New York: Duell.

Reeve, Arch (1945), 'Letter from Arch Reeve, AMPP Secretary Public Information Committee to Studio Publicity Directors', 25 April, AMPP Special Collection, Academy of Motion Picture Library, Beverly Hills, CA.

Reynolds, Robert (1944), *Congressional Record*, 7 March, Washington: US Congress: A1120.

Richardson, Bonnie J. K. (1999), 'ITC INVESTIGATION NO. 322–403: Assessment of the Economic Effects on the United States of China's Accession to the WTO. Statement by Bonnie J. K. Richardson, Vice-President, Trade and Federal Affairs, Motion Picture Association of America, Inc.', 23 February (downloaded from http://www.mpaa.org/legislation/press/99/99_2_23.htm on 12 September 2005).

Richardson, Bonnie J. K. (2003), Testimony of Bonnie J. K. Richardson, Vice-President Trade and Federal Affairs, MPA before the US Trade Policy Staff Committee on US–Australian Free Trade Agreement, 15 January (downloaded from http://www.mpaa.org/legislation/press/2003/2003_01_15.pdf on 12 September 2005).

Richmond, Ray (2005), 'Support Team: The DGA's African-American Steering Committee Offers Information and Guidance to Directors of Color', *Hollywood Reporter*, 5 March: S-4.

Rohter, Larry (1990), 'Black Panellist at NAACP Session Accuses Studios of "Jewish Racism"', *New York Times*, 13 July: C5.

Ross, Steven J. (1999), *Working-Class Hollywood: Silent Film and the Shaping of Class in America*, Princeton, NJ: Princeton University Press.

Rosten, Leo (1941), *Hollywood*, New York: Harcourt Brace.

Russo, Gus (2001), *The Outfit: The Role of Chicago's Underworld in the Shaping of Modern America*, London: Bloomsbury.

Sanchez-Ruiz, Enrique E. (2003), *Some Remarks on NAFTA and the Mexican Audiovisual Field* (downloaded from http://www.mexicanadecomunicacion.com.mx/Tables/FMB/mjc/mexican2/some.html#27 on 12 September 2005).

Sayre, Nora (1995–6), 'Assaulting Hollywood', *World Policy Journal*, Winter: 51–60.

Schatz, Thomas (1998), *The Genius of the System: Hollywood Film-making in the Studio Era*, London: Faber and Faber.

Schroeder, Alan (2004), *Celebrity in Chief: How Show Business Took over the White House*, Boulder, CO and Oxford: Westview Press.

Schulberg, Budd (1981), *Moving Pictures: Memories of a Hollywood Prince*, New York: Souvenir Press.

Schulberg, Budd (1992), *What Makes Sammy Run?* (3rd edn), London: Allison and Busby.

Screen Actors Guild (2004), *Casting Data Report 2003: Executive Summary*, 6 October (downloaded from http://www.sag.org/sagWebApp/Content/Public/diversity_reports_2003. htm on 12 September 2005).

Screen Writers of Hollywood (1936), 'Screen Writers of Hollywood: Advert', *Hollywood Reporter*, 9 May.

Segrave, Kerry (1997), *American Film Abroad: Hollywood Domination of the World's Movie Screens*, Jefferson, NC and London: McFarland.

Semati, M. Mehidi and Patty J. Sotirin (1999), 'Hollywood's Transnational Appeal: Hegemony and Democratic Potential?', *Journal of Popular Film and Television*, Winter (downloaded from http://www.findarticles.com/cf_dls on 12 September 2005).

Sharp, Kathleen (2003), *Mr and Mrs Hollywood: Edie and Lew Wasserman and Their Entertainment Empire*, New York: Carroll and Gaff.

Sherman, Len (1990), *The Good, the Bad and the Famous: Celebrities Playing Politics*, New York: Lyle Stuart.

Shindler, Colin (1996), *Hollywood in Crisis: Cinema and American Society 1929–1939*, London and New York: Routledge.

Sinclair, Upton (1933), *Upton Sinclair Presents William Fox*, Los Angeles: Upton Sinclair.

Sinclair, Upton (1936), 'The Movies and Political Propaganda', in William J. Perlman (ed.), *The Movies on Trial: The Views and Opinions of Outstanding Personalities in Screen Entertainment Past and Present*, New York: Macmillan.

Siwek, Stephen and Gale Mosteller (1998), *Economist Incorporated, Copyright Industries in the US Economy: The 1998 Report, Prepared for the International Intellectual Property Alliance* (downloaded from http://www.mpa.org/legislation/press/99/99_2_23.htm on 12 September 2005).

Sklar, Robert (1975), *Movie-Made America: A Cultural History of American Movies* (rev. edn), New York: Vintage Books.

Skouras, Spyros (1953), 'Speech' quoted from Manjunath Pendakur (1990), *Canadian Dreams and American Control*, January, Toronto: Garamond: 38.

Sorrell, Herbert (1948), 'Jurisdictional Disputes', United States House of Representatives, 80th Congress: 1874.

Speight, Kimberly (2005), 'SAG Candidates Heat up Election', *Hollywood Reporter*, 3 August.

Squire, Jason E. (1992), *The Movie Business Book: The Inside Story of the Creation, Financing, Making, Selling and Exhibiting of Movies*, New York: Fireside.

Staggs, Sam (2002), *Close Up on Sunset Boulevard: Billy Wilder, Norma Desmond and the Dark Hollywood Dream*, New York: St Martin's Griffin.

Stewart, Donald Ogden (1971), American Film Institute Oral History Programme, December: 94.

Street, John (2004), 'Celebrity Politicians: Popular Culture and Political Representation', *The British Journal of Politics and International Relations* vol. 6, no. 4, November.

Thomas, Bob (1969), *Thalberg*, New York: Doubleday.

Thompson, Kristin (1985), *Exporting Entertainment: America in the World Film Market 1907–1934*, London: British Film Institute.

Tosches, Nick (2000), 'The Devil and Sidney Korshak', in Nick Tosches, *The Nick Tosches Reader*, New York: Da Capo Press.

Towle, Angela Phipps (2003), 'NAACP Images Awards: Interview with Kweisi Mfume and Julian Bond', *Hollywood Reporter*, 7–9 March: S-6.

Trumbo, Dalton (1970), *Additional Dialogue: Letters of Dalton Trumbo, 1942–1962*, ed. Helen Manfull, New York: M. Evans & Co.

Trumpbour, John (2002), *Selling Hollywood to the World: US and European Struggles for Mastery of the Global Film Industry, 1920–1950*, Cambridge: Cambridge University Press.

Ulff-Moller, Jens (2001), *Hollywood's Film Wars with France: Film Trade Diplomacy and the Emergence of the French Film Quota Policy*, Rochester, NY: University of Rochester Press.

Valenti, Jack (1980), 'Webb-Pomerene', *Vital Speeches* no. 47, 15 October: 26–28.

Valenti, Jack (1982), 'Testimony before Subcommittee on Courts, Civil Liberties, and the Administration of Justice of the Committee on the Judiciary House of Representatives, Ninety-Seventh Congress, Second Session on HR 4783, HR 4794, HR 4808, HR 5250, HR 5488, and HR 5705: Home Recording of Copyrighted Works' (downloaded from http://cryptome.org/ hrcw-hear.htm on 12 September 2005).

Valenti, Jack (1997), 'Press Release: If You Can't Protect What You Own – You Don't Own Anything; Comments by Jack Valenti President & Chief Executive Officer Motion Picture Association of America before the House Subcommittee on Courts & Intellectual Property on WIPO Copyright Treaties Implementation Act and the Online Copyright Liability Limitation Act', 16 September (downloaded from http://www.mpaa.org/jack/ 97/ 97_9_16b.htm on 12 September 2005).

Valenti, Jack (2000), 'Interview' quoted from Kenneth Bowser, *Hollywood DC: A Tale of Two Cities*, Fremantle Corporation (Broadcast on Bravo cable network, November).

Valenti, Jack (2003), 'Valenti Testifies before Senate Commerce Committee and Calls on Congress to Support Efforts to Protect Intellectual Property', MPAA press release, 17 September (downloaded from http://www.mpaa.org/MPAAPress/ index.htm on 1 March 2005).

Valenti, Jack (2004a), 'Signing-off Speech', MPAA press release, 6 September (downloaded from http://www.mpaa.org/MPAAPress/index.htm on 1 March 2005).

Valenti, Jack (2004b), 'British Screen Advisory Council (BSAC) Interview with Jack Valenti, Former President and CEO of the Motion Picture Association of America (MPAA) and Motion Picture Association (MPA) interviewed by David Elstein, Chairman of BSAC', 11 October (downloaded from http://www.bsac.uk.com/ 2004.html on 12 September 2005).

Variety (1936), 'Guild Accepts 81 Bow-Outs! Must Pay Up Before Org Lets Loose', 8 May: 1–2.

Variety (1944a), 'Motion Picture Alliance for Preservation of American Ideals', 7 February: 1.

Variety (1944b), 'Time to Name Names', 14 March: 3.

Vasey, Ruth (1997), *The World According to Hollywood 1918–1939*, Exeter: University of Exeter Press.

Vaughn, Robert (1996), *Only Victims: A Study of Show Business Blacklisting*, New York: Limelight Editions.

Vaughn, Stephen (1990), 'Morality and Entertainment: The Origins of the Motion Picture Production Code', *Journal of American History*, June: 39–65.

Vaughn, Stephen (1994), *Ronald Reagan in Hollywood: Movies and Politics*, Cambridge: Cambridge University Press.

Vendel, Christine (2005), 'Spitting by Vietnam Vet Dismissed', *Kansas City Star*, 26 August (downloaded from http://www.kansascity.com/ mld/kansascity/news/local/12479774. htm%22 on 12 September 2005).

Walsh, Frank (1996), *Sin and Censorship: The Catholic Church and the Motion Picture Industry*, New Haven, CI and London: Yale University Press.

Walsh, Sean (2003), 'Interview', quoted from *Arnold Schwarzenegger in the Governator*, BBC Productions.

Warner, Harry (1948), Quoted from 'The Great Hollywood Anti-Trust Case Part 6: The Supreme Court Verdict That Brought an End to the Hollywood Studio System, 1948', *Hollywood Renegades Archive: The Society of Independent Motion Picture Producers* (downloaded from http://www.cobbles.com/ simpp_archive/ paramountcase_6supreme1948.htm on 12 September 2005).

Warner, Jack L. with Dean Jennings (1964), *My First Hundred Years in Hollywood*, New York: Random House.

Wasko, Janet (1994), *Hollywood in the Information Age*, Oxford: Polity Press.

Wasko, Janet (2003), *How Hollywood Works*, London, Thousand Oaks, CA and New Delhi: Sage.

Wasserman, Lew (1973), 'Interview with Joe B. Frantz', *Lyndon Baines Johnson Library Oral History Collection*, 21 December, LBJ Library, 2313 Red River Street, Austin, Texas, 78705.

Waxman, Sharon (2004), 'An Old Washington Hand to Succeed Valenti in Hollywood', *New York Times*, 2 July (downloaded from http://www.friends.ca/News/Friends_News/archives/articles07020401.asp on 12 September 2005).

West, Darrell M. and John Orman (2003), *Celebrity Politics*, Englewood Cliffs, NJ: Prentice Hall.

West, Darrell M. (2003), *Arnold Schwarzenegger and Celebrity Politics* (downloaded from http://www.insidepolitics.org/heard/westreport903.html on 12 September 2005).

Wheeler, Mark (2000a), 'Research Note: The 'Undeclared War' Part II: The European Union's (EU) Consultation Process for the New Round of the General Agreement on Trading Services/World Trade Organisation on Audio-visual Services', *European Journal of Communication* vol. 15, no. 2, Summer: 253–262.

Wheeler, Mark (2000b), 'Globalization of the Communications Marketplace', *Harvard International Journal of Press/Politics* vol. 5, no. 3, Summer: 27–44.

Wienart, Laura (2001), 'A House Divided? The Screen Actors' Guild Juggles a Number of Issues, from Infighting to Agents, While Trying to Put Their Organization Back in Order', *Back Stage West*, 8 February.

Wills, Garry (1987), *Reagan's America: Innocence at Home*, Garden City, NY: Doubleday.

Wills, Garry (1999), *John Wayne: The Politics of Celebrity*, London: Faber and Faber.

Wise, Robert, Norman Jewison, John Forsyth, Burt Lancaster and Kirk Douglas (1969), 'Joint Letter to the American Civil Liberties Union: Support for Voluntary Ratings Code', 14 April, AMPTP Archive, Academy of Motion Picture Library, Beverly Hills, CA.

Wright, Ben (2005), 'Fight Looms over Schwarzenegger's Plans', *BBC News America online*, 10 August (downloaded from http://news.bbc.co.uk/2/hi/americas/4136128.stm on 12 September 2005).

Index